MADOC
The Making of a Myth

MADOC
The Making of a Myth

GWYN A. WILLIAMS

Oxford   New York

OXFORD UNIVERSITY PRESS

1987

Oxford University Press, Walton Street, Oxford OX2 6DP

Oxford New York Toronto
Delhi Bombay Calcutta Madras Karachi
Petaling Jaya Singapore Hong Kong Tokyo
Nairobi Dar es Salaam Cape Town
Melbourne Auckland

and associated companies in
Beirut Berlin Ibadan Nicosia

Oxford is a trade mark of Oxford University Press

First published 1979 by Eyre Methuen Ltd.
First issued as an Oxford University Press paperback 1987

British Library Cataloguing in Publication Data
Williams, Gwyn A.
Madoc: the making of a myth.
1. Madog ab Owain Gwynedd 2. America—
Discovery and exploration—Welsh
I. Title
398'.352 E109.W4
ISBN 0–19–285178–0

Library of Congress Cataloging in Publication Data
Williams, Gwyn A.
Madoc: the making of a myth.
Reprint. Originally published: London: Eyre Methuen, 1979.
Bibliography: p. Includes index.
1. America—Discovery and exploration—Welsh.
2. Madog ab Owain Gwynedd, 1150–1180? I. Title
E109.W4W544 1987 970.01'4 87–11130
ISBN 0–19–285178–0 (pbk.)

Printed in Great Britain by
Richard Clay Ltd.
Bungay, Suffolk

In memory of
DAVID WILLIAMS

historian of Wales, France and America
magister

Contents

Illustrations

Map

Acknowledgements

The staffs of the National Library of Wales, the National Museum of Wales, the British Library Reference Section (British Museum), the British Library Map Room (British Museum), the Salisbury Library and the Arts Library, University College Cardiff; to the Librarians of Brown University Rhode Island, the Historical Society of St Louis and the staff of the State Historical Museum, Bismarck, North Dakota, for their invaluable personal assistance and photocopying services; to Mrs Mary Murray Brown of Mount Kisco, New York, for a photocopy of Morgan John Rhys's journal, and to the staff of the Historical Society of Pennsylvania, Philadelphia, the Veterans' Administration of the same city, and the University of Pennsylvania for their assistance; to the staff of the County Courthouse, Ebensburg, Pennsylvania, and the Cambria Historical Society of the same town, for lodging and unfailing encouragement.

To the Library of Congress for assistance over John Evans's map and to the Beinecke Rare Book and Manuscript Collection, Yale University, for permission to reproduce; to the British Library (Reference Division) for permission to reproduce John Dee's engraving of Queen Elizabeth and part of his Title Royal of 1580; to the National Library of Wales for permission to reproduce the watercolour of Iolo Morganwg, and for permission to reprint the Karl Bodmer watercolours from *People of the First Man*, ed. Davis Thomas and Karin Ronnefeldt, to E.P. Dutton, publisher (New York).

To the Cartographical Section of the Department of Maritime Studies, University of Wales Institute of Science and Technology at Cardiff for the map.

To the editors of the *Welsh History Review* and the *Bulletin of the Board of Celtic Studies* for permission to reproduce material which first appeared in the form of articles.

To the students of University College Cardiff in my course on 'The Atlantic in Modern History' for their heartening, if unconscious, encouragement.

'. . . But yet (sayd he) there is a Little Lock of LADY OCCASION, Flickering in the Ayre, by our hands, to catch hold on: whereby, we may, yet ones more (before all be utterly past and for ever) discretely and valiantly recover and enjoy, if not all our Ancient and due Appurtenances to this Imperiall Brytish Monarchy, yet, at the least, some such Notable Portion thereof . . .'

(Dr John Dee, *General and Rare Memorials pertayning to the Perfecte Arte of Navigation*, London, September 1577)

A brief note scholastical for the better understanding of the *Decorum* observed (or at the least *regarded*) in this *present Two-fold Treatise* . . . [to quote Dr John Dee, only true begetter of the historical Madoc and mechanicien of the Plat Politicall of the Brytish Monarchie in 1577].

Twofold this treatise certainly is. In one obvious sense, it tries to trace the history of a myth which lived for nearly four hundred years and which, at two moments in its colourful career, became what Indians called an idea-that-walks, an idea that became material force. In another sense, this book is not about a myth at all, but about the way people have used myths to make history. The peoples whom this myth touched have been marginal to the historical interests of the majority: Spaniards in North America, and Mandan Indians, the Welsh, a lost generation of democrats on both sides of the Atlantic. They are none the less important for that, not least because of the way they have demonstrated, often to their own pain and loss, just how ideas, no matter how fanciful or Utopian or even lunatic, can become material force.

My mind and spirit and many of my waking hours have long been forfeit to the late eighteenth century, when writing was often 'felicitous', as John Adams called Thomas Jefferson's, but when throughout the Atlantic basin men and women of very different experience and tradition were set in motion by similar impulses. In that time of the breaking of dynasties, I found that my own people, the Welsh, numerically tiny and marginal though they were, proved to have been a people of some panache and not a little significance in that Atlantic perspective. I found a kind of short-lived nationalism emerging among them, a buoyant, generous, non-exclusive kind, infinitely more felicitous than later variants of the species; I found a crisis which cracked a society, a strong and millenarian thrust of migration, a young man who rode the length of the American Republic, fought for a black church in Savannah and for Indian identity on the Ohio, and tried to launch a New Wales in Pennsylvania; I found an even younger man who, on a quest for the Lost Brothers, the Welsh Indians of Madoc, served as Spain's last conquistador in the New World, and penetrated further up the Missouri and into the American west than any white man before him, to save the Upper Missouri for Spain and, in due course, for the USA. All of them, I found, carried in their heads some vision of Prince Madoc who, they believed, had discovered America in 1170 and had left behind him on that continent a tribe of Welsh Indians.

At first, I tried to capture this almost incredible moment in its entirety, to convey the totality of the moment in a single book. I still think I was right to try, but now accept the argument that such an experience would prove incommunicable. I have had to select, to make what Sorel called a *diremption* — a slice out of a living reality. I have chosen to begin with the mythic. In order so to begin, I have had to move back in time and forward into what was to me a future. It has been long and often arduous but I have travelled in magnificent company, for I perforce encountered peoples and times and minds I never thought to meet. I hope this book conveys some sense of that encounter.

I have contracted many debts, some as desperate as those of John Evans who, on his search for Welsh Indians, set off up an unknown Missouri with one dollar and seventy-five cents in his pocket. I try to list them elsewhere. My wife Maria has crossed the Atlantic with me so often, once in reality and a myriad times in the mind, that we are now reconciled to the fact that our abiding home must lie some place a few hundred miles west of the Azores. I had the privilege of travelling with Wil Aaron and a team from BBC Wales from New Orleans to Bismarck, out of a Bay of Mexico spring and into a Missouri winter on a wild-track which has ensured that so long as we seven do not die, Madoc will not.

Most of my debts have been to the writers of books; to my fellow-townsman Thomas Stephens of Merthyr who wrote the best essay of historical criticism on Madoc and had to shout above the band at an eisteddfod to make himself heard; to Richard Deacon, Madoc's last defender, whose book is often wild and sometimes silly, but always challenging; and to the prickly but magnificent Bernard de Voto, now rather scorned and neglected, I understand, who could encompass a whole continent, landscape and people, in a single vaulting thrust of the imagination.

Above all, I owe a debt to the man under whom I served my apprenticeship to this sullen craft at Aberystwyth — David Williams, formerly the Sir John Williams Professor of Welsh History there. David Williams, a man of wit, industry and style, called himself a Voltairean Baptist and would clearly have been at home in his chosen eighteenth century. He rebuilt the history of modern Wales and wrote with equal power and panache on Wales, France and America, an Atlantic man, as was appropriate for a scholar of the age of revolution. The history of the Welsh may have been full of myths, but they have numbered giants among their historians. David Williams among them was *Ysbaddaden Chief Giant* and I dedicate this book to his memory.

Cardiff   Gwyn A. Williams

Prologue

At half past seven in the morning of 7 March 1778, they sighted America, about eight leagues of it, looming high, craggy and snow-covered through the mist and the squalls. Five weeks out from those Pacific islands they had named in honour of Lord Sandwich, First Lord of the Admiralty, they beat northwards along a strange coast which they knew was Drake's New Albion. Fog and weather hid from them the mouth of the great river whose presence the Spaniard Bruno Heceta had sensed three years earlier and which a later American was to name after his Columbia. It took them three weeks of hail, sleet and snowstorms. They found anchorage at last off what they thought was mainland but discovered to be an island. They were not to know that the far shore was that of a much larger island which was to take its name from one of their young gentlemen, George Vancouver. They came to anchor at about six o'clock in the afternoon of Sunday, 29 March, with huge flights of birds wheeling overhead and scores of canoes swarming around them, and Indians in wooden masks singing in wild concert and rhythmically beating the sides of the canoes with the butts of their paddles. On the third day, they warped the *Resolution* into the cove they named after her, and lashed her to trees with hawsers; the *Discovery* found her place a little distance away. Captain James Cook named the harbour King George's Sound. Five years earlier, the Spaniard Juan Perez, battling up from the handful of priests and soldiers who were creating California, had called it San Lorenzo. History, perhaps from shame, knows it by its Indian name of Nootka.

Two of the world's great ships under one of its greatest explorers had touched on an alien place. It was to prove a potent place. For on those crags the rivalries of three empires and two republics were to focus. Some sense of those distant but intersecting worlds was present in and around the ships. Beyond the headland lay Spain, that empire which took such an unconscionable time dying, the empire which in fact did not die until the homeland was throttled in a war of national liberation which, like all such wars, was also a civil war. To the last, tiny handfuls of laborious and dedicated men — scattered across the vast and unknown continent which they had acquired from France in 1763 and

1

which they called Louisiana — in New Orleans, St Louis and Santa Fe, struggled against odds to turn Spanish shadow into substance in one of the most haunting might-have-beens of the history of North America.

Behind them glimmered, like the sheen on its long silver rivers, that other ghost empire of the French, the network which laced the continent, the *voyageurs*, fur traders, woodsmen and mountain men, whom Spain and Britain had inherited. Masters of the Indians, the beaver, the unthinkable geography, they were paddling and portaging and huckstering their way across a continental mystery towards the Pacific, Nootka and the Great River of the West, the arcs of their passage crossing those of the Scotsmen out of Canada, working under many flags, threatening at any moment to resume their own.

British admiralty, British power, British skill, of course, were physically present at the anchorage in the persons of James Cook and George Vancouver, in the troops of trained and expert observers, and in William Bligh, the captain of the *Resolution*, whose best-known command was to be the *Bounty*. But the China ships of the Americans, their fur trade empire of Astoria, the epic of Lewis and Clark were present too, in the person of a twenty-six year old corporal of marines, John Ledyard, who had been born in Groton, Connecticut. 'It was the first time I had been so near the shores of the continent which gave me birth', said John, 3,300 miles from home. 'I was harmonized by it . . .'

For at Nootka, continental and oceanic vision could be brought into harmony. The Indians there, noted Cook, knew of iron, brass and copper. Where could they have got them except from Europeans, perhaps through the medium of other tribes? The Hudson's Bay Company? Cook and Ledyard both thought so; maybe Mexico or the free traders out of Canada, added the former. Here was Pacific confirmation of that 'short portage' across the western mountains which, geographers asserted, was all that lay between Nootka and the outrunners of the American fur trade curving in from the east.

Moreover, the sea-otter skins which Cook's men picked up at Nootka made them a fortune in Canton in China and sent a clutch of British, American and French merchants scrambling for the North-West and Cathay. Within eight years, in his drive to root his new United States in this trade, John Ledyard was to set out, 'with only two shirts and yet more shirts than shillings', to cross Russia and Siberia to get to Nootka from the west and thence traverse his continent from west to east. The Russians stopped him at Irkutsk, but it was thinking of this kind which was to make Nootka into a global cockpit. Twelve years after Cook's ships pulled in, surrounded by their singing Indians, incidents at Nootka threatened to precipitate a world war.

There was however, another presence at that windy, strange and chanting place, a presence which was marginal, slightly manic, and disturbing. David Samwell was surgeon's first mate on the *Resolution*. In August, after the death of surgeon William Anderson, an accomplished botanist, he was to be promoted surgeon of the *Discovery* and to inherit Anderson's books. For

Samwell was no less accomplished, a lively, keen and quick observer. He had already transcribed six Maori chants at Queen Charlotte Sound, the first written record of the language and of crucial importance to scholars; he was to compose an elaborate account of the death of Captain Cook, which contemporaries thought well of, because David was a skilful poet in more than one language. A big man, he bubbled with wit and humour, a good friend and an alarming enemy. An adventurer, he was a man of violence, given to brawls and throwing pots in pubs. He was given to women too, revelling in the 'nymphs' of the South Seas and laying any personable female he could. It was venereal disease which killed him in the end when, a sad and disillusioned man, he was looking after British prisoners of war in the Versailles of the French Republic.

In that March of 1778, having noted that Nootka nymphs turned near-white when scrubbed, he commented on the agreeable style of their singing and reported that the British sailors replied with a few tunes on two French horns. The Indians were hypnotized into silence but responded with another song, whereupon the tars opened up with fife and drum. The Nootkas' medicine man, however, a capering figure in a mask who flourished his rattle and squawked like a London potato-man, outlived his welcome. He seemed to think his presents were a reward for his singing; in reality, said Samwell in a caustic aside, he ought to have echoed that old Welsh fiddler on his out-of-tune instrument:

Haws nag ynnill Ceiniog wrthi
o fewn ei blwy gael dwy am dewi . . .

(Easier than earning a penny from it in his parish is getting twopence by shutting up . . .)

These lines were part of an *englyn* or four-line stanza in the old Welsh literary form; indeed, Captain Cook's whole voyage had been punctuated by periodic bursts of Welsh verse in the traditional metres, for David Samwell was not only surgeon's first mate of the *Resolution;* he was also the Welsh poet *Dafydd Ddu Meddyg* (Black David the Doctor) and was to become a fully-fledged member of the Order of Bards of the Island of Britain *(Gorsedd Beirdd Ynys Prydain).* And Nootka was to be a focus not only for portentous powers and principalities, but for a people who were numerically tiny, awkward and yet in some respects peculiarly potent; a people who had less of a state and an organized polity than the very Indians; a people who, apart from their language, lacked practically every attribute of a nation except for the perverse and persistent belief that they were one. This was a people who had already dislocated the European historical mind with their magic King Arthur and were now about to disturb the American continent with their tenacious memory.

For twelve years later there was a sudden demand for Samwell's Nootka reminiscences among his fellow Bards, in particular from Edward Williams *(Iolo Morganwg).* Iolo was a stonemason of Glamorgan in south Wales, a tramping artisan who literally tramped — he generally walked his horse from

3

charity. A man of highly original intelligence and of amoral, indeed unscrupulous, imagination, gifted poet, antiquarian, scholar and wit, he was also fabricator-in-chief to that new Welsh 'nation' of which men like himself and Samwell were exemplars. In 1791 he took Samwell's notes and immersed himself in a dedicated quest among mountains of maps, memoirs and texts in his little cottage at Flemingston in the Vale of Glamorgan. It was the tracks of fur traders, sailors and frontier nomads he was tracing, from the Mississippi to that bleak Pacific coast his friend had seen. For in the previous year, William Pitt had taken Britain to the brink of war with Spain over Nootka Sound.

Cook had opened up the lucrative China trade and the whale fisheries; rival traders went swarming to Nootka and the Pacific north-west even as the Russians inched south from Alaska. The Spaniards, thinly holding the Mississippi, New Mexico and California around their huge and mysterious Louisiana, were alarmed. They claimed the whole coast even though they occupied but a fraction of it. They struck back: in 1789 a British adventurer John Meares — half-explorer, half-pirate — had his Nootka ships and property confiscated. Spain re-asserted its ancient claim to exclusive sovereignty, and resurrected a quarrel as old as that papal decision of 1493 which had divided the New World between Spain and Portugal, as old as the first Elizabethan generation of British explorer-pirates.

The England of William Pitt, with its ships riding cock-a-hoop over every sea, its new economy beginning to run off the map of knowledge, its exports, merchants and adventurers flooding into every nook and cranny, and its initiative flowing back after the trauma of the American war and its first post-colonial crisis could hardly tolerate this.

> Your right so to do which you claim from the Pope
> We Britons don't value the end of a rope!
> It's a farce you may make your weak Subjects believe
> But our right's equal to yours from Adam and Eve.

sang the street wits and by May 1790, Britain was in the grip of a war fever, even as Europe was trying to live with the first tumultuous months of the French Revolution.

The navy was mobilized, troops dispatched. There were plans for onslaughts on Louisiana, Mexico, Guatemala. Francisco de Miranda was summoned for a liberation of South America; the self-styled 'General' William Augustus Bowles, an Irishman who had made himself a chief among the Creek Indians, was readied for operations against Florida in alliance with American dissidents and plotters in Tennessee. The separatist Allen brothers of Vermont and the agent Peter Allaire in Kentucky were alerted, in case the American republic proved troublesome. In the Nootka Sound crisis, the entire American continent became a cockpit of imperialisms.

For the tensions of that continent were multiple and explosive. The new republic of the USA had just forced through its novel constitution over last-ditch resistance. It was equipping itself with the instruments of a national commercial-imperial policy in a tumult of partisan conflict, as Republicans fought the Bank, the Debt, the land policy, the Atlantic and the 'Anglo Saxon' schemes of Alexander Hamilton and the Federalists. Whole sections in the west, south and north grew restless at alleged neglect as British and Spanish agents, empire-building adventurers, worked Kentucky, Vermont and Tennessee and fought over disputed lands which in theory lay within the frontiers of the new state trying to force its way in a world of mercantilist empires. In the old north-west, along the Ohio lands, warlike Indian tribes blocked the tide of settlement, as British posts on American territory buttressed them and the Montreal fur-traders who moved among them. Major George Beckwith, directed from Canada, could create a British fifth column within American government itself; Alexander Hamilton figured as Number Seven on his list. In the south the Spaniards built up the Creeks under the half-Scot Alexander McGillivray, and supported the tribes through their British company of Panton and Leslie in Florida, even as a rival British firm in the Bahamas sponsored General Bowles, and a host of ambitious Americans, including John Sevier and William Blount, dreamed of empires of their own. The 'men of the western waters' in Kentucky and Tennessee, driving endlessly west, needed access for their goods to the Mississippi and New Orleans which was blocked by Spain. They could intrigue to get it and many rallied to James Wilkinson of Kentucky who plotted with the Spaniards for secession, annexation, and independence. They could fight to get it, and fili-bustering schemes against Louisiana pullulated, all looking to the British for support.

To the British the Spaniards looked, too, with alarm. Even as American migrants pressed by the thousand ever harder on their river and Indian barrier, British-controlled traders were pushing further and further west through what was to become Canada. They were raising forts along the Assiniboine and the Souris rivers, and moving down among the Indians along the upper Mississippi, the Des Moines and the Minnesota rivers which were legally Spanish. They were curling down on the upper Missouri, the lifeline of the continent, and on Spanish maps and in Spanish nightmares were menacing Santa Fe and even Mexico itself. Nootka Sound and the Pacific were the logical terminus of a thrust which would give enemies the continent.

For everyone's maps told them that the largely unknown Missouri river threading through the 'American desert' of Louisiana was the quickest way west to the hub of wealth and power at Nootka; there was but a short portage from its headwaters over the Shining Mountains down to that South Sea. In the Nootka Sound confrontation all the sectional tensions of North America shuddered into continental crisis. For months the continent was alive with rumours of plots and wars. In October 1790 the Spaniards, abandoned by a French nation locked into revolutionary self-absorption surrendered and

5

the immediate threat subsided. But not until European war forced a temporary settlement of British-Spanish-American frontiers, in the Jay and Pinckney treaties of 1794-5 was there some relaxation, and even then there was little in the west. The 1790s were years of high imperial tension as, after Nootka, eyes riveted on the Missouri.

During 1792-3, while the Britisher Vancouver and the American Robert Gray were nosing their ships about the Columbia river, Nootka, Puget Sound and Vancouver Island, the great Alexander Mackenzie of the Canada fur traders drove Europe across the Rockies. Threading his way through the bewildering north-western wilderness, he moved down the great river which he, and William Clark and Thomas Jefferson, thought was the reality behind the Great River of the West, the river which Robert Gray had named the Columbia. It was in fact the Fraser. He was stopped by Indians, by the force of the river, by a breakdown in supplies and by a collapse in his men's morale. But he knew that Nootka, the Pacific and the China trade were within reach, and by sheer will-power he led his party overland across the mountains. They finally reached the Bella Coola river and villages with European goods, Indians who complained of a 'Macubah' and a 'Bensins' — Vancouver and his naturalist Menzies. And at eight in the morning on 20 July 1793, they reached the sea. Mackenzie mixed vermilion with melted grease and painted in large letters on a rock, 'Alexander Mackenzie, from Canada, by land'. A dream older than Columbus had come true. The Scotsman had made the classic first land crossing to the Pacific.

And he was now fully seized of the geo-political realities of empire. His vision (which he wrote into a book eight years later) was of a great British fur trust spanning the continent from ocean to ocean and reaching out to China, linking Hudson's Bay with the great river of the west. It was essential, however, that this British Canada should stretch south. For the real axis of this natural empire was the Upper Missouri of Spanish Louisiana.

No one was to read Mackenzie's book with closer attention than Thomas Jefferson, that American statesman who saw the continent whole. The man who was to send Lewis and Clark west needed little persuasion. Already in 1790 the American lieutenant John Armstrong had been probing about the Missouri mouth on the Mississippi, on direct orders from Henry Knox, secretary of war. His mission was abortive, but its objective was clear:

Devise some practicable plan for exploring the branch of the Mississippi called the Messouri, up to its source and all its southern branches, and tracing particularly the distance between the said branches and any of the navigable streams that run into the Great North River which empties itself into the Gulf of Mexico . . .

In the 1793 of Alexander Mackenzie Thomas Jefferson seized the opportunity of the botanical mission of the Frenchman André Michaux. This was another year of crisis for Spain, with the American envoy of the new French republic organizing an army in the west to attack Louisiana under the famous frontiersman George Rogers Clark. Michaux's expedition, financed by the American Philosophical Society in Philadelphia, was inextricably involved in these belligerent plans. Avoid the Spanish posts, Jefferson told the Frenchman, but get to the Pacific:

> As a channel of communication between these States and the Pacific ocean, the Missouri, so far as it extends, presents itself under circumstances of unquestioned preference . . . It would seem by the latest maps as if a river called Oregon [another name for the Great River of the West; Meares thought he had found it at Nootka] interlocked with the Missouri for a considerable distance and entered the Pacific ocean not far southward of Nootka Sound . . .

This mission, too, proved abortive, but it was in that same year that the Spaniards, threats closing on them from every direction, were galvanized into action. In St Louis and New Orleans they learned of men who had crossed the western cordillera from the headwaters of the Missouri and who had heard from Indians of a river that ran to the Pacific a mere hundred miles away. 'Perhaps in that country would be found the fur of which the traveller Cook speaks . . .' they reported to Spain. In the same crisis year of 1793, energized by an outsider, Jacques Clamorgan, a West Indian adventurer of Welsh descent, the merchants of the little frontier outpost of St Louis were mobilized into a *Compania Exploradora*, the Commercial Company for the Discovery of the Nations of the Upper Missouri, which over the next few years sent expedition after expedition up that mystery river striving to break through to the Pacific and win the reward offered by the Governor, even as Spain mobilized a naval force for Nootka.

The immediate occasion for the formation of the Missouri Company and Spain's last great effort in North America was the receipt of news even more startling than the perennial and generalized threat from the British and Americans and shadowy French. For in October 1792 two travelling men had reached St Louis. One, the Frenchman Vial, was brought in by Kansas Indians. He had finally made the trip direct from Santa Fe to St Louis, opening the Santa Fe trail and confirming Spanish officials in their fears about the vulnerability of the Mexican provinces. The other man was more striking still. He was a French fur trader, Jacques d'Eglise, who had set out up the Missouri in August 1790 at the height of the Nootka crisis. He had broken all the rules and regulations and had dared to make his way further up the Missouri from St Louis than anyone had ever gone before. Over 800 leagues from the city, he had found a mighty and wealthy tribe of Indians, the Mandans. There had been earlier rumours of this remarkable tribe but no one had ever reached them from St Louis. They were 5,000 strong, he said, living in eight great fortified villages; they had the finest furs; they lived in sight of a volcano and alongside the Missouri, which at that point flowed from the west or north-west and could take the largest boats.

7

Given what their maps told them, the Spaniards realized at once that these mysterious Mandans must be the very hub of empire, controllers of the route to Nootka and the Pacific. Moreover d'Eglise's news was alarming. The Mandans all had English goods; the English were only two weeks away to the north. They had Mexican saddles and bridles for their horses, too, so Santa Fe must be within reach. And not only were these Mandans crucial; they were miraculous. For Jacques d'Eglise reported that their fortified villages were like cities compared to other native settlements. They were much more civilized than other Indians. And, the final marvel, these Mandans 'are white like Europeans'.

Here at last was confirmation of all those stories of white and civilized Indians which had been filtering back along the Missouri for years and which had cartographers scratching 'White Padoucas' across their vague sketches of the country near the Shining Mountains and the South Sea. All those eyes in all those imperial capitals, trading posts and cottonwood cabins, straining at their inadequate maps for the route to the Pacific, could hardly have missed them.

Half a planet away, certainly, other eyes full of other dreams did not miss them. This was no imperial capital or trading post or log cabin in a new world. This was one cottage among a cluster huddled on a bluff over a little river in a vale in south Wales, which was so old and had been so repeatedly colonized that it was like a palimpsest scrawled over by countless generations of hands. It was a vale which had greeted the Romans as newcomers, which had witnessed invaders and intruders without number but which was now experiencing something of a native revival. It was as a leader in that revival that the stonemason Edward Williams *(Iolo Morganwg)* bent over his maps, shuffled the notes of Captain Meares and David Samwell, the American travels of Coxe and Bossu and Carver, the accounts of Spanish explorers, drew lines from Nootka Sound to the 'White Padoucas' and scribbled calculations on the scraps of paper which blew around his Flemingston cottage like a blizzard conjured by a druid. As befitted such a man in such a country, the dream he cherished was old, an old dream resurrected by the old quarrel with Spain, older than those of French fur traders and American imperialists, perhaps older even than the dream which Alexander Mackenzie had fulfilled. But in pursuit of that dream, his mind was working in precisely the same way as those of Alexander Mackenzie and Thomas Jefferson and Lieutenant-Governor Trudeau of St Louis.

And when his calculations were done, his finger came down without fail on that empty place on the map out of which Jacques d'Eglise had come scrabbling breathless down the roaring river. That was where they were. That was where they had to be . . .

2

Dream and dominion

That empty place on the map was the homeland of the First People. The Mandans thought they were the First Men and their original country the heart of the world. The river they lived on, flowing into the Missouri, they called Heart River. In a sense, they were right. A hundred miles to the north-east, just west of Devil's Lake, is the geographical centre of the North American continent.

Like those remote Britons of the west whom Caesar heard tell of, the Mandans thought they had grown out of the ground. To explain their coming, they borrowed from the cosmology of their neighbours, the Hidatsa, with whom they were closely enmeshed. The People had lived in the underworld, but a grapevine grew tall through a hole into the sun. One day, they started to climb the vine, but it broke under the weight of a fat woman and only half of them got through into the heart of the world.

This borrowing from the Hidatsa is characteristic, for the ethnic entity called *Mandan* is elusive. This is a people who have lived more in myth than in history. After a span in which they loomed like ghostly giants in the minds of white traders, the great French explorer La Vérendrye reached their country (though perhaps not the Mandans themselves) in 1739. By the 1780s, Canadian traders were getting through to them from the north and in the brief interlude between the two smallpox epidemics of 1781 and 1837 which destroyed them, they emerge into the light in a sequence of reports from fascinated visitors, David Thompson the Welsh-Canadian, Lewis and Clark (who picked up Sacajawea at their village), Prince Maximilien, George Catlin and Karl Bodmer of the brilliant sketches and paintings. The smallpox of 1837 practically wiped them out; they lived on as a handful of survivors among the Hidatsa. On the Fort Berthold reservation today, their ceremonial grounds lost under Garrison reservoir, hardly any full-blooded Mandans or Mandan-speakers survive. And while someone is trying to transcribe their tongue into a literary language, their distinct identity is fading fast, though they still cherish their traditional shrine which white men call the Ark of the Lone Man.

Even before the smallpox epidemic of 1781, they had begun to dwindle, but in their time they had been a potent people and, even more remarkable, a focus for the myths of many other races. For they were the dominant group in a cluster of Upper Missouri tribes who were earth-lodge dwellers and who seemed to early explorers and traders, accustomed to eastern Indians, creatures from another world. North and south of Heart River were more recent arrivals. To the north were the Hidatsa, whom the Mandans called Minnetarees and the French, perhaps misreading a sign, Gros Ventres, Grovanders, Big-Bellies. Like the Mandans, they spoke a language of the Siouan family, and linked to those great traders the Assiniboines, they were kin to the Crows in the west; they were a heterogeneous people, and at one time seem to have occupied territory ranging from the Missouri up into Manitoba and east to Devil's Lake. To the south were the Arikara whose language was Caddoan but who shared in the earth-lodge culture.

For these were the most easterly of the Plains Indians, situated at the point where the forests yielded to the prairies and at the trading cross-roads of the continent. They were sedentary, living in large, fortified villages. Their lodges, which could range in circumference from twenty to sixty-five feet, had once been oblong and were now round. They were partly sunk in the ground and built around a heavy framework of timber ten feet high; around the timber frame, the women (for this was a matrilinear society in which the women built and ran the lodges, cultivated the ground and handled the bull-boats) piled layers of willow, clods of earth and dirt into a beehive shape, oddly reminiscent of some Celtic settlements. The lodges were roomy and held the best buffalo horses (for fear of the thieving Sioux), whole families of ten people and more (occasionally up to forty), box-beds with skin curtains, poles for weapons and equipment, and maybe the bull-boats — round skin and wickerwork craft similar to Welsh coracles, which needed careful handling on the tricky Missouri.

The tribes were concentrated in a few large villages, often built on the buffalo-backed bluffs of the Missouri, with the lodges running in streets, sometimes in hundreds, ringed by a palisade and a ditch. With their drying frames for grain and vegetables, the poles carrying medicine symbols, the sweatlodge in which the young men purified themselves before the sacred ceremonies which were held in the massive medicine lodge facing the open space used for dances and rituals around the shrine of the Lone Man, with the platforms for the dead outside and the circles of human and buffalo skulls, these earth-lodge villages must have seemed veritable 'cities' to awestruck visitors from nomadic tribes.

Not that the Mandans and the others were immobile. Some time in the eighteenth century they got horses and became great buffalo hunters, their Buffalo Dance capturing the imagination of Catlin and Bodmer. In winter they moved to smaller lodges; the rotting of the timber forced some movement. But their base was agricultural. The rich soil of the Missouri bottom grew corn, beans, squash, pumpkins, sunflowers and tobacco in abundance. They made the best pottery, which was nothing like as beautiful as that of the south-west, but gems in this world. They were superb craftsmen in leather. They never became carriers like the Crees, but they dominated the trade between the Plains and Rockies tribes to the west and the Indian culture to the east which was in turmoil under the impact of Europeans. And they were critically placed on the route to the Pacific.

Before the smallpox epidemic of 1781, the Mandans were one of the few peoples who did not fear the Sioux on their massive and terrifying migration westwards. In their fortified villages, they could laugh at them. But the terrible smallpox of 1781-2 wiped out half the tribe. They moved north from Heart River and settled on Knife River, closely packed among the Hidatsa, and it was there that white traders finally established continuous contact and built them into a mythic people.

For even among these — to the whites — startling earth-lodge peoples, the Mandans were mysterious. They were certainly the oldest of the cluster. Anthropologists place their arrival on the Missouri at various dates between 900 and 1400. By the time Catlin visited them, they had a taboo against settlement south of Heart River, and to cross the Missouri had become a significant ritual act. But their own legends placed their origins 'lower down' and there were persistent reports of an early migration from the south (modern anthropologists think they came from the east). Catlin thought he could trace evidence of Mandan settlement all the way down the Missouri and even among the mysterious mound-builders of the Ohio, whom archaeologists today identify with the Middle Woodland peoples of before 400, who may also have built the stone 'forts' which run down to Mobile Bay on the Gulf of Mexico. Indeed a later tradition among the Hidatsa identified the Mandans as 'Gulf-people' because of their alleged origins on the Gulf of Mexico.

This, however, may represent the absorption of other people's myths into Indian tradition, which could be peculiarly plastic. Certainly, from their first encounters, white men found Mandans unique. Even La Vérendrye, who was disappointed when he reached Mandan country, strikes a familiar note:

> The fortifications are not characteristic of the Indians . . . Most of the women do not have the Indian features . . . The tribe is mixed white and black. The women are fairly good looking, especially the light coloured ones; many of them have blonde or fair hair.

Observer after observer commented on the 'whiteness' of these Indians; it was this above all which made them into a people of myth. Many of them, without doubt, were fair of skin and hair. Their hair was often brown, sometimes red; it turned grey. Their eyes were sometimes blue. There were cases of albinism. The Hidatsa, the Crows and the Arikara showed similar characteristics but far less frequently. Ethnologists can offer perfectly normal genetic explanations and have no hesitation in pronouncing the Mandans native Indian, but the impact of those fair skins and that unusual way of life on white men was

11

often unhinging.

And there was much in Mandan culture to stimulate speculation. Once, said the Mandans in a story which has a familiar ring to anyone acquainted with tales of 'white Indians' among Europeans and Americans, a strange people came to the other side of the river with tools and weapons of metal such as no one had ever seen. Cautiously the Mandans approached the river bank, to be startled by shouts in their own language. 'We are you,' called the strangers. 'You are we. We are the same people . . .' About the same time, they said, their language changed from Old Mandan to New. Then there was their great Okipa ceremony, which was the focus of the ritual year and as elaborate as any Sun Dance. At this ceremony, which lasted several days, the Buffalo Dance was danced and the young men subjected themselves to ordeals, while an actor personifying the Evil One was rebuffed. But the key to the ceremony and to Mandan cosmology was the Lone Man. At the heart of every Mandan village was his shrine — a palisade of cottonwoods, bound with a willow thong, inside which was a red cedar, the 'holy canoe' to some observers. Here offerings were made and dances performed; the big medicine lodge looked out upon it. The Oikpa began when the willow leaf was full, 'because the twig that the turtle dove brought home was a willow with full-grown leaves.' Mandan cosmology centred on a Flood. Gourds shaped like up-turned tortoises were central to the ceremony; so were four tortoise-shaped bags which held water from the four quarters of the world at the time the Flood subsided. When the willow leaf was full, the whole village rushed to life as a man was seen coming from the hills to the west. He was covered in white clay so that he seemed a white man. He marched into the village, opened the medicine lodge and started the ceremony. For this was the Lone Man who had brought all good things to the people and who had saved them during the Flood (the willow thong on the shrine was said to mark the water level), landing his 'big canoe' on a mountain to the west. That this tradition would start white minds racing is clear. The Mandan shrine became not only a 'big canoe' but an Ark. Later still, but in a process which is impossible to date, there was a subtle shift of emphasis and the Lone Man became a White Man who, in his 'big canoe', had brought the people across a Great Water.

Another Mandan story, however, is painfully easy to date and cannot have been earlier than the late eighteenth century. It was an addition to the creation myths. In the early days, the people were suddenly attacked by fierce wolves who threatened to destroy them. The Lone Man 'crossed the river' to save them. In good eighteenth-century fashion he captured the young wolves and taught them to eat only animals. The old wolves, however, were incorrigible. So the people killed them and threw them into the Missouri. As they floated downstream, the rotting bodies turned into white men.

The first of the old wolves to get through to their country was the Frenchman La Vérendrye in 1739 — although geographical evidence on the village he then reached and the absence of any reference to a medicine lodge, a

12

ritual arena or a Lone Man shrine strongly suggest that the people he encountered were actually the Hidatsa. What brought him out of Canada (and across the British Hudson's Bay Company routes) were stories he had heard at Lake Nipigon in 1728, and which had been elaborated over the next few years. To the south-west, and along that Great River of the West which must flow to the Pacific, were Indians who were civilized and lived in large villages. They were white; their language and their songs sounded like French and they had beards. The Assiniboines called them *Ouachipouenne*, but at Fort Charles on Lake of the Woods, La Vérendrye first applied to them the name *Mantannes*. Kindred tribes further south he called the *Panana* and the *Pananis* (these were probably the historic Mandans and the Arikara, the latter being related to the Pawnees or Panis).

There had been a myriad myths about Indians ever since Columbus, but by the eighteenth century most of them focused on the Missouri, probably as a consequence of the focusing of rival imperialisms on that north-western mystery. Baron La Hontan had written early in the century of a great salt lake to the west along whose shores richly civilized Indians lived; he had spoken of a Long River whose imaginary course sometimes coincided with the actual Missouri. Bénard la Harpe had penetrated into the Plains in 1719, while Etienne de Bourgmond had got up the Missouri as far as the mouth of the Platte. The Platte, however, remained for many years the limit of penetration from undernourished Louisiana, and beyond it lay the mythic Great River of the West and Cathay. There the magic tribes flourished, helped along by La Hontan's imagination, and by the fictional journeys of Moncacht-Apé, created in 1758 by Le Page du Pratz, who in 1718 was one of the founders of New Orleans. His Moncacht-Apé followed a Beautiful River which flowed west, and came across a tribe of white Indians with untrimmed beards who were stunted of stature. Another story said that 1,000 miles beyond the Platte de Bourgmond was going to trade with a populous nation of little men with big eyes sticking out an inch beyond their noses, who dressed like Europeans and wore boots studded with gold. They, too, lived beside a lake and had much gold and many rubies, no doubt obtained from the Spanish mines of New Mexico which had to be close. The Crees reported such a people, too, three and a half feet tall and haters of Indians, white, bearded and living in fortified towns beside a lake. Another Frenchman placed them fifteen days beyond the Arikara; they worked metals and traded with the Comanches. Others, however, reporting a similar people, said they were not dwarfs at all but the best looking people on the continent, living along the Great River of the West. By mid-century, stories of white, bearded, civilized Indians living in style somewhere in the vicinity of the Missouri were commonplace and, as they filtered back into Canada, St Louis, and the English colonies which became the USA, they fused with other myths and acquired a life of their own.

The reality behind them were clearly the Mandans, who must also surely know the best route to Nootka and the Pacific. The way to them up the Missouri however was arduous. Long after Louisiana had passed to Spain by the Peace of Paris of 1763, knowledge had advanced no further than in de Bourgmond's day. The river itself ferocious, endlessly shifting course, was a frightful struggle for boats and pirogues battling up stream against the current and having to be dragged and poled along much of the time. The Lower Missouri tribes, the Otos, Omahas and Poncas were neatly parcelled out among the sedate St Louis merchants, led by the Chouteau family. They could be troublesome enough, since each tribe was anxious to monopolize trade, and the troubles got worse as the cheaper and better British goods started to come through from interlopers west of the Mississippi. There were worse threats. After 1760, the Sioux began to arrive in strength on the Missouri and to cross it, well advanced in their cultural transformation into Plains Indians. They were well stocked with British goods, pro-British, belligerent and savage. They blocked the Missouri as effectively as the Spaniards blocked the Mississippi to the Americans. And beyond them, the Arikara, while much more genial, were equally stubborn. Not until 1787 did Joseph Garreau get to the Arikara from St Louis and he behaved so badly that he alienated them. The first hard news the Spaniards got of the Mandans was from Jacques d'Eglise in 1792 and he found them already well supplied with British goods.

It was probably in the 1780s that the Hudson's Bay Company, its rival the North West Company and some independent traders from Canada set up a trade from the north with the Mandans. When d'Eglise reached the villages he found a Frenchman Ménard there, gay, boastful, with an Indian wife and half-Indian himself. He claimed, though he probably exaggerated, that he had been there for fourteen years. No one knows how he got there. British traders may have reached the Mandans in 1785. James McKay certainly got there in 1787, in the service of the North West Company and moving south from their far western post at Fort Espérance on the Qu'Appelle River. McKay was a forceful, stubborn and imaginative man, who in the quest for a Pacific route was to draft Instructions for explorers which President Thomas Jefferson copied for Lewis and Clark. Born in Scotland in 1759 to a family which claimed ancestors among the Irish nobility (and at least one king), McKay had migrated in 1776, his uncle having gone to North Carolina two years earlier. The Scotsman became an expert wilderness man in the fur trade; he met Piegan Indians and explored the Canadian north-west with much success. He must have been one of the first white men since La Vérendrye to see the Mandans. By 1793, he had moved to Spanish Illinois and switched his allegiance.

The Spaniards had need of him. By the early 1790s, British visits to the Mandans were becoming frequent and even regular. In 1793 René Jusseaume, a hardened, tough, wily, illiterate but highly skilful operator, took some free traders to them, with goods supplied by the North West Company. Though two men were killed by Sioux on the way back, Big John McDonnell sent nine

Norwesters there within months. North West posts at the mouth of the Souris River on the Assiniboine, and a little further up the latter river at Rivière-Tremblante, together with the Hudson's Bay Company's post at Brandon House nearby, soon became bases for the trade. Late in 1794, Jusseaume, now in the service of the North West Company, not only took goods to the Mandans; he built a small fort there and instructed his *engagés* to fly the Union Jack once a week — in Spanish territory. Jacques d'Eglise had first reported the British presence in 1792 and had thrown the Spaniards into a burst of passionate energy: the creation of their Missouri Company. When the same man brought news of the British fort among the Mandans in 1795, there was another spasm. The Missouri Company organized the most massive expedition Spain ever sent up the Missouri and appointed James McKay to command it.

Their alarm was in part the product of a geography as mythical as those Byzantine tribes of white Indians along the Great River of the West. For they feared not only a British blockade of the route to the Pacific; they were afraid that the British would attack Santa Fe from Canada. The airline distance from Winnipeg to Santa Fe is 1,100 miles; a militarily feasible route would be several hundred miles longer. Moreover, they thought the British would be able to go most of the way by water. To our minds, in which North America is plotted out as neatly as any land-surveyor's plat, this is lunacy. But as so often in the history of Spain, the Spanish illusion was simply an extreme example of a general predicament.

No one has yet gone up the Missouri beyond the river of the Sioux, reported Governor-General Miró from New Orleans in 1785, but the Arikara say that two hundred leagues beyond their villages is a large cascade which falls over a high mountain they call *La Montaña que Canta*, the Mountain-which-Sings ...

It is necessary to bear in mind that the chain of mountains that starts from Santa Fe, a little to the east of it and which goes to the province of Quivira [Kansas], according to report, forms the high land between New Mexico and this region. Many of the rivers that rise to the east of these mountains empty into the Arkansas River, of which I spoke above, and the greater number into the Missouri. Those that rise to the west flow into the River of the North or Bravo [Rio Grande] which, your Excellency knows, empties into the Gulf of Mexico. The Missouri cuts this chain of mountains to the north of the source of the aforesaid River Bravo, verging towards the west, a quadrant to the north-west and according to all signs, this is the region where the cataract or cascade is formed, of which the Arikaras speak. And passing these mountains, it should flow as far as the other chain of mountains which passes between the Colorado River and the province of Teguayo [an area placed near the Pacific at this date].

The rivers to the east of this mountain to the north of Teguayo must empty into the Missouri which, as it seems, has its source here, because to

15

the west of these mountains, the Sea or Bay of the West [Pacific] almost washes its base . . .

In this extraordinary *mélange* (the Spaniards at New Orleans did not know that their compatriots in Santa Fe had learned about the eastern slopes of the Rockies) the American west is made into a relatively small country. All the major rivers symmetrically rise from a single mountain chain, running north-south about 500 miles beyond the Arikara. The source of the Missouri is not far from Santa Fe and indeed within striking distance of the Pacific. This picture was confirmed when Vial got through to St Louis from Santa Fe in 1792 and claimed that, had the Kansas not captured him, he would have done the trip in twenty-five days (he would have been extraordinarily lucky if he'd done it in fifty). In this geographical balance, the Missouri is placed much further south than it actually is and New Mexico is thrust much closer to it than the Almighty had intended. Hence the rooted fear that British traders on the Missouri spelled a deadly threat to the wealth of New and indeed old Mexico.

European geographical theory was symmetrical, never more so than in the century of Mozart. Every watershed was thought to have rivers running to the four points of the compass, and by the eighteenth century it was understood that there had to be 'a height of land' somewhere to the west of known American territories. The dream of a north-west passage linking Atlantic and Pacific persisted. Now it took varied forms: a mingling of east and west flowing rivers; or an inland sea, the Sea of the West, which somehow gave on to the Pacific; or a strait curving in from the South Sea — the Strait of Anian or of Juan de Fuca; or a Great River of the West, an Oregon. As knowledge was patchily accumulated, it was fitted together, sometimes in sheer fantasy, more often with the eye of logical and symmetrical theory; there was a Great River of the West because there had to be one. The picture gradually built up through the reports of traders and travellers, and the essays of thinkers — the Jesuit Charlevoix, Bossu, Daniel Coxe, Jonathan Carver.

What was absent from this thinking were the Rocky Mountains. Although they had been touched on by a number of people, their real character as massive chains of mountain ranges was not conceived. La Vérendrye had seen the Turtle Hills of North Dakota in his day and had noted that many of them shone by night and day. These Shining Mountains became the 'height of land'. But they were only a hand's span. And they had to be the source of the major rivers of the continent. It was a rooted belief that the sources of the Mississippi and the Missouri were close to each other. All the other great rivers — the Arkansas, the Red River of the South, the Rio Grande — had to rise in the same chain, and were so located in book after book as information, guesswork and fantasy came in to be subjected to theory. The Colorado was thought to run south-west, evidently from the same watershed. Gradually the Inland Sea began to yield to that Great River of the West which was thought to exist in parallel, though it survived for a long time as a lake linked to that river. It was in 1765 that the partisan leader Robert Rogers projected a route to the Pacific via the Great Lakes and the head of the Mississippi 'and from thence to the River called by the Indians Ouragan' which flowed into the Pacific. Seven years later, after more hard experience and after learning from his lieutenant Jonathan Carver, Rogers modified the scheme. The plan now was to go up the Minnesota, cross a twenty-mile portage to the Missouri, go up that river to its source and then take a thirty-mile portage to the Oregon which ran to the Strait of Anian.

Through most of the century, the distance across the watershed remained short; Jefferson still thought it was 'one day's portage' in 1803; Daniel Coxe had made it half a day. The work of the British explorers injected a little more realism into the concepts of distance, but the classic expression of their thinking — Jonathan Carver's *Travels* of 1778, building on the labours of the French and his own experiences — still retained the traditional view, although in more sophisticated form. Though the span from them to the Pacific was now wider, the Shining Mountains still stretched their single-chain length from north to south, with the Mississippi, Minnesota and Missouri rising within easy reach of each other, a Bourbon river running north, a Colorado running south-west and an Oregon running due west to the Pacific near the Strait of Anian. New Mexico was once again close up to the watershed and the portage across the latter from Missouri to Oregon was still short.

The Spaniards were working to an older knowledge, in which distances were shorter and more frightening still. But most maps had Indians called Padoucas (which was what the French called the Comanches) scattered across the area, sometimes confused with the Pawnees; and, of course, at the strategic centre, those Padoucas were white. For the British to be among those Mandans who clearly *were* the White Padoucas, thus spelled doom for Santa Fe and for the silver empire of Mexico below.

But this was simply one threat among many, for the vast but thinly held Louisiana of the Spaniards, to them essentially a defence zone for the Mexicos, was circled by a great arc of menace.

One storm-centre was the south-east, within striking distance of New Orleans and the Floridas. At the peace of 1783, the British had ceded the Floridas to the Spaniards, with the northern frontier of West Florida fixed at the juncture of the Mississippi and Yazoo rivers on the 32° 26' parallel. In its peace treaty with the Americans, however, Britain had established the southern frontier of the new republic at the 31° line. The disputed zone included Natchez, which was full of Protestant British-American Loyalists who preferred Spanish sovereignty to American. With population building up rapidly in the raw frontier state of Georgia, and in the turbulent settlements along the Holston and the Cumberland rivers, the whole area became a jungle of plots and counter-plots. Thrusting frontier speculators and empire-builders like William Blount, James O'Fallon and John Sevier launched land speculation schemes at Muscle Shoals, Chickasaw Bluffs and Yazoo,

17

dreamed of attacks on New Orleans and of British aid. The Spaniards rallied the Indian tribes, notably the Creeks, under Alexander McGillivray, the son of a Scottish Loyalist and a Creek woman, a chief who lived high like a planter on his estate, a Freemason of sophisticated tastes with an Indian wife and a susceptibility to manic and homicidal rages. Behind him was the Scottish Loyalist fur-trading firm of Panton, Leslie and Company, based in Florida, with their Spanish licence and British goods, buttressing Creeks, Chickasaws. Choctaws and even Cherokees, and periodically turning the Indians loose on the Georgians, the Cumberland and even the Kentucky settlers. Against them, the British firm of Miller and Bonnamy in the Bahamas with the support of Lord Dunmore, conjured up 'General' William Augustus Bowles, the handsome and dramatic Irishman who waged a long guerrilla against Spain as a rival Creek chief and tried to exploit the Nootka Sound crisis. Across this troubled scene flitted shadowy British and French agents and adventurers of infinite variety; until the Pinckney Treaty of 1795 settled the borders in favour of the Americans, this southern frontier was a cauldron.

Further north, in buoyant Kentucky and what became Tennessee, navigation of the Mississippi, stopped by Spain, was the critical issue. The western settlers, multiplying alarmingly, needed the river and New Orleans, for their natural outlet was the Caribbean, the American South and Europe. During the negotiations between John Jay and the Spanish emissary Gardoqui in 1786, Congress had shown itself ready to abandon their claim to free navigation of the Mississippi in order to secure the 31° line and a mercantile entry into the Spanish empire. The 'men of the western waters' were incensed and threatened secession. An engaging and plausible Irishman, James Wilkinson, had established himself as a Brigadier-General and a merchant and land speculator in Kentucky. In 1787 he submitted a memorial to the Spaniards offering to engineer Kentucky's secession from the USA and its alignment with Spain, in return for the Mississippi navigation and a personal pension. The Spanish Council of State was cautious, authorizing only a Spanish response to a Kentucky initiative, but they paid Wilkinson a salary of $2,000, and for years Kentucky was riddled with sedition even as the Cherokees fought back against the incoming settlers and the Spaniards directed Shawnees and Lobos against the frontier villages and the Wilderness Trail.

But if the first half-horse, half-alligator Americans in Kentucky could not intrigue their way on to the Mississippi, they could perhaps fight their way there? Scheme after scheme of military conquest was mooted and during the crisis of the French Revolution acquired reality. The already fierce conflict within the USA between Federalists and Republicans assumed a whole new dimension under the impact of the Revolution, and when the flamboyant Citizen Genet, a Girondin, arrived as French representative, large crowds greeted him everywhere and Democratic Societies of revolutionary temper mushroomed so rapidly that George Washington feared for his head. Genet

18

issued licences for privateers wholesale and unofficial sea war broke out between America and Britain, which was already being denounced for its commercial stranglehold and its refusal to give up its posts in that north-west which had formally been ceded to the USA. Moreover, Genet mobilized an 'army of the French republic' in the West to attack Louisiana under the command of the frontier hero George Rogers Clark now lapsing into alcoholic incoherence. Through 1793 and into 1794, the Spanish authorities in St Louis went into another paroxysm of alarm as reports came in of American freebooters massing in Kentucky. Hardly less alarming was the news of a strong federal army mobilizing along the Ohio to avenge the shattering defeat which the American general St Clair had suffered at the hands of the Ohio Indians late in 1791.

For the old north-west was another jungle. The British refused to give up their posts in that vast territory north-west of the Ohio which had legally become part of the new USA, citing as their reason the American failure to compensate dispossessed Loyalists. Those posts protected the fur trade fiefs of the Canada merchants and the Six Nations of the Iroquois under their remarkable chief (another half-Scot) Joseph Brant, who could rally Indian nations further west. Even as Major Beckwith tried, with some success, to organize a British party within the American government and pored over cabinet secrets slipped to him by Alexander Hamilton, the Ohio lands became another cauldron. The Indians, with covert British support, inflicted a catastrophic defeat on the American army in 1791 which, like an early Custer Massacre, turned all the tribes aggressive and insolent.

By 1794 a regular war fever against Britain had built up in America, fuelled by the passionate internal conflict. To stop the rot, Washington and the Federalists took the desperate decision to come to terms with the British through their emissary John Jay. The struggle to ratify the Jay Treaty during 1794-5 rocked the republic, but a revulsion of popular feeling against the French Revolution, with the English expatriate William Cobbett helping to create an American Tory press (and a gutter press in the process), carried the Federalists through into a phase of conservative reaction, the Alien and Sedition Acts against American radicals and the distinctive *Jacobins* immigration from Britain, Ireland and France. There was a violent swing into a war-fever against France. The Jay Treaty recognized America's dependence on British commerce, but finally forced the British to evacuate the north-west posts. A decisive sector of the fur trade passed into American power, carrying it deep into the west, and the Indians, abandoned by the British, were demolished at the battle of Fallen Timbers in 1794 by the federal army under Anthony Wayne. At the Greenville peace talks of 1795-6, the Indians of the old north-west began to pass out of history. Once again, St Louis was shaken with alarm.

And west of the Ohio and the Wabash and the Illinois, report after report spoke of the British fur trade, superior in its skills, its organization and its goods, pressing down into Spanish territory beyond the Mississippi, along the Des Moines and Minnesota rivers, taking command of the terrible Sioux, penetrating among the Omahas, the Otos, the Poncas, tribes which had been formally allotted to the cosy collective of St Louis merchants, and even reaching the Osages, those imperial Osages who posed a permanent threat to St Louis from the west. Outflanking them all, finally, were the Canada traders moving into the Mandans and driving for the Pacific.

After the Nootka Sound confrontation of 1790, Spanish Louisiana moved through crisis after crisis, through the war against atheist and republican France in unnatural alliance with Britain in 1793, a war which unsettled its predominantly French inhabitants, screwed St Louis into permanent alert and brought the most dismal news from Europe; through the temporary settlement with the USA in the Pinckney Treaty of 1795, when Spain lurched out of the war in disarray; and into the renewal of war in 1796, this time as an ally of France against the traditional English enemy. American turbulence, the endless British pressure, and the strain of maintaining an empire with hopelessly inadequate resources ran as a permanent descant to this general disharmony, all the way through to the final solution in 1800-1803, when Napoleon took back Louisiana and sold the continent to the Americans.

The Spanish response to this permanent crisis could be called futile or heroic according to taste; quixotic perhaps?

At the end of 1791 Hector, baron de Carondelet, took over the governorship of Louisiana. A French-speaking Fleming who was related by marriage to the celebrated colonial family of Las Casas, Carondelet had been transferred from San Salvador, had no experience of America and no English. American historians generally find him 'unrealistic'. He was a fighter. When he heard in 1794 that one Elijah Clarke of Georgia was planning an attack on the Floridas, he had to be physically restrained from leading an expedition personally into the wilderness. He had precious little to fight with. In letter after letter, he bombarded the home government with requests for arms, troops and money, and drove his subordinates into direct and aggressive action.

His agents moved resolutely into the south-eastern tribes. General Bowles, returning from London with ambitious schemes after his Nootka trip, was captured, the Creeks were regained, Indians persuaded to break their treaties with the USA. For the first time, Spanish influence penetrated the Cherokees in depth. Carondelet organized a great assembly of the southern tribes and Indian war once again ravaged the frontiers. Settlers and federal government responded in kind. When George Rogers Clark began to mobilize his French republican army in Kentucky, Carondelet massed his gunboats, ordered St Louis to set up a raiding base at Cap Girardeau and re-activated the Wilkinson conspiracy, entering into negotiations with a Secret Committee of the West and manipulating customs dues on the Mississippi to win support.

On the far frontiers he was no less aggressive, although he was shrewd in his discrimination. The St Louis officers were told not to tackle British and

Americans simultaneously, but to play one off against the other. Inducements to migrate were to be offered to traders and settlers, but no British or American Indian merchants were to be allowed past the Mississippi. When the perennially troublesome Osage Indians turned nasty, Carondelet proposed to mobilize friendly Indians to wipe them out. He responded enthusiastically to the formation of the Missouri Company and to the grandiose imperial vision of the adventurer Jacques Clamorgan; he argued their case strongly to the home government and dispatched one of the strongest fleets Spain ever sent up the Mississippi to support these plans, crush *Jacobins* and destroy British forts. It was the decision of the government in Spain to quit the war, rally to the French and cede to the Americans which undercut him. After the Pinckney Treaty of 1795 he became increasingly an anachronism, and in 1797 he was replaced by the more supple and conciliatory Gayoso de Lemos.

Throughout Carondelet's time in office, therefore, Louisiana lived in permanent crisis. Nowhere was that crisis more tangible than in the capital of Upper Louisiana, the little frontier outpost of St Louis, *San Luis de Ylinoia*.

St Louis and its cluster of dependent settlements rose like a knife-edged reef out of a sea of perils. The townships were tiny. In 1798 St Louis itself had less than 1,000 people — mostly French — dominated by the Chouteau family which had created it. Despite its turbulence and exposure, Auguste and Pierre Chouteau had imposed a measured style and a quasi-aristocratic ambience on the place; the trade of the Osages and nearby tribes was ritually allotted in annual shares. St Louis lived by that trade. 'It has very few farmers', reported Lieutenant-Governor Trudeau in 1798, 'and those who follow that calling cultivate blindly without the least knowledge except what custom teaches . . .' If only Americans were more law-abiding, how welcome they would be as immigrants!

The only successful centre of immigration was New Madrid, a hundred miles south of St Louis below the junction of the Ohio and Mississippi, and a sub-delegacy of its own. It had been created in 1789, with Spanish permission, by Colonel George Morgan, who had served with both George Rogers Clark and the celebrated Irish soldier, Governor O'Reilly, who had imposed Spanish authority on Louisiana after its transfer from France. Morgan's settlement on the west bank of the Mississippi was full of Americans; over 340 newcomers took the oath of allegiance there between 1791 and 1796 but thereafter the inflow dried up. With less than 600 inhabitants in 1798, it was a natural centre for the infiltration of undesirables, but was also well placed as an observation post against the Americans. Carondelet wanted to station the galleys there.

The other settlements were even smaller and rigidly controlled by their commandants. St Geneviève was halfway between New Madrid and St Louis, often flooded and nicknamed *La Miseria*, was the Nob Hill of Upper Louisiana; 'numerous and notable families' lived there closely interlocked by marriage, a small universe of cousins in a population of less than 600. A

21

couple of miles away was an offshoot, Nueva Borbon (Nouveau Bourbon), created originally for a hundred French Catholics, aristocratic refugees from the Revolution and survivors of the disastrous Scioto fraud on the American Ohio. They persisted in planting the lowlands despite floods which lost them two harvests out of five and despite the example of the Americans who were moving in.

Between St Geneviève and New Madrid was an even newer settlement at Cap Girardeau, created for strategic reasons. Louis Lorimier, a French trader and part-time spy, had become heavily involved with the Shawnee, Cherokee and Lobo Indians, settling many who fled from the land-hungry Americans on the western side of the Mississippi. He was allowed to bring over about thirty American families and start planting them out in the beautiful and fertile but empty country at the Cape and inland around the San Francisco river. Lorimier, who was commandant of Cap Girardeau but at daggers drawn with commandant Thomas Portell in New Madrid, found it difficult; in their raids and their endless wars with other tribes, the Osages kept the whites pinned to the river.

The Osages were no less active in the immediate vicinity of St Louis, shooting men, kidnapping women and stealing horses in the outskirts. They had depopulated the Maramec valley and threatened the mines at Las Salinas. They pressed hard on a handful of settlements which had sprung up around the capital: a village named after Carondelet, a few miles down river, with a couple of hundred poor Creoles and French; San Fernando and Marais des Liards (Cottonwood Swamp) a score of miles west, where the men were hard workers and good hunters (they needed an Irish priest, said Trudeau) and San Carlos (St Charles) a little to the north, which looked more hopeful.

This cluster of habitations, with less than 3,500 people, ringed by powerful and troublesome Indian nations to the west and north, among whom British trade and British influence were penetrating deeply, confronting large and restless American populations across the river, was the target for hostile immigration schemes and empire-building enemies. It was no less the lynch-pin of imaginative imperial plans concocted by adventurous newcomers and belligerent officials down in New Orleans, many arduous weeks away. The very hinge of western destiny, the Gateway City was earning its Arch long before it even became American.

In July 1792 Carondelet appointed Don Zenon Trudeau as Lieutenant-Governor to command this harassed community and to walk the knife-edge. It is difficult not to sympathize with this man, for Spain in North America was fortunate in her last servants. A Franco-Spanish officer of the old school, Trudeau was honest, painstaking and impeccably correct. He proclaimed free trade at once and cleaned out corruption. He was punctilious in the performance of his duties, running the town well, maintaining good relations with the Church (and improving its tone), urging better cultivation on the settlers, fighting down his anger and contempt to deal with what must have seemed to him an infinity of treacherous and bloody-minded Indians, warding off threats from all quarters, looking for immigrants who would not be subversive, and paying warm courtesy visits to Judge Turner the American justice for the new north-west whenever he came up in his official barge to Kaskaskia and Cahokia across the river. Intelligent, perceptive and hard-working, Trudeau impressed men who could judge other men (the Scotsman James McKay named his eldest son after him). But while he was acutely aware of immediate realities, he lacked imagination, and his endless crises ground him down into an ineradicable pessimism. It is easy to see why; he had to face a mortal crisis practically every month.

No sooner had he established free trade and issued permits for seventeen merchants with their 115 *engagés* to go up river to the tribes, than the Osages and the Iowas cut loose on more of their endless raids, and Jacques d'Eglise came in with his startling news of the Mandans and of British penetration to them. This British menace became a permanent theme in Trudeau's correspondence with Carondelet. 'We are not able to trade with the Indians of the Mississippi,' he reported in November 1792. 'This year, it is full of Englishmen from Michilimackinac. At least 150 canoes from there each loaded with two to three thousand pesos worth of merchandise . . .' Entrenched on the Des Moines and the Minnesota, the British were sending goods, medals, banners and rich presents through all the tribes, right down to the Lower Missouri nations, Otos, Omahas and Pawnees. Despite the wars between the Osages and the Sauk and Fox nations, the British were getting through to the former. News of the American defeat in 1791 had turned all the tribes tough. Not only were the ferocious Sioux, committed to the British, ranging the Missouri; Black Bird, a chief of the Omaha, had built himself up by his medicine into a power among the lower tribes and was ordering them to stop the Spaniards.

Jacques d'Eglise, whose report on the Mandans had thrown St Louis into excitement and alarm, tried to reach them again in 1793 and was stopped by the Sioux blockade. Trudeau had learned nothing more of the Mandans by the May of that year, but was hoping to get information from an experienced Canadian *mozo*, who must have been James McKay. In that same month, he submitted a highly intelligent and penetrating report on British superiority to Carondelet. The answer was clear — more and better goods, more and better traders, support, more support. But from where was Spain now to dredge up that support?

By that spring, however, Trudeau's mind had been wrenched back nearer home, for the Osage threat suddenly erupted into something approaching full-scale war. The powerful Osage nation, to the west of St Louis, was credited by the Spaniards with 1,300 warriors. Together with their neighbours, the Little Osages, they killed and pillaged up to the very doors of government house in St Louis, and plagued the lesser tribes, many of whom were refugees from the Americans who had sought Spanish protection. After one raid in

January 1793, their chiefs, whom Trudeau thought appalling hypocrites, came into St Louis weeping, blaming their young men, and bringing back their Spanish medals. At that moment, a couple of hundred men of the Sauk, Fox, Kickapoo, Mascouten and other nations were in town. They surrounded the Osages in their quarters and threatened to kill them. Trudeau managed to smuggle them out to a nearby loft, but for ten days he had personally to stand guard over the door, pleading with the Indians for hours without a break. In the end, he got the chiefs drunk on brandy and smuggled their intended victims out by night.

The Chouteaus had the trade of the Osages; they had to be pacified, which infuriated not only the other tribes but also the settlers who were being driven from their lands. The response from Carondelet in New Orleans was characteristic. Build forts on the Des Moines and Minnesota at once, he ordered; garrison them and throw the English out. Mobilize the Indians against the Osages, cut off all trade with them and suspend all free trade to make sure. By August he was calling for massed Indian raids to hit the impregnable Osage village to wipe it out as its braves were returning piecemeal from the summer nunt. And what about those Mandans?

Trudeau was at his wits' end. News of the proposed war on the Osages leaked out and there was a dreadful fear that the merchants who were already on their travels would be massacred. Lorimier had gathered numbers of Indians at Cap Girardeau, but they would not move without white support and St Louis could not spare even twenty men from its garrison of fifty. By the autumn, the war plan was abandoned and in the following year the Chouteaus' offer to build and garrison their own fort among the Osages and to keep them happy was gratefully accepted.

But by this time the St Louis merchants were in full revolt against the suspension of free trade, and in October 1793, in a concerted move, they presented petitions to Trudeau calling for a re-organization of trade, the distribution of the tribes by lot and the election of a new syndic of merchants. Furthermore they called attention to the Mandans, and to the imperative need to create a Company for the Discovery of the Nations of the Upper Missouri. Their plan was breathtaking in its imperial scope; from the careful and prudent merchants of St Louis it was quite startling in its audacity. For the plan, of course, was not theirs. It originated in the man they now elected as their syndic, Jacques Clamorgan. This was the man who was to prove the driving force behind Spain's last imperial enterprise in North America. He was Trudeau's opposite in almost every respect: as the situation got worse, his plans got bolder.

Clamorgan was an outsider. He had come to the Illinois in the 1780s and had contacts with Canada; he had traded with Pierre Lacoste at Michilimackinac. He bought property in St Louis in 1784 and worked for Gabriel Cerré. He had a vaulting imagination and ambition to match. His plans, if they had been carried into effect, would have wrenched the

24

continental fur trade into Spanish hands. The key to the necessary but absent resources was Canada. He was probably alive to that possibility as early as 1793; by 1794, he was certainly aware of the choice which the Jay Treaty, clearing out the British from the American north-west, would force on the Canadians. By that year, he was already in contact with the great Canadian firm of Todd and McGill. But his schemes could be unfolded to the St Louis merchants only in stages; they took fright too easily. Trudeau, who had reluctantly to support him, was soon disconcerted and it was on Governor Carondelet that Clamorgan came to rely.

Like the more famous Manuel Lisa after him, Clamorgan blazed through the world of St Louis like a comet. In the tight little universe of the Chouteaus, he was, to quote one commentator, a man who 'had been, among other things, a slave trader in the West Indies, merchant, land speculator, explorer, keeper of a negro harem, church warden and bachelor father of four children . . .' By the end of his time in St Louis, he was vainly claiming a million arpents of land which he said had been promised him. After Louisiana passed to the USA, he served briefly as a judge, and a petition to Congress on his behalf called him, with some justice, a precursor of Lewis and Clark. He ended his days obscurely in Mexico, a remarkable man who, like several other remarkable men, have faded from history in the darkening twilight of Spanish North America.

Who was he? The name Clamorgan is unique and would be strange in any language. Any language, that is, other than Welsh. It is so similar to Glamorgan, a county in south Wales with ancient roots (*Morgannwg*, *Gwlad Morgan*, Morgan's land) that it sounds like a pseudonym. Indeed, in the Spanish records, it is sometimes written Clan-Morgan and even Llan-Morgan, which sounds even more Welsh! Trudeau at times simply called him Morgan and his name appears to have been Charles Morgan. He seems to have originated in the West Indies, and was sometimes called a Portuguese. Perhaps he had lived or been born in a Portuguese possession. The best and most common guess is that he was a West Indian of Welsh descent.

Through the winter and into the spring of 1794, he was busy dragging the St Louis merchants after him into the proposed Missouri Company, preparing an exploratory expedition up the Missouri, and pressing on Carondelet a scheme to transplant 6,000 German and Dutch Catholics from the USA into Louisiana. He ran into trouble at once. The merchants wanted the Lower Missouri tribes parcelled out as usual; Jean Munier claimed to have discovered the Poncas and wanted their trade. In 1794 Jacques d'Eglise demanded a monopoly of the trade with those Mandans whom he had first reached. The Chouteaus viewed the dramatic Missouri Company with alarm and Trudeau himself was soon worried.

Trudeau, in any case, was never able to stop worrying. The Osage war had faded, only to be replaced by the threat of the French mission of André Michaux. Although Britain and Spain were now allies against France (though they did not know this at St Louis until April 1794) the Canadian traders were soon back north of the Missouri and west of the Mississippi. And early in 1794 urgent messages came through from Carondelet, reporting that George Rogers Clark was massing his 'French' army in Kentucky, while Anthony Wayne was mobilizing federal forces for the great campaign beyond the Ohio Carondelet was sending the galleys to New Madrid and he demanded action.

Drained of resources, Trudeau could do nothing but call on Lorimier and his Indians at Cap Girardeau. Through the early months of 1794, Lorimier lived a situation at the Cape which bordered on the fantastic. The summons from the Spanish Father to his Children went out to six tribes; the objective was a pre-emptive strike at the Americans with 2,000 Cherokees, Mascoutens and Lobos, backed by the New Madrid gunboats. The Children proved an unruly bunch, fighting among themselves, stealing Lorimier's whisky and prone to panic. When Lorimier had got 300 together and was feeding them with the utmost difficulty, he took them, with his thirteen-year-old son, to the mouth of the Ohio and started raiding American settlements.

But the enemy was waging skilful psychological warfare, threatening that the French of Louisiana would join the Americans and kill all the women and children left behind; they offered a prize for Lorimier's head. During May and June, pleading orders from their Great Chief at Detroit (who was British), the Indians decamped en masse and thronged the streets of St Louis. 'How is it possible for us to be steadfast and tranquil?' said Pacane, chief of the Miami, to Lorimier. 'If there were none of these merchants who are babblers like evil birds, we would go where it pleases us to go.'

Fortunately, spies in Kaskaskia reported that the French army project of George Rogers Clark was collapsing and Lorimier was strictly ordered not to harass the American Judge Turner as he passed upstream in October, with fourteen soldiers and eighteen crewmen, in a barge flying its American flag and blowing its bugles. Those bugles, however, heralded the next, inevitable crisis. The American victory over the Ohio Indians at Fallen Timbers and the Jay Treaty threatened to shift the balance of power on the Spanish frontier. The British were pressing down on the tribes harder than ever, despite the wartime alliance. And Clamorgan, angered by the resistance he was encountering, drove forward with renewed energy. He denounced the claims of Munier and d'Eglise, bombarded New Orleans with projects and, with Trudeau trailing luke-warm behind, won the ear of Carondelet.

On 5 May 1794 the Missouri Company was formally instituted, with Clamorgan as Director and he and Antoine Reihle as the leading members. Trudeau joined to give it official sanction, but there were only nine shareholders. Most St Louis merchants held aloof, following the lead of the Chouteaus; the lower tribes were distributed by lot as usual and the company had to restrict its operations to the largely unknown land north of the Poncas, though it was promised a ten-year monopoly. But Carondelet enthusiastically rallied and offered an official reward of 2,000 pesos (later raised to 3,000) to the first Spanish subject to reach the Pacific; a certificate in Russian from the

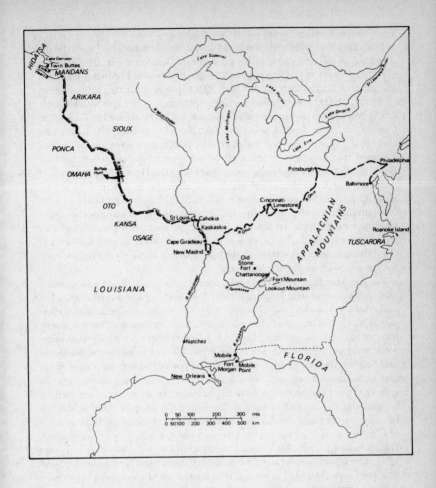

Madoc's America and John Evans's Journey, 1793-1797

Tsar's coastal settlements would be acceptable as proof.

It was precisely this ambition that Clamorgan cherished. By June 1794 the planning of the first phase of his great project was complete. The first two expeditions were in fact two stages of a single movement. The first consisted of one pirogue loaded with goods worth 30,000 pesos, supported by another as escort with 6,000 pesos. It was a small group, the men's wages totalling only 8,000 pesos, and its purpose was essentially a reconnaissance. To lead it, Clamorgan chose Jean Baptiste Truteau, the schoolmaster of St Louis, who had some experience of the fur trade. His instructions were precise. It was assumed that he might be harassed by the Lower Missouri tribes, because Black Bird of the Omahas was running amok again. He was to avoid them, if possible, but if he were held up in any way, he was to send an urgent message back to St Louis, because by 15 April 1795 the second boat was to go out without fail, under one Lecuyer. This was to be the substantive expedition heading for the Pacific. Its big boat, as well as the usual presents for intervening tribes, was to carry 25,000 pesos' worth of goods; it would drop off some men at the Arikara, and then go through the base which Truteau should by that time have established among the Mandans.

For the Mandans were Truteau's objective. He was to build a fort among them, with several large buildings (precise details were laid down), make a full survey of the Missouri and its people, keep the Indians simple, and levy what prices he chose. Above all, however, he had to find out how far the Rocky Mountains were from the Mandans, whether there were rivers running west, whether there was a Sea of the West. He was to locate the Shoshone and Snake nations and impress upon all the power and benevolence of Spain and its Missouri Company. This was a full imperial programme, but its controversial beginning was reflected in orders to stop any others trading beyond the Poncas and to keep a close watch on Jacques d'Eglise and his brawling *engagé* Garreau who was reported to have offended the Indians.

D'Eglise in fact set out independently once again and took Clamorgan's Instructions with him, for Truteau had actually left with eight men on 7 June 1794. The schoolmaster ran into a prolonged nightmare. He managed to steal past the Lower Missouri tribes and after sixteen weeks was hoping to meet the Arikara near the Grand Detour. In fact, afraid of the Sioux, the Arikara had shifted upstream and it was the Sioux whom Truteau ran into. At first they were Yanktons who knew Truteau and were reasonably friendly, but almost at once Teton Sioux arrived and they were traditional. They spat on the Spanish Father, terrorized his men and pillaged his goods, which were in any case too few for his mission. Only the presence of the Yanktons prevented a massacre. Truteau managed to get away, cached his goods and went looking for the Arikara on foot. When they could not be found, his men, with winter fast settling in, panicked. Truteau picked up his goods and moved down river, looking for a safe place between the Sioux and the lower tribes. He thought he'd found it, but the Omaha came upon him. The blackmail started again, to be turned into sheer extortion when the wily Black Bird arrived, to fix himself in the Frenchman's mind as the worst scoundrel he'd ever met. Black Bird worked up a rage over the St Louis attempt to bypass him. When Truteau finally got away to the Poncas, who had just stripped Munier, Black Bird sent them word that the Frenchman meant to poison them. The Poncas had begun their death dance before Truteau managed to calm them.

Eventually, in the spring of 1795, he managed to reach the Arikara, who were genial but just as stubborn. D'Eglise, who had passed him early on and had given him some help, was stuck there too. Persistent to the last, Truteau managed to send messages on to the Mandans and, in Arikara company, met some Cheyennes and got some information. The original plan, however, was failing miserably. The boat he sent back to St Louis was threadbare.

Worse was to follow. For the Lecuyer expedition, sent out like clockwork in April 1795, was a total disaster. It reached the Poncas but was promptly pillaged without mercy. Lecuyer himself seems to have joined in, taking two Indian wives in a couple of weeks. News of the collapse reached St Louis quickly, for Clamorgan at once sent out another boat under Antoine Breda to try to save the day. It was too late. The Missouri was littered with the debris of the first major Spanish enterprise; the Sioux and Arikara blockade was intact and the Lower Missouri tribes were arrogant, spoiling for more trouble.

The first news of the disaster reached St Louis in June 1795. Trudeau, already facing a resurgence of the Osage troubles and more threats from the British and Americans, was appalled. His 2,000 pesos' contribution to the company had been borrowed from Auguste Chouteau; how would he ever pay it back? The shareholders were plunged into gloom. The very next month, Jacques d'Eglise came home. He reported more fully on the company's losses. Not only that, he brought with him two deserters from the Canadian companies who told the Spaniards of the British fort which René Jusseaume had just built among the Mandans.

The Missouri Company shuddered into crisis, for Jacques Clamorgan, unabashed, promptly proposed a third expedition, twice as powerful as the others and vastly more ambitious. He devised even more optimistic projects: an alliance with Canadian merchants, an inflow of Canadian goods and traders, the building of a chain of forts from St Louis to the Pacific, gunboats to go up the Missouri to drive the British out. The bulk of the shareholders recoiled in horror. So did Trudeau, who resigned with them, denounced Clamorgan as a megalomaniac to Carondelet and transferred his fragile hopes to Jacques d'Eglise. Undeterred, Clamorgan won Carondelet's support and, ultimately, that of the Spanish Council of State. In August 1795 he sent off up the Missouri the greatest expedition of them all, under the redoubtable James McKay.

And with the Scotsman, as his deputy sailed another of those remarkable men whom Spain succeeded in enlisting in its last days in North America. A newcomer, this was the man whom McKay personally chose to make the final thrust for the Pacific. When he had first appeared in St Louis during the previous winter, however, this man must have seemed to Trudeau (a hard-working camel if there ever was one) the last straw sent to break his back.

For in the midst of all his other troubles in the winter of 1794, Trudeau had been confronted with an apparition. Around Christmas, a complete stranger had suddenly appeared in the streets of St Louis. A British subject, he had crossed the icy Mississippi from the American side in the dead of winter. His manner, his language and his mission were so outlandish that the town officers immediately arrested him as a British spy, clapped him in the stocks and threw him into prison.

In so far as he could be understood, for he spoke no French, the stranger said that his name was John Evans and that he was a Welshman. He said, further, that he had come to St Louis to find a companion to accompany him up the Missouri. He was going to make contact with that celebrated and powerful tribe of Welsh Indians who lived on its upper reaches. Those Indians, he said, were descendants of a Welsh colony which had been established six centuries earlier on the shores of the Gulf of Mexico. He stated, finally, that the colony had been set up by followers of a Welsh prince, Madoc, who had discovered America in the year 1170, three hundred years before Columbus.

3

Imperial Madoc

The story of Madoc, says Bernard de Voto, 'became by far the most widespread legend of pre-Columban discovery. In the United States, it became our most elaborate historical myth and exercised a direct influence on our history.'

De Voto, who was an idiosyncratic but superbly evocative historian of the American continent and himself a master of geo-political mythology, cites in explanation the Celtic character of the Welsh people.

> It is a race for whom the insubstantial world has always been more real than the visible one, for whom the little people have always shaken their milk-white arms in a ring by moonlight and the towers of Avalon have always glimmered in the sunset — and a people who, though they have always gone forth to battle, have always died.

A thoroughly disconcerted Welshman, whose only memory of milk-white arms shaking in a ring by moonlight is that of pitch-and-toss gamblers during the Depression which snapped the mainspring of his people in their industrial heartland, dispersed half a million of them and precipitated the multiple crises of identity in which they now live, may perhaps be forgiven the suspicion that Bernard de Voto has become hopelessly confused among his Celts. He would, however, recognize some validity in the American's final comment on a people who have 'always fought but always died' as an explanation of that people's susceptibility to myth. It was a functional susceptibility, a condition of survival.

A talented but marginal people, with the former characteristic perhaps a product of the latter, the Welsh, as the English called them, the *Cymry* as they called themselves, emerge into history from the wreck of Roman Britain as self-conscious heirs of the British. As late as the tenth century, their great polemical poem, *Armes Prydein*, focused anti-Saxon minds not on a 'Welsh' but on a 'British' identity. As the British language rapidly evolved into *Cymraeg* (Welsh) during the breaking of 'the Britains' and the making of the island nation, and as two western peninsulas of Britain, inhabited by mixed kindreds developing intensely localized monarchies and

31

a distinctive Christianity out of persistent Romano-British memories (which infuse the later story-cycle of *The Mabinogion*), were marked off by English settlement behind Offa's Dyke, the slowly-forming 'Welsh' fell heir to an already old and developed aristocratic culture which acquired vibrant life in their magnificent Heroic Age poetry, the first 'Welsh' poetry, traditionally attributed to such as Aneirin, Taliesin and Llywarch Hen. It is a hard, mosaic, jewelled tradition, infinitely remote from that 'Celtic Twilight' which later Welshmen tried to live up to after the English invented it. (There are striking parallels among the hill peoples of the Spanish world, particularly in their 'Snowdonia' of an Asturias.) The language and the culture remained dynamic and complex for centuries, concentrated in the poetry but also strong in its prose, folk-tale, romance, learned religious text and chronicle, a beginning in science and medicine. It was as alien domination strengthened that secret, occult, mythic traditions — the 'Merlin' complex, from *Myrddin*, bard and guru to Arthur — themselves grew stronger, just as the very language itself tended to become the half-secret code of a necessarily subversive and marginal freemasonry on the borders and within the bounds of the precocious monarchy of the English lowlands.

For political unity these Welsh signally failed to achieve. Until the discovery of its mineral resources, their country was poor, the better lands easily subjected by 'the landless Saxon pirates', the people cabined in their pastoral and often transhumant uplands. Wales was a country with a hollow heart. The central massif ribbed a sparsely populated mountain polity (for the Welsh were thin on the ground) into intense localisms and finely nuanced particularities — the local *bro* in Welsh is as powerful as the *patria chica* of that other country with a hollow heart, Spain. The open lowlands of the south-east, Gwent and Glamorgan *(Morgannwg)*, running through to the plains of Dyfed (Pembrokeshire) in the south-west were increasingly subject to influence and controls radiating out from the rapidly organized English lands, as was the easier country of the south generally. The avenues of penetration into north and west were much more narrow; the ring bastions of mountains in the north-west, with the granary of Anglesey behind, could shelter and nourish an independent polity in Gwynedd.

The multiple piratical kingdoms, forming and re-forming around four recurrent dynastic groupings and occasionally throwing up an overlord reminiscent of the High Kings of Ireland, achieved a certain social coherence, fairly sophisticated codes of law and highly complex poetic disciplines which nurtured shadowy guilds of lawmen, remembrancers and poets — poets who were 'bards' because they had specific social and political functions and recognized duties in society. That institution which was 'remembered' and revived as the *eisteddfod* — the only 'national institution' the Welsh had before the 1880s — a disciplined competitive festival, uniquely Welsh-national in scope, though with many local exemplars, focusing on the arts with a complicated and difficult poetry as its prime 'mystery', served the function of an embryonic national academy. But at no time was this cultural unity translated into political cohesion.

In the age of the Vikings, this polity experienced a crisis of dissolution and legitimacy. Its kings fell subject to the Anglo-Saxon crown even as several princes became quasi-Norsemen themselves, before they were all overwhelmed by the Norman invasion, which tore much of the east and south away into a distinctive and culturally hybrid Welsh March, precipitated in reaction a native attempt to create a miniature Welsh feudal state centred on Gwynedd, produced the first and last native Prince of Wales in Llywelyn ap Gruffydd of Gwynedd in the thirteenth century, and finally subjected the whole country to Edward I — who had to take action against the 'bards', the people's remembrancers.

Kings gave way to princes to lords to gentry as Welsh social structure began to approximate to the English pattern in the colonial centuries, a process punctuated and accelerated by the rebellion of Owain Glyn Dŵr (Glendower) in 1400, the first visibly 'national' rising which, like all such struggles in such countries, was also a civil war. From colonialism, the Welsh were liberated by the accession of the Tudors, part-Welsh in descent and widely regarded as Welsh. Hailed in Wales as a Welsh *revanche* (it was not for nothing that Henry VII unfurled the Dragon at Bosworth and called his son Arthur) the Tudor century witnessed the first of the recurrent Welsh explosions into English society, an administrative rationalization and integration of Wales into the English shire and gentry system, an enriching of economic and cultural life, and the advent of the Protestant Welsh Bible, even as the old language stammered before the Renaissance and increasingly fell victim to political discrimination and social scorn. The upheavals of the revolutionary seventeenth century decimated the multitudinous lesser gentry of Wales (itself a product of its rooted kindred structure and critical to a separate identity) and integrated landowners into the broad and flexible oligarchy of the eighteenth century, leaving a few strongholds of Puritan Dissent inching from the borderlands towards the west as nuclei of an alternative society. An ambiguous process of 'anglicization' virtually removed its 'natural' élite from the Welsh world. In this process, the language and the culture associated with it became archaic and remote, and threatened to disintegrate, even as it remained a massive but unrecognized and prestige-less presence in popular life.

The alternative society was born of the eighteenth century population explosion and the war that lasted a generation. The phenomenon which in Welsh history goes under the name of the 'revival' was in fact a complex of contradictory movements: a major evangelical drive for literacy associated with the circulating schools of Griffith Jones, which must have turned a majority of the adult population technically literate in Welsh at least for a time; a Methodist movement whose origins were independent of that in England; rationalist and democratic stirrings within renascent Old Dissent;

33

and an upsurge of interest in Welsh antiquities, literature and language. The population explosion precipitated crisis in rural Wales, enormously accelerated by the pressures of the Revolutionary and Napoleonic Wars as the coal and iron industry stretched into the country striking deep roots in the south-east, and as the first large towns appeared in the Welsh landscape. In little more than two generations, during the nineteenth century, there was a social revolution, a spectacular shift of the centre of population to the industrial south-east and the emergence of a 'nation' (like the Czechs, its spokesmen thought of it as a 're-emergence') which formed along a religious and a language line which was also a class line as most of the people seceded from Establishment, many of them into the Nonconformist sects, and as the whole country, south and east in particular, was more closely integrated into British society and British nationalism: an ambiguous, contradictory, and minority 'nation' which equipped itself with institutions after the advent of democracy in the 1880s, even as there was another explosion of the Welsh into English society.

In such a people with such a history, the question of identity had been ambivalent almost from the beginning. From the days of Asser who spent half his time at the court of Alfred, there were Welshmen who found fulfilment in the wider world even as others assiduously cultivated their *bro*. From the beginning, but particularly at the moments of most intense and abrasive contact with external forces — the emergence of the nations of Britain, the coming of the Normans, the Tudors, the impact of industry — there had been 'explosions' of Welsh people, Welsh ideas and Welsh writing in both languages into those external worlds: the legend cycle which grew from the Welsh Arthur, the fabulous and Arthurian *British History* of Geoffrey of Monmouth, the historical geography and sociology of Gerald the Welshman, the myth of the pure, original British church of which Protestantism was a rebirth.

The Madoc legend seems to fit into this tradition and in this sense, Bernard de Voto's final comment is just. A small and talented people, rarely enjoying parity of esteem and generally treated with contempt, even as their distinctive contribution to the life of a much larger neighbour runs in uneasy harness with an obsession with their own identity, needs even larger myths to redress the balance. In the early middle ages, a chieftain like Emrys, ringed by his 'bawling bards' chanting genealogies and singing praise in intricate word-play, his rule stretching no further than his sword could reach and his stolen gold shower, could call himself Ambrosius Aurelianus and 'wear the purple'; King Arthur and Prince Madoc are recognizable as his spiritual heirs.

It is therefore essential to understand that the story of Madoc first emerged in fact not from this marginality of the Welsh but, on the contrary, from their momentary centrality. It comes straight out of the heartland of buoyant Elizabethan enterprise, from the hub of the first English — or to be

34

more precise and indeed historically accurate — the first British imperialism. Its emergence can be pinpointed. The Madoc story first appears in print in 1583, in a pamphlet *written by an Englishman* to promote a British colonization of America. More generally, it is a product, and a characteristic product, of the climacteric moment of 1576-85 which was to debouch into the launching of the first Virginia colony, in what Dr John Dee, a Welsh intellectual mentor of the enterprise, was the first to call 'The British Empire'.

Dee, like so many others, was the product of a distinctive movement. With the accession of Henry VII, the Venetian ambassador thought the Welsh had recovered their independence. Certainly, there was a striking inflow of Welshmen into all fields of English life. A story current at the Tudor court had St Peter reduced to despair by a sudden influx of Welsh into heaven, driving everyone mad with their incessant talk. He arranged for an angel to stand outside and to shout in a loud voice, *'Caws Pôb!'* (toasted cheese). (Evidently the original Welsh rarebit.) The Welsh thundered out in a stampede after their national delicacy and the gates were slammed behind them, to everyone's intense relief. The influx was influential: the great house of Cecil took its origin from Dafydd Seisyllt, an immigrant adventurer from the borderlands, and there were many other lesser imitators.

The impact was no less marked in the intellectual field. For a Protestant England, particularly under its 'red-headed Welsh harridan' Elizabeth, had to struggle for its Protestantism, for its independent 'empire', and for its place in the sun, in particular against that powerful Counter-Reformation Spain which was monopolizing the newfound lands in America.

Intellectually and emotionally central to this enterprise was the assertion of an aboriginally independent and imperial British identity. The historical roots of this island polity, of necessity, had to be sought in remote ages, in the time of giants when Albion was an empire and its Christianity free from Rome. The mythical history which established Brutus the Trojan as the progenitor of Britain, Joseph of Arimathea as the founder of its independent Christianity and, buried at the same Glastonbury, Arthur of Britain as its great hero, grew under the Tudors to become quasi-official doctrine in the reign of Elizabeth.

The twelfth-century *British History* of Geoffrey of Monmouth, with its Welsh and Breton roots and its gigantic King Arthur straddling the European and much of the extra-European world, appeared at much the same time as the original British and Welsh legends of Arthur were being transmuted into the most celebrated of European story-cycles: under the Tudors it became an ever-extending heartland of patriotic ideology. Similarly the struggle to derive the purity and primacy of Protestantism from an originally impeccable British autonomy, a pre-Constantine insular Christianity enshrined in John Foxe's *Acts and Monuments*, gained power from the struggle of the new clergy in recalcitrant Wales, where people looked on the new order as *ffydd y Saeson* (the English religion). Welsh intellectuals, led by a bishop of St David's, fought an ultimately successful battle by reaching back into Celtic Christianity and its conflict with Roman St Augustine: 'the Pope came late into Wales and that by the sword of the King of England.'

When the *British History* came under attack in the sixteenth century from Polydore Vergil of the Italian school, most Tudor intellectuals rallied passionately to its defence. This was particularly true of men like John Leland and John Bale, practitioners of the new chorography, the detailed and antiquarian study based on geographical surveys which was to culminate in a comprehensive British history. Welshmen were to the forefront: Sir John Price of Brecon, the *History's* ablest defender, and the learned Humphrey Llwyd of Denbigh who was a corresponding member and protégé of the seminal Netherlands school of geographers. Chorography's finest achievement, the magnificent *Britannia* of William Camden, was inevitably rooted in this Welsh scholarship. The new 'British-ness' unavoidably took much of its tone and colour from those Welsh who had been its first celebrants and were still its most direct inheritors. The Tudor monarchs and their servitors necessarily devoted much time to genealogies tracing their line back through Welsh and British kings to Arthur and Brutus. In this 'Britain' and its 'British', the Welsh, with their 'British tongue', could recover a respectable identity, and the English create a new one, under those Tudors who *were* the 'Return of Arthur' prophesied by Merlin.

It is no accident that this British and Arthurian cycle reached its climax — in learning, poetry, public ritual and propaganda — in the late 1570s and 1580s, the days of Spenser's *Faerie Queene*, when relations between Britain and Spain degenerated into open war, when the excommunication of Elizabeth and invasion threats brought down repression on English Catholics, and when the voyages of Drake and Hawkins, Gilbert and Raleigh initiated a conscious policy of American colonization and the building of sea-power in the crisis which culminated in the Spanish Armada. It was to this 'imperial' construction that the 'Worthiness of Wales', to quote one of its English celebrants, and Welshmen like Humphrey Llwyd and John Dee were central.

Dr John Dee was an astounding man, a brilliant polymath. Born in London of Welsh parents, he cherished his roots in Radnorshire in south-central Wales. Like many scholars of the Renaissance, like Kepler after him, he inhabited a world which was at once half magic and half science. He became notorious as a sorcerer — a 'caller of devils' — with his metaphysics and mysticism, his 'angelic conversations' with spirits and his astrology — the 'Arch Conjurer' of England. He was once imprisoned under Mary on a charge of trying to 'enchant' the Queen, and when he left for Prague in 1583 a crowd sacked his library at Mortlake as the den of a black magician. He was also a brilliant speculative scientist and mathematician, a worthy successor to the great Robert Recorde (also from Wales); a geographer and polymath whom Elizabeth dubbed 'hyr philosopher' and who built up a European reputation.

Born in 1527 and ten years older than the celebrated Richard Hakluyt, who was to translate several of Dee's ambitions into achievement, he went to Cambridge and became one of the original foundation fellows of Trinity in 1546. He moved to Louvain, because English humanism was inadequate in science, and established friendship with some of the seminal minds in mathematics and geography, Gemma Phrysius, the Fleming who was Cosmographer to the Emperor; Gerard Mercator the map-maker, another Fleming who removed to Duisburg; the great Portuguese Pedro Nuñez, and Abraham Ortelius of Antwerp. Dee was to be courted by emperors and princes all over Europe. The lectures of this twenty-three-year old at Paris were a sensation. He returned to England with navigational devices such as the *balestila* or cross-staff, was fêted by men in power (particularly by the circle of Sir Henry and Philip Sidney and the Dudleys) and taken up by the Queen; he published an augmentation of Recorde's *Grounde of Artes*, a mathematical textbook which ran to twenty-six editions by 1662, and wrote his own seminal Preface to the English translation of Euclid. He built up a massive library at Mortlake to which all the world, including Elizabeth, came to marvel, mingled with the 'mechanicians', and established himself as the thinker behind many of the exploration and colonization ventures of the English in their search for the North-East and North-West passages to Cathay.

Dee strongly supported the British school of chorography, though he lacked the stamina to carry it through to a *Britannia*. A key figure here was Dee's fellow Welshman, the older Humphrey Llwyd, who was a Denbigh man and MP for his home town, and personal physician to the Earl of Arundel. Llwyd was a serious and distinguished geographer and antiquarian, though most of his work, which was directly inspired by savants of the Low Countries, was still unpublished at his death in 1568 and was sent to Ortelius in Antwerp. This included an essay on *Mona* (Anglesey, reputed heart of Druidism) which was published in Ortelius's *Theatrum*, a map of Wales which was printed by Ortelius in 1571, and the *Britannia Descriptionis Fragmentum*, printed in Cologne in 1572 and in English, as the *Breviary of Britayne*, by Dee's friend Thomas Twyne in 1573. Appropriately, Llwyd had been put in contact with the important centre of Antwerp through Sir Richard Clough, a London merchant of Denbigh origin, and Sir Thomas Gresham of the Merchant Venturers.

For Dee himself was enmeshed in the commercial and imperial speculations of Elizabethan England, as scientific adviser to the Muscovy Company and the Company of Cathay, and to a small host of explorers who were thrusting now for the North-East, now the North-West Passage. He

37

corresponded eagerly with navigators and ship-masters, with Mercator and Ortelius, pouring out treatises, maps and instructions in his characteristic blend of crisply practical technological and scientific arguments, imperial fantasy, erudition and speculation, the oriental occult. The decisive moment came with the opening of a great cycle of semi-official exploration, colonization and piratical enterprises from 1575.

Even as Martin Frobisher, armed with Dee's advice, launched his successive explorations into the North-West and others tried to reach Asia through the Arctic seas of the North-East, Sir Humphrey Gilbert published his *Discourse* April 1576 on a north-west passage, to begin the first serious essay in American colonization. Dee worked carefully through Gilbert's *Discourse*, recalled an imperial discourse of his own on Atlantis (as he called America) and during six days in August 1576 he wrote the first of four major books calling on Elizabeth to establish, or rather re-establish, a great British maritime empire in the northern latitudes.

The first volume of his *General and Rare Memorials Pertayning to the Perfect Arte of Navigation* was devoted to the 'Brytish Monarchie' and its 'Incomparable Islandish Empire'. He argued strongly for the creation of a 'Pety Navy Royall' of sixty tall ships, supported by taxation and the mobilization of British resources for imperial expansion. He hinted at the unassailable evidence he was soon to produce on British claims to northern Atlantic dominion. He followed up this 'Hexameron Plat Politicall of the Brytish Monarchie' with a volume of *Tables Gubernatick* for the Queen's navigators (now lost), another volume which he burned (possibly as politically or theologically dangerous) and a fourth, which he completed in the early summer of 1577, the *Great Volume of Famous and Rich Discoveries* on British projects to the north-east and Cathay. As a rider, he fulfilled his promise in the 'Pety Navy Royall' by presenting the evidence for an early British empire in the north. He grounded himself in the mythical northern conquests of Arthur and another legendary British king Malgo, in the enormous extension of those conquests (to include Greenland) which had been projected by writers later than Geoffrey of Monmouth, and in a skilful deployment of the recently published and widely accepted evidence of the Zeno brothers' apocryphal fourteenth-century journeys into Arctic regions which multiplied the number of legendary islands in those parts. Arguing from the naval power called for in his first volume and from a hundred-mile limit of sea-jurisidiction, he summoned Elizabeth to rebuild a great British maritime empire in the high latitudes extending from the Orkneys through Iceland and Greenland to the shores of Atlantis.

Throughout this period, when the Elizabethan court was treading very carefully indeed in the shadow of Spain, secrecy and security precautions controlled men's minds. In response to pressure, however, Dee published the first volume of his great work, in a strictly limited edition of a hundred, in August 1577. It was graced by a gorgeous, allegorical (and partly occult) engraving of Elizabeth at the helm of an imperial ship, restoring the twenty kingdoms of the 'Brytish Empire'. By November Sir Humphrey Gilbert was closeted with Dee, and the very day he had spoken with the Doctor presented the Queen with nakedly anti-Spanish proposals for American and West Indian expeditions. Before the month was out, Dee himself was summoned to Court and expounded to Elizabeth her 'Title Royal' to dominion overseas. At her command, he prepared two treatises in 1578 on that title and on the limits of British empire. Both are now lost, but if a similar plan he presented two years later was in truth a summary of them, they would have supported sweeping claims to sovereignty over much of North America and the North Atlantic, in the name of illustrious precursors from Arthur forward. In particular, they would have argued for a British claim to much of the eastern American coast north of the actual Spanish settlement of *La Florida*, a term which the Spaniards, under their Papal warrant, extended to the entire coastline. In June 1578 Gilbert got his royal patent for colonization.

It is precisely in this context that the name of Madoc first enters the historical record. Gilbert's first voyage set out in the autumn. Heavily armed, it was clearly heading far more to the south than its official destinations of *Norumbega* (the New England area) and *Hochelaga* (the area of the St Lawrence and New York) would suggest. It proved abortive, but by the summer of 1580 Gilbert had returned to the attack. Simon Fernandez, the Azores pilot and pirate Simao Fernandes, who often based himself with his fellow John Callice in Cardiff and Penarth in south Wales, and had entered the service of the fiery Protestant imperialist Sir Francis Walsingham, went on a quick and successful reconnaissance of *Norumbega*. He was duly despatched to Dee who worked on his chart. Gilbert, raising funds by the assignment of estates in the proposed colony, promised Dr John Dee vast grants of land north of the 50° latitude, which would have given him much of present-day Canada and control of the north-west passage to Cathay. On 3 October 1580 Dee once more went to Court. This time he presented formal and powerful claims to the Council, evidently serviced by a small team of cartographers. One set has been lost, but a summary statement survives. It was a superbly executed map, with a full and formal 'Title Royal' carefully worked out on the back.

And it is there, taking formal precedence over every other claim, ranking ahead of Arthur and Malgo and later voyages, real and mythical, from the Zeno brothers through the Thornes to the Cabots, that Madoc first appears. Warrant number one runs: 'The Lord Madoc, sonne to Owen Gwynedd, Prince of Northwales, led a Colonie and inhabited in Terra Florida or thereabowts'; the claim therefore was to *Terra Florida*. In the summation this claim, which was based on a colonization venture attributed to the son of an authentic prince of Gwynedd (who died in 1169), was used to establish British title to 'all the Coasts and Islands beginning at or abowt Terra Florida

39

. . . unto Atlantis going Northerly', and then to all the northern islands extending as far as Russia.

This abrupt, bare and startling statement is the first direct, authentic and public reference we have to Madoc as a discoverer and colonizer of America.

It was not at once followed up. The Queen was warm but the hooded-eyed Burghley, though he seems to have moved a little from his initial scepticism, was evidently reluctant to use the claim. It is very difficult to know how much use was made of Madoc before 1584. The younger Richard Hakluyt, for example, began his career in these years with a volume *Divers Voyages touching the discoverie of America*, which was published in 1582 in support of Gilbert. He had heard of the Madoc story from Dr David Powel, personal chaplain to Sir Henry Sidney, who was in touch with Dr John Dee and knew of a manuscript history of Wales compiled by Humphrey Llwyd in which the Madoc story figures. Hakluyt did not use Madoc in his *Divers Voyages*, but this may have been for security reasons or because of the technical nature of the book; he was certainly using Madoc as a central argument in his *Discourse of Western Planting* a mere two years later. Whereas most of the other claims in Dee's 'Title Royal' could be construed as offering no *direct* challenge to Spain, Madoc's *Terra Florida* obviously ran into head-on collision not only with Columbus but with the Papal Bull of 1493 and the Treaty of Tordesillas of 1494 which had divided the New World between Spain and Portugal.

Hakluyt's book did not appear until 1582, for 1581 was a year of penury and frustration for Sir Humphrey Gilbert, though John Dee's enthusiasm overflowed into another enormous work: four volumes calling for the Christianization of America. During 1582, however, Gilbert's preparations for colonization assumed a new dimension of reality. A complex of related enterprises clustered around him. Central to the Gilbert project was a remarkable proposal to solve the problem of English Catholics by 'evacuating' them across the Atlantic. Sir George Peckham and Sir Thomas Gerrard were the moving spirits and they secured the support of many Catholic gentry and sympathizers. Entering into the customary assignment agreements with Gilbert, they proposed to establish a hierarchical colony of Catholics on the American mainland out of harm's way and out of the way of the ferocious recusancy fines which had been imposed in 1581.

This at once aroused the Spaniards, who had already wiped out a French settlement north of Florida in the 1560s. Their ambassador Mendoza weighed in with heavy threats against the English Catholic 'traitors'; they'd get their throats cut like the French. Florida was the entire North American coast, granted to Spain by the Pope. There was only one authority to whom a perturbed Peckham could turn. In July 1582 he visited Dr John Dee specifically over the question of lawful title to America. He was evidently reassured, for during August and September Peckham and Sir Francis Walsingham presided over a major inquiry in depth into the possibilities of settlement in *Norumbega*. A key witness was David Ingram, one of a hundred men put ashore on the Gulf of Mexico by Sir John Hawkins in 1568. He claimed to have walked 2,000 miles of the North American continent and his report was astounding. He, too, duly trod the familiar path to Dr John Dee's house at Mortlake; his narrative appeared in print in 1583.

In June of that year Gilbert's fleet sailed, equipped with yet another map from Dee. It failed. In September, Edward Hayes returned with news of its misfortunes and of the death of its leader. The Catholic scheme, however, went ahead. Peckham was joined by Philip Sidney and, promising Dee further huge grants of land in the new colony, he published a *True Reporte* on Gilbert's discoveries late in 1583, resuming the argument in favour of colonization. This project was also stillborn, but by this time Gilbert's half-brother Walter Raleigh had taken up his mission. Supported by Richard Hakluyt's *Discourse of Western Planting* in 1584, it was Raleigh who finally got the first English colonists into America in the shortlived Roanoke settlement of his *Virginia*.

With this thrust, Madoc, too, moved from the confidential parchment of Dee's 'Title Royal' of 1580 into public print and into historical discourse.

Sir George Peckham's *True Reporte*, which may have been written by his son George, was dedicated to Sir Francis Walsingham and carried a preface dated 12 November 1583. Sustained by the customary galaxy of commendatory verses allegedly written by persons of distinction, it was a long argument in favour of the principle of colonization, laced with biblical and classical references. In the third chapter, the essay had to get to grips with the bitterly disputed problem of 'lawfull tytle' to North America. Here Madoc, once again taking primacy over all others, reappears. Since this is, in fact, the first appearance of the Madoc story in print, it is worth reproducing in full.

> And it is very evident that the planting there shall in time right amplie enlarge her Majesties Territories and Dominions (or I might rather say) restore to her Highnesse auncient right and interest in those Countries, into the which a noble and woorthy personage, lyneally descended from the blood royall, borne in Wales, named Madock ap Owen Gwyneth, departing from the coast of England, about the yeere of our Lord God 1170 arrived and there planted himselfe, and his Colonies, and afterward returned himself into England, leaving certaine of his people there, as appeareth in an auncient Welch Chronicle, where he then gave to certaine Llandes, Beastes, and Fowles, sundrie Welch names, as the Lland of Pengwyn, which yet to this day beareth the same.
>
> There is lykewise a Fowle in the sayde Countries, called by the same name at this daye, and is as much to saye in Englishe, as White-headde, and in trueth, the sayde Fowles have white heads.
>
> There is also in those Countries a fruite called Gwynethes which is

41

likewise a Welch word. Moreover, there are divers other welch wordes at this dite in use, as David Ingram aforesaide reporteth in his relations. All which most strongly argueth, the saide Prince with his people to have inhabited there. And the same in effect is confirmed by Mutuzuma that mightie Emperor of Mexico, who in an Oration unto his subjects, for the better pacifying of them, made in the presence of Hernando Curtese, used these speeches following.

My kinsemen, freends and servaunts, you do well know that eighteen yeeres I have been your King, as my Fathers and Grandfathers were, and alwaies I have beene unto you a loving Prince, and you unto me good and obedient subjects, and so I hope you will remaine unto me all the daies of my life. You ought to have in remembraunce, that eyther you have heard of your Fathers, or else our divines have instructed you that we are not naturallie of this Countrie, nor yet our Kingdome is durable, because our Forefathers came from a farre countrie and their King and Captaine who brought them hither, returned againe to his natural countrie, saying, that he would sende such as should rule and governe us, if by chaunce he himself returned not etc.

These be the verie words of Mutuzuma, set downe in the Spanish Chronicles, the which being thoroughlie considered, because they have relation to some straunge noble person, who long before had possessed those Countries, doo all sufficientlie argue, the undoubted title of her Majestie: For as much as no other Nation can truelie by any Chronicles they can finde, make prescription of time for themselves, before the time of this Prince Madocke. Besides all this, for further proofe of her highnes title sithence the arrivall of this noble Britton into those partes . . .

and Peckham went on to cite the Cabot voyages, arguing that further proof was 'needeles'.

Several features of this text need to be noted. It was, above all else, a challenge to Spain in America. The Madoc story, launched in 1583, was to live in men's minds for nearly 400 years and to suffer many a sea-change. Never at any moment in its long history did it lose this, its aboriginal meaning. Peckham has only one voyage and return, which leaves a residual colony. The voyager is identified as the son of an authentic prince of Gwynedd of the twelfth century. No explanation is offered of his departure and nothing is said of his fate. The voyage, however, is dated and an unidentified old Welsh chronicle cited as evidence. Madoc does not return to his colony (clearly he could not, if he were to be identified as the Founder of Mexico in Montezuma's discourse); the colony is not located with any precision and nothing is said of its destiny. The proofs of its existence reside in the linguistic evidence of David Ingram, the celebrated speech of Montezuma and the fact that no other nation in its chronicles claimed such a discovery.

What a weak and wispy performance! This is the work of a man who has grasped at a useful story, but whose grasp of it is insecure.

The link between Montezuma's speech and the old Welsh chronicle is effected by the evidence on language provided by David Ingram, who initiated a long tradition. Ingram gave his evidence before the Walsingham-Peckham inquiry of 1582, in answers to questions and in a 'relation'. Ingram said he had been put ashore by Sir John Hawkins on the Gulf of Mexico in 1568 and had walked by Indian trails all the way to Maine, to be picked up by a French ship. Years of retelling his story had elaborated fantasies of elephants, pillars of gold and red sheep; penguins are mixed up with flamingoes. Hakluyt published Ingram's narrative in the first edition of his celebrated *Principall Navigations*, but dropped it from the second. Scholars believe, however, that the story is based on some core of truth.

The Welsh linguistic evidence is slight but shattering. There was a fruit called *Guiathos* (which becomes *Gwynethes* in Peckham), a greeting *Gwando* (*Gwrando* is Welsh for Listen!) and, of course, there was the penguin — 'They are exceeding fatte and very delicate meate, they have white heads, and therefore the Countrey Men call them Penguins (which seemeth to be a Welsh name). And they have also in use divers others Welsh words, a matter worthy the noting . . .' Worth noting indeed! *Pen* (head) plus *gwyn* (white) equals penguin (white head). QED. The only snag here is that (*pace* Sir George and David) penguins have black heads. Later writers translated it as 'white rock'; in any case no speculative linguist worth the name is to be deterred by such little local difficulties. By the twentieth century, at least fifteen Indian languages had been identified as Welsh, often by linguists of such uncommon capacity as to be able to recognize the Welsh language without knowing it.

In fact this alleged resemblance of some Indian words to Welsh was noted by several travellers and there had been a curious reference in Humphrey Llwyd's *Breviary of Britayne*, published in 1573 but written some time before 1568, when, dealing with the character of the Welsh language, he comments under the heading 'Mexicani':

I am not ignorant that the Spayniardes have in use LL as have the Germanes LH . . . But neither of thease expresseth ours . . . I take it rather, that the Mexicani, whiche inhabite the newfounde worlde, do use that Letter, which the Spayniardes expresse by LL, but bycause I was never amongste them: I doubt whether it be so or not, for ours is sharpe in the hissinge . . .

This, while entirely negative, was later made the basis for some hugely entertaining linguistic speculation. It indicates that alleged similarities between Indian tongues and the Welsh (British) language had become a subject for discussion.

The story of Montezuma's famous speech, of course, had by that time passed into general circulation and there was a wealth of intriguing information for Peckham to draw on. The origin legends not only of the Aztecs but of the Maya of Yucatan and even the Incas, all had white, bearded demi-gods or gods as founders, and monuments and sculptures to them were found inland. Spanish writers commented freely on the cross and other apparently Christian symbols they encountered. During the Spanish settlement of Florida, which was in part motivated by the search for the legendary Fountain of Youth associated with the island of Bimini, a raid by Ayllón netted an Indian captive on the coast of what became Carolina. He told many wonders to his captors (probably in an effort to get away from them). What struck the Spaniards, including the chroniclers Peter Martyr and Oviedo who questioned him in Spain, were his stories of white people with long brown hair in his homeland of Chicora near Cape Fear (he also had men with tails and giant chieftains). After Ayllón got his patent in 1523, Spanish expeditions penetrated as far north as Cape Breton in 1525, and in 1524 the Governor ordered a specific search for the *gente blanco* (white people) which scoured what became South Carolina for 150 leagues inland. In 1528 another hunt for the whites occupied one expedition on its four-months' tramp through the back country, and there were Spanish searches as late as 1661. Some of these later expeditions may have been occasioned by stories of 'white Indians' stemming from the Lost Colonists of English Roanoke, but the earlier ones resulted from direct contact with Indians and may well have had legends like those of St Brendan and Madoc in mind. For some apparent references to the Madoc story (a version of which had passed into European discourse very early) occur in Spanish sources *before* any publications by Peckham, Powel or Hakluyt. Columbus apparently referred to one stretch of sea near the Sargasso as *Mar di Cambrio (Cambria* being the Latin for Wales) and on one early Spanish map of the Gulf of Mexico (1519), a caption (probably inserted later) apparently labels Mobile Bay *Tierra de los Gales* (Land of the Welsh). The most northerly Spanish coastal settlements on the Atlantic were to be disputed by English colonists and, indeed, had probably been the target area for Sir Humphrey Gilbert. The Spaniards called the lands Guale, after an Indian chief, and used the expression *lengua de Guale* for the language. English colonists pronounced this phonetically as *Wallie* — which could hardly have done the Madoc story any harm!

It was relatively easy, then, for Peckham to mobilize 'evidence' from 'Montezuma's Mexico'. He had interrogated Ingram himself on the language. But where did he get his 'ancient Welsh chronicle' with its story of Madoc? It must have been from Dr John Dee whom he had consulted on title in July 1582. However Dee's own words in his 'Title Royal' of 1580 — that Madoc had led a colony to 'Terra Florida or thereabowts' — were certainly taken from a manuscript history by Humphrey Llwyd. Some nine years before his death in 1568 Llwyd had been composing an English version from old Welsh texts of chronicles narrating the history of Wales from the Arthurian Cadwaladr to the 'last of the British blood' to rule in Wales, LLywelyn ap Gruffydd. The chronicle, which ended in 1294, was prefaced by a translation of Sir John Price's Latin description of Wales and Llwyd dated the finished text at London on 17 July 1559.

This manuscript passed to Sir Henry Sidney, President of the Council of Wales and the March. His personal chaplain, David Powel, moved in the Welsh geographical and chorographical circle, centred on the Court, to which John Dee belonged. Its focus was Blanche Parry, mistress of Elizabeth's household, who was Dee's 'cousin' and came from the Welsh-speaking part of Herefordshire (home county of the Hakluyts) which had produced the Cecils and where one of Burghley's kinsmen still lived. Powel had himself published a primer in cartography in 1573 and was a friend of Dee. The latter's mind had been directed to Madoc in late 1577 after his work on his *Famous and Rich Discoveries* had provoked a remarkable letter from Gerard Mercator which, citing a lost geographical text, drew his attention to alleged survivors of 'the race of Arthur' who were still active in the northern waters in the later fourteenth century. A copy of Llwyd's original manuscript which survives is a copy made for John Dee, who in his own hand corrected some of Humphrey's errors and inserted marginal references. In September 1583, however, Dee, captivated by the 'angelic conversations' of Edward Kelley and the mystical Polish Prince Laski, left for Prague. It was then that the Sidneys asked David Powel to publish Llwyd's history. Powel did not restrict himself to Llwyd's material. He got some evidence on Glamorgan from the Stradling family, through Blanche Parry, and raided other sources in order to augment Llwyd.

It was this work of Powel's which appeared hard on the heels of Peckham as a *Historie of Cambria* in 1584, in time for Hakluyt to cite its section on Madoc in his *Discourse of Western Planting*. Powel was a conscientious scholar. Although his portraits of individuals were drawn entirely from the very Arthurian *Hollinshed's Chronicles*, he very carefully distinguished (through the use of different founts and other devices) between Llwyd's work and his own 'augumentations'. In this, the first printed history of Wales the section about Madoc specifically attributed by Powel to Humphrey Llwyd and therefore dating from some time near 1559 (though corrected by John Dee some time between 1577 and 1580) would seem to be the first authentic emergence of the Madoc story into history:

> Madoc another of Owen Gwyneth his sonnes left the land in contention betwixt his brethren, and prepared certaine ships with men and munition, and sought adventures by seas, sailing west, and leaving the coast of Ireland so far north, that he came to a land unknowen, where he saw manie strange things. This land must needs be some part of that countrie of which the Spaniards affirm themselves to be the first finders sith

45

Hanno's time; for by reason and order of Cosmographie, this land, to the which Madoc came, must needs be some part of Nove Hispania or Florida. Whereupon it is manifest, that this countrie was long before by Brytaines discovered, afore either Columbus or Americus Vesputius lead anie Spaniardes thither. Of the viage and returne of this Madoc there be manie fables fained, as the common people doo use in distance of place and length of time rather to augment than to diminish: but sure it is, that there he was. And after he had returned home and declared the pleasant and fruitfull countries that he had seene without inhabitants; and upon the contrarie part, for what barren and wild ground his brethren and nephews did murther one another: he prepared a number of ships, and got with him such men and women as were desirous to live in quietnes, and taking leave of his freends tooke his journie thitherward againe. Therefore it is to be presupposed, that he and his people inhabited part of those countries; for it appeareth by Francis Loves [Lopez de Gomara] that in Acusanus [Acusamil] and other places, the people honoured the crosse; whereby it may be gathered that Christians had beene there, before the comming of the Spaniards. But bicause this people were not manie, they followed the maners of the land they came unto, and used the language they found there.

Humphrey Llwyd in this passage, which justifiably became a classic, was more tentative than many later celebrants of Madoc. He has the civil wars in Wales and the two voyages which became standard and he notes that there were many popular legends about them. This would appear to be the *hard, irreducible core* of any Madoc story: Madoc, son of the great prince Owain Gwynedd, sick to death of civil war between his brothers, sailed off on a sea venture. He discovered an unknown land and saw many marvels. He returned and took people of like mind with him to found a colony. He and his people disappeared. Llwyd makes the overt and specific assumption that this handful ('some pretty company' in the words of a later writer) had been absorbed by the natives and had lost their language.

Llwyd was one of the scholars who initiated the serious, scientific study of place-names and he would have no truck with any of the linguistic fantasies of such as David Ingram. It is not the language of Mexico and Florida which catches his attention, but Spanish reports of Christian-like ceremonies (for some Indians, the cross represented the Four Houses of the Sky). This is clearly the evidence which, in his mind and those of many others, wrenched Madoc's journey towards *Nova Hispania* (New Spain) and *Florida* (unified in a single, convenient 'Mexico' by many writers). For if Madoc left the Irish coast 'so far north' then the unknown lands he reached — 'must needs be . . . by order of Cosmographie' those which the Spaniards claimed to have discovered. It is that 'must needs be' which is central to Llwyd, as is the existence of an *unspecific* popular tradition susceptible to fantasy.

46

David Powel himself, however, was much more representative of what was to become the major interpretation of the Madoc story. He locates Madoc's landfall without hesitation in *Mexico*, anchoring it there firmly in Montezuma's speech and the language of the 'Mexicans'. He added to Ingram's little collection the words Corroeso Island (Curaçao, identified with the Welsh *Croeso*, Welcome) a river Gwyndor *(Gwyndŵr)*, the cape of Bryton *(Cap Breton*, purloined from the Celtic cousins of the Welsh with their sister language). It was he who first related 'penguin' to a rock as well as a bird. The two voyages he left unchanged, but Powel adds that, on his second voyage, Madoc 'went thither againe with ten sailes, as I find noted in Gutyn Owen'. Powel therefore reinforces Llwyd's account of a popular Madoc tradition by this reference to an authentic Welsh writer of the fifteenth century (who might well have written before Columbus) and by stating that Llwyd's work was essentially based on a chronicle by Caradoc of Llancarfan.

Gutyn Owain certainly existed and was a man of some distinction. He was appointed to the commission set up to establish the Welsh pedigree of Henry VII. A gentleman from the Oswestry region who worked at Basingwerk abbey, he was a *pencerdd* or master-poet. Scholar, genealogist and chronicler, he wrote verse, several calendars and a pedigree book, and transcribed several of the *Bruts* or chronicles, compiling one of his own times to 1471; he made the earliest copy of a Welsh Book of Heraldry. He is believed to have written most of his works in the period 1470-1500. He probably did not live into the 1500s and may have died around 1498. It is an open question whether anything he wrote on Madoc could have been composed before or after news of Columbus's journeys had reached Wales.

Welsh scholarship, however, despite many false starts and alarms, has not been able to find any trace of Powel's 'ten sails' or any other Madoc reference in Gutyn Owain's surviving manuscripts (which, while a critical point, does not necessarily mean that such Madoc manuscripts never existed). Much the same is true of Caradoc of Llancarfan, the alleged source of Llwyd's history. He was mentioned by Geoffrey of Monmouth around 1135. Geoffrey, closing his *British History* at the year 689, passed his material on England to the English chroniclers Henry of Huntingdon and William of Malmesbury, and his Welsh material to Caradoc, with the duty of continuing the British history of his own people. Although earlier versions of *Brut y Tywysogion* (Chronicle of the Princes) were attributed to Caradoc in the sixteenth century, there is no evidence that he carried out Geoffrey's commission. Caradoc is associated with lives of the early British-Welsh saints Gildas and Cadog and, in particular, with Glastonbury and its Arthurian legends. Humphrey Llwyd certainly had an old Welsh manuscript to work on. Along with the surviving chronicle of his which passed to John Dee, there was a genealogy, traced through the maternal line, with the inscription: 'This much was written out of the Bryttishe bok wher the

History of Humfrey Lloid is in Welsh written'. It is difficult to relate anything on Madoc to Caradoc, however, since he is believed to have died in 1156.

On these two sources of the Madoc story, then, Gutyn Owain and Caradoc of Llancarfan or his continuator, the fairest and indeed most scholarly verdict would be 'not proven'. Modern Welsh scholarship has not been content with a scholarship so thin-blooded. It has fallen upon any and every alleged manifestation of the Madoc legend with a cold and correct ferocity. Its prime motive drive has been shame. For, after the sixteenth century, the quest for Madoc assumed manic proportions. It has been devilled by Iolo Morganwg's eighteenth-century fabrications, by wishful misreading of documents, by misguided and often paranoid Welsh patriotism and by sheer fantasy. At times, the excesses have been lunatic.

Resistance to the legend grew rapidly in the nineteenth century, particularly among the Welsh themselves, to reach a climax in the work of one of the most formidable critical intelligences in Welsh (or any other) history, Thomas Stephens of Merthyr Tydfil. His work on Madoc could serve apprentice historians as a very model of totally destructive historical criticism. In revulsion against fantasy and, in particular, against an alleged native propensity to fantasy attributed to the Welsh in English racial mythology, modern Welsh scholarship, in sharp contrast to American, has however gone far beyond rational analysis of the speculations of early geography. It has itself become something of a positivist excess, which seems to exclude even the historical analysis of myth.

It has, in consequence, swept the field virtually clear. Moving back from Gutyn Owain towards Caradoc, it has tackled three poets contemporary to Owain Gwynedd and his sons, who have been subjected to the most tortuous and forced misinterpretation in the service of Madoc. *Not a single line* of their work can be used in support of the story. This is the first statement, and the most important one, to be made about the Madoc story as transmitted by Humphrey Llwyd. In the authentic medieval chronicles, prose and verse of Wales which survive, there is *not a single trace* of a Madoc who found America, a Madoc who sailed to distant lands or even a Madoc who was the son of Owain Gwynedd (though he might have figured in Owain's *teulu*, a word meaning warband or retinue which today means family, or among the imposing ranks of Owain's multitudinous bastards).

This is clearly a vital, perhaps the most vital, statement which scholarship has to make about the Madoc story. It is not, however, the only statement that scholarship has to make. It is certainly not the only statement that scholarship *needs* to make.

It is a striking fact that the Madoc canon, as it developed in the seventeenth and eighteenth centuries, used as its reference not twelfth century material but material from the fifteenth century. For in that century, there *are* traces of some tradition of Madoc a seafarer in Welsh writing. Upon three writers

48

cited by the seventeenth century and a fourth quoted by the eighteenth, modern Welsh scholarship has once more directed the fire of its seagreen fury. Of Cynwric ap Gronw, a 'source' used in the seventeenth century, we know nothing beyond his probable existence. The stories attributed by the eighteenth century to Ieuan Brechfa, a Carmarthenshire writer, turn out to be forgeries or cannot be found. No one has yet found 'ten sails' or anything else in Gutyn Owain.

We are left with one poet, Maredudd ap Rhys, who lived about the middle of the fifteenth century and who wrote verse (probably around 1440) about a Madoc son to Owain Gwynedd. This verse was to achieve immortality in the pages of Hakluyt's classic, *Principall Navigations*, and to run a remarkable career through Welsh, English, Latin, French, Dutch and several generations of British and European writing. The poet was thanking his patron for the gift of a fishing net and his thanks include such expressions as — 'Madoc the bold . . . true whelp of Owain Gwynedd, would not have land . . . nor great wealth but the seas . . . A Madoc am I to my age and to his passion for the seas have I been accustomed . . .'

All the poem actually suggests is that this Madoc was a lover of the sea and presumably of fishing. The poet also cites St Peter in this context but, to quote a celebrated Welsh scholar, 'no one has based thereon an argument for the prior discovery of America by the Apostle.'

True enough, but at this point, scholars do protest too much. 'A Madoc am I to my age' is incomprehensible without the assumption that some tradition of Madoc a seafarer existed. Thomas Stephens himself, whose devastating critique of the legend has itself acquired near-legendary prestige, stated quite categorically (and without doubt accurately): 'it is quite evident that in the middle of the fifteenth century, when this poem was written, there was a distinct Madoc tradition.' There is certainly not the slightest reason to assume that the grave and learned (and careful) Humphrey Llwyd was a liar on this point.

Such a tradition certainly seems to have left less imprint on the surviving materials than one might perhaps have expected. The problem is to grasp what its nature might have been. A closer and less *a priori* hostile examination, directed less at the demolition than at the understanding of a myth, unearths a small but cogent corpus of evidence, some of it tentative and speculative, some but recently discovered outside Wales, which strengthens the argument for the existence of a Madoc tradition or traditions which could well have proved susceptible to a Columbus revision in the sixteenth century, but which had also entered European discourse much earlier and might even have lodged in serious, scientific hypotheses.

The most riveting evidence, which remains difficult to date with precision, comes from Flemish (Dutch) sources. Flemings were planted in twelfth-century Wales, in southern Gower and southern Pembroke, and were mercenaries everywhere. Their priests and poets were one channel for the

49

transmission of Arthurian stories from Wales and England into Europe. More generally, Flanders, one of the earliest centres of industrial specialization in medieval Europe and one pole of the vital Italy-Low Countries axis, was also the meeting place of Germanic and Romance languages. It produced an influential vernacular literature relatively early. In particular, the most successful version of the celebrated medieval satire *Reynard the Fox* was the Flemish.

Its author was one Willem, who is difficult to identify. Identification is made the more difficult by the Dutch poets' convention of referring to an earlier author and an even earlier Celtic source, who might have been mythical. The Flemish version of the story of Gawain (Gwyn), for example, was attributed to a Celtic poet Penninc whose work was said to have been 'completed' by Peter Vostaert. Nevertheless, it also seems true that Latin versions of Welsh stories were made by priests and then translated into Dutch. The patron Lodewijk van Velthem ordered several such translations, and versions of the legends of Merlin and the Holy Grail derived at least ultimately from Welsh sources, were fairly common through the twelfth and thirteenth centuries.

No story was more successful than Willem's *Reynard*, which followed the original French and German classics. No one knows where Willem came from, though in 1938 a memorial was erected to him on the Dutch-Belgian border near Hulst. Some scholars have identified him as a premonstratenser from the Abbey of Drongen near Ghent, which held estates at Hulst and Hulsterloo in Dutch Flanders; a *Willelmus clericus* lived near Hulsterloo in 1269. There is another apparent reference to Willem in the work of his near-contemporary Jacob van Maerlant, who spoke of a *priester* Willem Utenhove of Ardenbourg who had written a bestiary; the *Reynard* itself mentions Hoeckenbroeck in Ardenbourg. The writer was certainly a cleric, though he carried the charge lightly and seems to have joined the international fraternity of troubadours as a wit, humorist and satirist. A Latin verse translation of his *Vos Reinaerde* was made by a Bruges cleric in 1272 and it is assumed that Willem himself wrote in the early or mid thirteenth century or possibly a little earlier.

Reynard's appeal, despite some echoes in Chaucer, was largely confined to the central French, Dutch and German lands. Even more striking, then, is the established fact that Willem was also the author of an apparently well-known work called *Madoc*. Introduced as *Willem, die Madocke makede* (Willem the author of Madoc), he refers to the fact himself in a prologue to *Reynard* which, in the most scholarly English translation reads:

> Willem who laboured to indite
> Madoc in many a wakeful night . . .

Jacob van Maerlant refers to the *Madoc* in his *Rijmbybel*, which seems to have been composed around 1270. In an early nineteenth-century French version of Willem's *Reynard*, the Belgian editor Delepierre renders this Van Maerlant reference to his own work:

> Want dit is niet Madocs droem
> No Reinaerts no Artus boerden . . .

Van Maerlant, who had himself written romances around Merlin and the Grail, renounced such nonsense and set to work on huge and indigestible epitomes of secular and biblical history in verse. In his work, therefore, to quote the version of a modern Dutch scholar in English translation, there would be no 'Madoc's dream, neither Reynard's nor Arthur's pranks . . .'.

This establishes that there was a Madoc romance, perhaps associated with Arthurian stories, written (or 'completed') by Willem which was evidently quite well known and in circulation probably by the early or mid thirteenth century. There are snippets of information which suggest that Willem travelled widely in France and Britain including Wales. A 'jongleur-bardh Willem' was known to the English writer Walter Map. Map was another Herefordshire man, who referred to 'my compatriots the Welsh', and was a friend of Gerald the Welshman. Attached to the court of Henry II, a justice in Herefordshire and Archdeacon of Oxford, Map was a lively, pungent writer, whose *De Nugis Curialum* was full of folk stories, gossip and racy yarns fully in the spirit of Willem and his fellows. Very knowledgeable on Wales and in close touch with the Dutch, he has been credited with some of the Arthurian romances and a *Lancelot du Lac* attributed to him was translated by a Brabantine at the request of van Veltham in 1255. Map himself was dead by 1210, but he recorded his acquaintance with a young poet Willem, proud as a peacock, who sang like a nightingale and who, he said, left for the court of Marie de Champagne.

No copy of Willem's *Madoc* has been found, though Delepierre commented in 1837, 'ne pourrait-on croire que ce roman était le récit des aventures de Madoc, fils d'Owen Gwynedd, prince de Galle, qui vers l'an 1170 découvrit l'Amérique?' (Was not this roman possibly the story of the adventures of Madoc, son of Owen Gwynedd, prince of Wales, who around 1170 discovered America?) In the seventeenth century, a fragment of a reputed French copy of the work is said to have been found in Poitiers. This is very late, and it could therefore have been composed after the sixteenth century stories of Madoc had passed into circulation (though why anyone in seventeenth century France should go to the trouble of that kind of fabrication is beyond conjecture!) A local scholar, however, believes that the fragment belongs to the late fourteenth century or even earlier and relates to the *romans de Guillaume le Jongleur* which were current in Provence and Champagne in the thirteenth century. The author identifies himself as *Guillaume qui fait Reynaud*, which certainly sounds familiar!

The manuscript, itself an incomplete précis, tells a romantic story. Its Madoc is not related to Owain Gwynedd, but is a member of a noble Welsh family whose grandfather was 'half a Viking' (Owain Gwynedd's father in reality, Gruffydd ap Cynan, sailed with the Norsemen of Ireland and the Isle of Man). A famous sailor, this Madoc went on a mission to the court of France disguised as a monk (Owain Gwynedd in reality did send clerical emissaries to the French court). Madoc, whose lover dressed her legs in fishnets, went sailing to find the Fountain of Youth, landed on an island called Ely to look for the lodestone (magnet) which he could safely use because the nails of his ship were made of stag horn. Sailing out from Ely, he found an island paradise bathed in sun, and returned to Ely for more ships to launch a new kingdom of love and music. Willem mentions an island surrounded by very large fish, identified as one of the magic isles of *Gwerddonau Llion* and a 'treacherous garden in the sea' reminiscent of explorers' stories and sailors' yarns of the Sargasso Sea and the 'warm sea in which plants do grow', an untraceable Madoc reference attributed to Cynwric ap Gronw.

This story, if it is in any way authentic, seems to combine both the traditions of romance and some of the characteristics of medieval speculative geography. It would clearly belong to the familiar Quest genre of voyages to the Isles of the Blessed, the Fortunate Isles and Antillia of the Seven Golden Cities which intersected with the many 'sightings' of those fly-away islands which peopled late medieval maps.

Moreover it evokes many echoes. The nails of horn figure, of course, in geographers' warnings about deadly magnetic islands in the sea. They also figure in stories about a half-magic ship *Gwennan Gorn*, found in north Wales and often associated with old harbours at Abergele and Afon Ganol whence versions of the Madoc story have the hero leaving. Arresting evidence of a popular tradition comes from a report of 1582, which tries to explain the by then traditional name of *Ffrydiau Caswennan* for the dangerous race of Bardsey Sound off the coast of Gwynedd, and does so in onomastic terms, in terms of a ship *Gwennan Gorn* built by Madoc with stag horns for nails, which nevertheless ran into trouble — *Cas Gwennan* (Gwennan's Woe). In 1582 this explanation was said to have been handed down 'by word of mouth through the ages'.

Equally striking is the name of Ely for Madoc's base which Willem said he had actually visited during his stay in Wales. Ely was a name once applied to Lundy Island in the Bristol Channel. Lundy, as *Ynys Wair*, was identified in early Welsh writing with the Fountain of Youth. The island was usually cited as the starting point for Madoc's second journey in later versions of the legend and there is some evidence of a local but late Madoc tradition.

More striking still, Lundy has vivid associations with the Northmen and with the long traditions of seaborne enterprise on the Irish Sea and the Western Approaches. The Irish had been great sailors of the northern and western seas since at least the days of the Christian missionaries and St Brendan. So had Welsh monks during the Age of Saints, in a movement

52

which was a sector of the general seaborne culture of Celtic Christianity. A Welsh monk had served as bishop in Spanish Galicia (itself Celtic) in the early middle ages and the premier Welsh shrine, St David's, on its peninsula, a 'barbarous and remote corner' in terms of the land-mass and of Tudor Protestantism which tried to move it inland, had been a hub of the western sea-routes. The Irish had reached Iceland and possibly even Greenland before the arrival of the Northmen, and Irish as well as Welsh stories credit Madoc with a brother Rhiryd who was lord of Clochran in Ireland; both were great sailors and both disappeared at sea. It is intriguing that the most successful seventeenth century popularizer of the Madoc story, Sir Thomas Herbert of York who had access to sources apparently not available to sixteenth century writers and which have since been lost, had his Mexicans reporting the arrival of their ancient founders (Madoc and his men, of course) in *curraghs*.

No less striking is the fact that Ireland, with its Viking enclaves, became a traditional asylum for princelings displaced in the endemic civil wars of medieval Wales. Several Welsh adventurers, of whom Gruffydd ap Cynan of Gwynedd was simply the best known, sailed with Danes and other Northerners. The Norsemen, and particularly the Icelanders with their admixture of Celts, were masters of the northern seas to Greenland and beyond to Vinland in America, as they were of the Irish sea; Viking bases in the Isle of Man and on the Irish coast were factors in the political struggles of Wales, whose coasts the Vikings ranged and ravaged and trafficked over. Geoffrey of Monmouth, writing in the twelfth century and steeped in Celtic source material, had his King Arthur conquer Iceland as well as the Orkneys and Ireland itself, taking the homage of the kings of Norway for good measure ('truths' which a later English writer used in order to 'explain' Norse and Danish settlements in Britain in terms of their *British* inheritance!). Benjamin Franklin de Costa, the most expert (though also the most credulous) historian of allegedly pre-Columbian discoveries in nineteenth-century America, suggested that Madoc might have sailed because he had heard of Vinland through Norse and Irish sources (Adam of Bremen the German chronicler had reported Vinland or Wineland around 1070; he had learned of it from the king of Denmark).

Most riveting of all, in this context, is the fact that a Welshman who was 'half a Viking' figures in the historical record of the Icelanders themselves. Their *Orkneyinga Saga* (the Earls' Saga) makes frequent reference under the years 1139-48, to a 'Freeman of Wales' who repeatedly harassed their settlements in the Southern Isles, as well as Tyree and the Isle of Man. In revenge, Sweyn and Holdboldi savaged Wales. The Freeman ran to Lundy, where the Icelanders tried but failed to block him in. At much the same time, the Saga reported that one of the Icelanders' leaders quit his people for months on end, which he spent closeted with a Welsh cleric.

It is difficult to impose much coherence on all this, particularly in view of

53

the geographical scatter. At the very least however one can surely argue that that very scatter, the appearance and re-appearance of themes common to the stories of several peoples on the western seaboard of Europe, certainly the Irish and the Icelanders and possibly the Bretons, the clear affiliation of many elements and the evident existence of Welsh popular traditions such as those of *Gwennan Gorn*, do strongly suggest that a persistent and not excessively inconsistent body of folklore existed.

It is possible to go further. The Icelanders' Freeman of Wales was sailing the Irish Sea and the northern waters and turning Lundy into a raiding base at a critical moment. The years which had seen Gruffydd ap Cynan use Northmen from Ireland to win Gwynedd, and which had seen Wales almost succumb to the Normans, had also witnessed the planting of the Flemings in Wales. They were followed by years of a revival of the Welsh, who fought the Normans to a frontier between March and *Pura Wallia*, which lasted for 150 years, which saw the work of Geoffrey of Monmouth and the Arthurian stories pass into European discourse, and set Owain Gwynedd, son to Gruffydd ap Cynan, in power. They also saw the Freeman on his western viking. Walter Map encountered his 'jongleur-bard' Willem and wrote of his departure for Marie de Champagne's court before 1210. By the middle of the thirteenth century, Willem's *Madoc-roman* was apparently almost as well known, at least in Provence and Champagne, as his *Reynard the Fox*.

It is conceivable that *Madoc*, as a romance, was better known in France than it was in Wales; it is certain that *some* Madoc story about a seafarer entered a common European stock of stories relatively early.

It is also possible that, as in many such stories in Welsh poems, folk-tales and *The Mabinogion*, legends about Madoc were anchored to historical individuals. If a Freeman of Wales could make forcible entry into the *Orkneyinga Saga*, he would certainly find a place among the story-tellers, even if only as a nine-days' wonder. Indeed, it is quite possible that a historical person, the Freeman or someone like him, *did* make a journey sufficiently dramatic to lodge in folklore. It is not inconceivable that, if the Freeman or some such person did make some memorable voyage, he also collected people of like mind, sailed off again to regain his 'unknown land' with its 'many marvels' and then disappeared *(which is all that the original Madoc story, reported by Humphrey Llwyd, actually said)*.

Moreover not only did some story about Madoc a seafarer enter European literature during the thirteenth century; it may well have lodged in serious scientific speculation. This Madoc fragment of Willem's, in its simultaneous 'southern' atmosphere of sun-drenched islands, seas of weed and isles of *Llion* and 'northern' hints of semi-Vikings and Lundy, and above all in its concern for stag-horn protection against the deadly powers of magnetism, irresistibly calls to mind one of the most celebrated of the 'lost texts' of early geographical speculation which was also concerned with the perils of the Pole and also, apparently, trapped in a north-south contradiction. This was the fourteenth century English *Inventio Fortunata* which haunted the sixteenth century. No one did it haunt more than Dr John Dee and Richard Hakluyt the younger, who hunted for it in vain. They first heard of it, at least in an immediately exciting context, from Gerard Mercator. For he in turn cited it from yet another 'lost text', which proved even more startling. This was the *Itinerary* of Jacob Cnoyen of s'Hertogenbosch. Cnoyen was himself Dutch (Flemish) and among *his* sources, there apparently figures a 'Willem of Ghent'.

Which raises an interesting and possibly crucial question: just when did that Arch Conjuror, Dr John Dee, conjure Madoc?

The moment can be located with some precision. In Dee's writings of 1576-7 there is no mention of Madoc. So Arthurian are those writings that it is difficult to believe that Dee would have omitted the Madoc story had he been in possession of it. Madoc certainly appears in his 'Title Royal' of 1580 and may have appeared in the lost Titles which Dee submitted to the Queen in 1578. The earliest possible date for Dee's insertion of Madoc into English discourse lies, then, between June 1577, when he was finishing his great imperial work, and August 1578, when he went to the Queen at Norwich. The critical moment for Dee's acquisition of Madoc was his reception of the letter which Gerard Mercator addressed to him in April 1577.

In 1576-7, Dee based his British empire on two sources, both mythical or semi-mythical. The first was a litany of Arthur's fabulous conquests which first appeared in print in 1568, in the *Archaionomia* of William Lambard. Lambard, a celebrated jurist and author of standard historical texts on the courts and justices of England, had immersed himself in Saxon documents and had translated them into Latin. He was an Arthurian patriot and revelled in the power and sovereignty which the kings of England had 'inherited' from their British predecessors. Speaking of Arthur, and using an 'ancient text', he wrote, 'His kingdome was too little for him and his mind was not contented with it'. So he subdued 'all Scantia (now called Norway) and all the Islands beyond Norway, to wit Iceland and Greenland which are appurtayning to Norway'; Lambard went on into a sonorous chant, listing all the kingdoms conquered by Arthur, which ranged through the whole of Scandinavia, the Baltic and the Arctic, into Lapland where he placed the eastern boundaries of Arthur's British empire. The western frontier stretched to the Pole. Among the names was a 'Windland' (in other versions written Winland or Wyneland) which some authors have identified with the Vinland of the Icelandic settlements in Newfoundland (and a few with Gwynetland or Gwynedd, with benefit of Madoc!) Lambard 'explained' the Danish and Norse invasions of England in these terms. The subject Norwaymen had intermarried with the British and, weary of their bony fiords, had come to England to claim their British citizenship.

This roll-call of Arthurian conquests reverberates through the sixteenth century. It appears as a marginal insertion in a different hand in the

Itineraries of William Worcestre, an Arthurian antiquarian of the late fifteenth century who knew of Bristol sailors' attempts to discover the mystery island of Brazil, before Columbus's voyages, and was familiar with the Icelandic voyages of both the men of Bristol (several of whose merchants and sailors were of Welsh descent) and those of Norwich and the east coast where he spent his last years. Lambard duly registers in Hakluyt's *Principall Navigations* and he dominates Dee's *Famous and Rich Discoveries*.

This text seems to have some points of contact with Dee's second source, the alleged northern journeys in the fourteenth century of the Zeno brothers of Venice. Central to Lambard was his inclusion of Greenland among Arthur's conquests. Geoffrey of Monmouth in the twelfth century had been content with Iceland and the homage of Scandinavia and the rest of the 'Six Islands of the Ocean Sea'. The Norse settlements in Greenland had probably disappeared by the early fifteenth century, but the Icelanders certainly had a wide knowledge of those regions. This knowledge informed the early fifteenth-century maps of the Dane Claudius Claves Swart which were the first to depict Greenland, and were themselves the basis of sixteenth century attempts to map the polar regions. A Claves map was, without doubt, the foundation of the map which accompanied the remarkable Zeno story published in Venice in 1558. Most scholars believe that the journeys of the Zeni were apocryphal; some argue for a few 'buried truths' in them.

The Zeni created a new slate of imaginary late fourteenth-century islands in the north, an Estland, a Friseland which seems to be a duplicate of Iceland, a Drogeo near what is assumed to be the American coast, an Icaria nearby and, above all, an Estotiland, in the far west, sometimes identified by scholars with Newfoundland, whose inhabitants traded with Greenland, knew European arts and at the court of whose king there was a Latin book (which they could not read). The Zeni spoke of much ruder people inland. Lambard also talked of the rude inhabitants of the northern lands which Arthur had conquered, but referred to 'Christians living in secret among them' who made his task of conversion easier. It is difficult not to remember the Irish monks whose relics the Norsemen found in those regions, and the fragile successor Christianity of the Icelandic settlements in Greenland.

Many of the leading geographers of the age were convinced. The imaginary islands of the Zeno brothers appear on Mercator's great world map of 1569, which the Frobisher expeditions took with them on their Arctic ventures. Hakluyt did not include the Zeni narrative in the first edition of his *Principall Navigations*, but he did in his *Divers Voyages* of 1582 and, with Ortelius's support, published it in the second version of his *Navigations*. Dee fused it with Lambard. It is not clear whether the latter could have had direct prior access to the Zeni narrative, which was published in 1558, figured in the Mercator map of 1569 and was best known in England from the 1574 edition of Ramusio's collection of voyages: Lambard published in 1568.

It is possible, however that Lambard (and conceivably even the author of the Zeni narrative) drew on another source, the mysterious but evidently familiar *Gestae Arthuri* (Deeds of Arthur) cited by Jacob Cnoyen in his *Itinerary*.

We know of these texts only from the letter which Gerard Mercator addressed to John Dee in April 1577. Dee had originally written in January 1577 to Ortelius in Antwerp about the geography of the northern and sub-Arctic regions, in connection with the Frobisher expeditions beyond Greenland; the Fleming had called on him in March, shortly before Frobisher set out on his second voyage. While completing his *Famous and Rich Discoveries*, Dee further questioned Gerard Mercator about his mapping of the Polar regions. The reply he received evidently excited the doctor.

For, in response, Mercator said that he had drawn his material on the north from the *Itinerary* of the Dutchman Jacob Cnoyen, and he transcribed the relevant section virtually word-for-word in Old Dutch and Latin. When Hakluyt in 1580 (sceptical of some of Dee's arguments on the Arctic) tried to get hold of the original text, however, Mercator reported that he had lent it to a friend (probably Ortelius) and that it had disappeared. No one ever found it again.

Mercator said that Cnoyen had 'travelled the world like Mandeville but described what he saw with better judgement' and wrote 'in the Belgic language'. Cnoyen's description of the northern lands was broadly in accord with current geographical notions, which had the Grand Cham's Eastern lands approaching the tenebrous region of North Norway near the Pole and which envisaged Greenland as a peninsula. Cnoyen however, referred to the Little People in the North (Eskimos or *Skraelings* as the Icelandic settlers in Greenland and Labrador called them, to be followed by Mercator) and noted that there had also been mention of these people in the *Gestae Arthuri*. There was 'a beautiful, open land' nearby, between the Oriental Province of Darkness and a Province of Bergi, each of them surrounded by the dread indrawing seas which flowed together into the celebrated Polar whirlpool. Cnoyen explicitly stated that 'these facts and more about the geography of the North are to be found in the beginning of *Gestae Arthuri* etc.'

He went on to describe a great circumpolar range of mountains to the north, through which multiple channels cut, flowing together to form four indrawing seas at the Pole. It is not clear whether Cnoyen drew this material from *Gestae Arthuri* or not, but after a break in the manuscript (the text was badly damaged by fire) he suddenly has Arthur's great army in the north conquering the islands around 530AD. No fewer than 4,000 of Arthur's people had gone into the indrawing seas and had never returned. In 1364, however, eight 'of these people' appeared at the court of King Magnus of Norway. Among them were two priests, one of whom had an astrolabe. This man was 'descended in the fifth generation from a Bruxellensis: One, I say: the eight were sprung from those who had penetrated the Northern Regions in the first ships'.

Then, in a section which might or might not have been derived from the testimony of those eight people (or might simply be a continuation of the *Gestae Arthuri*) Cnoyen goes into detail about Arthur's expeditions. The great army had crossed from the northern islands of Scotland to Iceland, but had been warned by four returning ships of the perils of the indrawing seas. So Arthur instead peopled all the islands between Scotland and Iceland as well as an island called *Grocland*, on the lip of these indrawing seas (he found people twenty-three feet tall there). The four ships bringing the warning had claimed that they knew where the 'magnetic lands' were, and in the following year twelve of Arthur's ships, carrying 1,800 men and 400 women, tried to get through the high rocks into the dread seas; half the people were lost but they apparently succeeded.

Cnoyen then abruptly returned his narrative to the eight survivors of 'these people' at Bergen in 1364. The priest with an astrolabe reported that in 1360 an English Minorite from Oxford, who was a good astronomer, had come to the northern islands. He had left his party, penetrated alone into the polar regions and written up his report into a book *Inventio Fortunata* (which began at latitude 54° and went on to the Pole). This book he had presented to Edward III.

The Minorite went into great detail about the circumpolar mountain chain, the multiple channels flowing together into four indrawing seas, the four large land areas they formed, two inhabited and two not. At the Pole itself, there was the great whirlpool and a huge, black, magnetic rock-island thirty-three miles in circumference. The Minorite also mentioned a 'fair, level land' under the North Star, a narrow arm of land which was nearly all wooded, where he met twenty-three people not above four feet tall, sixteen of whom were women. He spoke of a sea which froze to the east but was free to the west because of the strength of the current, mentioned ship-timbers and other evidence of humans he had found, and talked of high plateaux and trees of Brazil wood. Moreover, according to the priest with the astrolabe at Bergen, the English Minorite had made five further journeys into the northern regions.

A book *Inventio Fortunata*, which covered the Polar regions, had without doubt existed and had been used by earlier scholars. Its material appears on the first great globe made in 1492 by Martin Behaim, a German cosmographer based at Lisbon. Another German, Johann Ruysch, who had sailed from England (probably from Bristol), used it for his world map of 1508. John Day, writing his famous letter from Bristol to Columbus in 1497, had mentioned it. Both Ortelius and Mercator used it for their maps, though the latter, who had his own ideas about the magnetic pole, did not make the *Inventio's* great black rock magnetic. No copy of this English book was available to Dee and Hakluyt and it became the 'ghost book' of the century. In Dee's own writings, the Oxford Minorite was not identified, but the doctor was acknowledged as the source for the entry in Hakluyt's *Principall Navigations* which named the astronomer as Nicholas of Lynn, a celebrated Oxford mathematician. Hakluyt himself seems to have suspected that the real author might have been the contemporary friar Hugh of Ireland (Nicholas of Lynn was a Carmelite, not a Franciscan).

The information in Mercator's letter was (characteristically) a blend of fantasy and genuine geographical knowledge. Some of the detailed topography, the references to *Skraelings* (the Minorite's encounter with Eskimos seems plausible) and other particulars are strikingly reminiscent of the Icelanders' descriptions of Greenland and the neighbouring areas of America, especially of Markland (Labrador) and possibly even of Vinland. A leading Icelandic-Canadian scholar felt able to identify some of the places mentioned as Hudson Strait, Fox Basin, Baffin Island and other locations in the Canadian Arctic, while a British scholar saw the currents of the Davis Strait in the indrawing seas. The whirlpool at or near the Pole was a conventional belief of long standing; Gerald the Welshman had spoken of one. None of this knowledge would have been strange to the Icelanders who had been ranging those regions for several hundred years.

What is striking is that the ordering and placing of this knowledge was achieved by the author of the *Inventio*, the author of the *Gestae Arthuri* and by Cnoyen in much the same manner and, by the last two, located in an Arthurian context. It is not clear whether Cnoyen obtained his story of the eight persons at the court of Bergen at first hand. It is not impossible; the city was a staple of the Hanseatic League and also a centre for English merchants. It was from 1342 that the Norwegians began to make desperate efforts to re-establish contact with the Icelanders in Greenland who were said to have abandoned the Christian religion and to have turned to the peoples of America. Ivar Bardarson served as administrator of the remote Greenland see from 1342 to 1362; it was he who found the Western Settlement deserted in 1342. In 1354, King Magnus issued an urgent order to Poul Knutson to take the great royal ship, the *knorr*, to Greenland to rescue the Christian religion there. In 1347 the Icelandic annals mention a Greenland ship which had sailed for Markland but had been driven to Iceland without an anchor; the ship and its crew were taken to Bergen. In 1363 or 1364, Ivar Bardarson got back to Norway from Greenland. There is, then, nothing inherently implausible in the story of the arrival of eight persons at Bergen in 1364.

But who made them descendants of Arthur's people? In the Cnoyen narrative, when the priest with the astrolabe had finished his report to the

King of Norway, 'the other 7 that were with him testified that they had also heard such things said by their elders but had never seen them'. This comment, however, may simply refer to the priest's account of the climate and nature of the Polar regions. Because of gaps in the text, it is not possible to relate the priest's narrative very precisely to Cnoyen's or that of *Gestae Arthuri*. A close reading of the material suggests that Cnoyen used the priest as a major source and supplemented him with the *Gestae;* the latter was said 'also' to mention the Little People. Whenever he appears in the text, as far as it is possible to tell, the priest is used to provide geographical detail or to report on the Oxford Minorite (from whom he had obtained the astrolabe in exchange for a testament). It is noticeable, however, that this priest is singled out as somebody different; he was a fifth-generation descendant of a Fleming (Flemings crop up in these narratives as often as those elusive Britons!) Either Mercator or Cnoyen drew attention to his difference from the others — 'One, I say' — though all eight were also in some sense descendants of Arthur's people. The reference by 'the other seven' to 'things said by their elders' suggests a distinction between the priest and their own native leaders and also carries a hint of 'ancient histories' and origin legends. It would be remarkable if Icelandic survivors or strays from remote settlements in Greenland or adjacent parts (which is what one assumes these eight people to have been) had come to think of themselves as 'descendants of Arthur', perhaps at the prompting of others (the progenitor of this priest would presumably have joined the people, if the story is true, in the early thirteenth century), particularly since there appears to be no trace of such stories in other Icelandic records. It is not, however, entirely to be ruled out as a possibility; there was, after all, a Celtic strain there.

It is far more likely, however, that Cnoyen himself gave them this identity and that his mind was governed by his own reading at home in one of the cultural marts of Europe and, in particular, by the *Gestae Arthuri*. No one knows anything about this text. It was certainly rather late. Its Province of Bergi (reported as Berga in the Ruysch map) was the *pianura de Bargu* similarly described in the *Travels* of Marco Polo. It also, quite clearly, drew heavily on the Icelanders' experience of the north. There had evidently been a massive extension of Arthur's mythical conquests in the north since the days of Geoffrey of Monmouth. William Worcestre, the Bristol man who was as familiar with the Bristol ventures out into the western and northern seas in quest of Brazil (which might have taken some men to America before Columbus), as he was with the Bristol and Norfolk trade with Iceland (and conceivably Greenland), was certainly immersed in Arthur's conquests. He had a French book which cited older texts about them. The listing of Greenland among the extended roll-call of such triumphs among his papers, however, was the work of another hand. That list reappears, of course, in William

60

Lambard's celebrated 'ancient manuscript', which turned up in the *Principall Navigations*. This might have been based on the *Gestae*, since it includes lands north of Norway 'even under the North Pole', but it makes no mention of *Grocland*. Richard Hakluyt, annotating Mercator's letter to Dee in 1580, thought that Grocland was simply a duplicate of Greenland — 'Grocland to me seemeth to be our Groenland' — and, when he repeated the remark in his comment on Arthur's peopling of Grocland, referred directly to Lambard (who might, of course, himself have been thinking along the same lines). Mercator however, as well as Ortelius in his *Theatrum* of 1570, believed in Grocland and boldly located it as a large heart-shaped island well to the west of Greenland.

So did John Dee in his map of 1580, and it was Dee who would have been most excited by this new information. 'Gestae Arturi . . .', he noted on Mercator's letter, 'A rare testimony of great importance to the Brytissh title to the Septentrional Regions, Atlantis in particular'. He went on eagerly to incorporate the new material into the structure he had already built out of Lambard and the Zeni. That new material, however, also stopped him in his tracks. Having carefully rebuilt Arthur's old empire in the north, he was now suddenly confronted with direct 'evidence' of a British colonization of the Arctic and sub-Arctic at the cost of thousands of lives and with British survivors of Arthur's people apparently still active in those regions as late as 1364. Those 'five generations' of the priest with the astrolabe clearly confused him as they did others. Marginal comments on the letter calculate the possibilities.

> 8 men being of the generation of them which went in King Arthur his tyme to these places discovering . . . I mean in the 25 generation at the least, after King Arthur his tyme allowing longer Ages than now the generall rate is: at betwene 25 and 30 years to a generation . . .

Hakluyt dropped Mercator's report — that the priest with the astrolabe was descended in the fifth generation — from his *Principall Navigations*, but it quite evidently lodged in Dee's mind. These people could not possibly have been survivors from Arthur's time. Where then did these British or Welsh come from?

It was certainly at this point that John Dee turned to Humphrey Llwyd's manuscript history of Wales. He had a copy made and carefully underlined and annotated it. He was already at odds with Mercator over northern sea routes and he found discrepancies in the great map-maker's interpretation. Mercator took care not to endow the *Inventio's* great black rock at the Pole with magnetic power. Johann Ruysch, however, had stressed its menace. 'Here the ship's compass does not hold, nor can ships containing iron turn back . . .' Mariners had become familiar with compass variation before the fifteenth century, but early geographical texts and travellers' tales had been full of horror stories about menacing magnetic islands, against which the use of horn rather than iron for nails was the best defence. Such treatises, particularly the Arab, had located these threats in *southern* latitudes. One had been placed in the 'sea of weed' towards the Caribbean. Moreover, there was a book *Inventio Fortunata*, also full of alarms, which appeared to operate in a context radically different from that which figured in Cnoyen. Both Bartolomeo de las Casas and Columbus's own son refer to an *Inventio Fortunata* for floating and burning islands west of the Azores (sometimes associated with the Irish St Brendan) in a decidedly southern climate. The most distinguished British historian of these early years of exploration suggests that there must have been two different books with the same title. This seems eminently reasonable. But, while the books which cite the English *Inventio Fortunata* invariably do so in a northern and polar context, it is not entirely certain that its English (or Irish) author wrote *only* about the Pole. His book may have been based on personal experience for the north, but he might well have constructed a compendium, much as Cnoyen himself seems to have done. The possibility of confusion in the mind of Dr John Dee cannot be ignored. For in his search for more recent Arthurian venturers in the northern seas, he may well have unearthed stories about Humphrey Llwyd's Madoc which were charged with precisely this north-south tension. Testimony attributed to Dr John David Rhys suggests that he certainly did.

Rhys was a celebrated physician and grammarian. Born in Anglesey and a student at Christ Church Oxford, he spent many years in Italy and travelled to Venice, Crete and Cyprus. He took a doctorate at Siena, taught at Padua, published a book on Italian pronunciation at the latter place and a very popular Latin grammar at Venice. Back in Wales in 1579, he practised as a physician at Cardiff, settled in Breconshire, married a Herefordshire woman and published a notorious Welsh grammar in which he tried to impose Latin rules on a Celtic language.

He, too, was steeped in Arthurian erudition and was a close friend of John Dee, whose genealogy he traced back to the early kings of Wales. He apparently left a report which, unfortunately, lacks any verification or confirmation whatsoever, but which might possibly reflect something of the travail into which Mercator's letter undoubtedly plunged the 'Brytish Philosopher'. According to Rhys, in this alleged report, Dee came to feel that Mercator had been deceived. The priest at Bergen could not have been one of Arthur's people; he must have descended from a survivor of Madoc's expeditions. Rhys asserts that Dee, in pursuing Cnoyen, came across references to a map earlier in date than 1400 which showed the track of both Madoc and the Oxford astronomer and indicated, far out in the Atlantic, an island of *Gwerddonau Llion* which Madoc had discovered. At one point, according to Rhys, Dee was apparently speculating that Madoc might have reached Bermuda or an island in the Bahamas.

Moreover, among the sources of Cnoyen's narrative were listed not only Nicholas of Lynn and the priest with the astrolabe, but Cnoyen's fellow-Dutchman, a Willem of Ghent.

There is no trace of any of this outside Rhys's alleged testimony, but taken at face value it sounds remarkably reminiscent of the Poitiers fragment attributed to Willem and his *Madoc:* the sea of weed, the nails of horn, the isle of *Llion*, that Fountain of Youth which sixteenth-century Spaniards sailing for Florida associated with Bimini in the Bahamas.

Without necessarily accepting any of this testimony attributed to Rhys, there remains the highly plausible supposition that John Dee, in the hunt for Madoc into which Mercator's letter had precipitated him, might well have come across earlier Madoc stories kin to Willem's. Indeed, Cnoyen's own story may carry some echo of legend. If the ambivalent priest with the astrolabe is set to one side, there were seven unambiguous 'descendants of Arthur' at Bergen in 1364. Seven survivors of an Arthur expedition were a theme in Welsh writing. In one of the Welsh Arthur poems attributed to Taliesin in the thirteenth century, a work which seems to have some connection with the celebrated and Arthurian *Culhwch and Olwen* of *The Mabinogion*, there are stories of Arthur leading raids in his great ship *Prydwen* into the eight *caers* (strongholds) of the Otherworld. The poem, *Preideu Annwfyn*, chants a litany:

> Three freights of Prydwen went we into it,
> Save seven, none came back from Caer Siddi . . .

> And when we went with Arthur . . .
> Save seven, none came back from Caer Feddwyd . . .

> And when we went with Arthur, sad journey,
> Save seven, none came back from Caer Fandwy . . .

> When we went with Arthur, sad contest,
> Save seven, none came back from Caer Ochren . . .

And, perhaps, when we went with Arthur to the four indrawing seas, save seven, none came back to Bergen in 1364?

Whatever the nature, provenance and atmosphere of the Cnoyen text, it not only focused Dee's mind on Madoc but, within that mind, located Madoc in a *northern* complex of exploration. The relevant section of Humphrey Llwyd's manuscript actually has Madoc 'leaving the coast of Ireland northwards' — an ambiguous phrase which Dee himself interpreted in a marginal note: 'Madoc sonne to prince Owen sayled to the land north of Ireland . . . afterward above 400 year was judged to have byn . . . (in the lands) . . . first by the Spaniards and others discovered'. Whatever the truth or falsity of John David Rhys's report, the 'Arch Conjuror' has Madoc's voyage growing out of the Arthurian penetration of the northern seas.

In his 'Title Royal' of 1580, the emphasis is entirely northern. After Madoc, come the Thornes (for Newfoundland), Sebastian Cabot (for Labrador), Martin Frobisher (for Meta Incognita in the sub-Arctic), and Stephen Borough (for islands in the Scythian Sea). Dee claimed Novaya Zemlya, discovered by Borough, as an Arthurian conquest and as one of the four islands around the Pole listed in the *Inventio*. Mercator's letter was central to the whole presentation, knitting it together. Alongside Cabot and Borough were listed St Brendan, Greenland and Iceland from Lambard, King Malgo from Geoffrey of Monmouth, and a whole sequence of Arthurian conquests from Cnoyen, the *Gestae Arthuri* and the Zeno brothers. Arthur had sent colonies into all the islands between Scotland and Iceland,

> whereby it is probable that the late named Friseland is of Brytish ancient discovery and possession. And also seeing Grocland beyond Groenland got its inhabitants from Arthur it is credible that the famous Ilande Estotiland was by his folke possessed . . .

Moreover, 'The Latin book in the King's Library in Estotiland by no history (yet heard of) can most probably be ascribed to any other mens bringing thither than by the foresaid colonies sent by King Arthur'. There follows a direct reference to the Oxford friar and the *Inventio* (which Dee, following one rendering in Mercator's letter, thought had actually been called *Inventio Fortunae*). His map plots all the familiar names — Iceland, Friseland, Greenland, Icaria, Grocland, Estotiland and Brendan. And at the head of the list is Madoc, curling down *out of the north* to *Terra Florida*.

Furthermore, in all future British claims to *Florida*, Madoc is indissolubly coupled with the Cabots, John and Sebastian, who were thought to have followed a similar trajectory, sailing into the north (which by then must have been fairly familiar!) and then driving south to the Spanish lands. Sir Thomas Herbert in the seventeenth century has his Madoc sailing far to the north of Ireland, hitting Newfoundland and then 'ranging the coast' to the Gulf of Mexico. Dee and Herbert were at least logical.

Dr David Powel however took a very different tack. He was even less able to resist the pull of Mexico and those Welsh-speaking Mexicans. He rewrote Llwyd's original phrase into a 'leaving the coast of Ireland so far north' in order to direct his Madoc unambiguously into the south-west. Richard Hakluyt followed him and so did most later commentators. This sudden sortie from the Irish Sea (usually from Lundy) to the south-west certainly managed to plant Madoc firmly in Mexico, but it came apparently out of a blue emptiness. At the heart of the Madoc myth, at its very origins, there is therefore a certain contradiction, an initial blankness.

It is a paltry sort of scholarship, however, which would confront one blankness with another. Myths, after all, have been the very stuff of history; at important moments, they have been the very motor of history. Of no time has this been more true than of those dramatic and frustrating years when Europeans were confronted with the 'discovery' and settlement of a new world. Such evidence as we possess on the origins and emergence of the Madoc myth is singularly frustrating, contradictory and often deceptive. Nevertheless its general import seems clear enough.

Circulating through late medieval and early modern Wales there probably *were* stories about a Madoc, generally though not invariably associated with the family of Owain Gwynedd, who was renowned as a seafarer and who was credited with the discovery of suitably marvellous islands. We may in fact be confronted with a successive reworking and reshaping of old stories. If the Poitiers fragment bears any genuine resemblance to thirteenth-century stories, they would have been legendary in tone, though probably anchored to historical personalities such as the Icelanders' Freeman of Wales. Such stories seem to have left no trace in the Welsh historical record. This is not too difficult to understand. Bards and storytellers had a great wealth of oral material to draw on, to which the enigmatic triads of Welsh literature were probably mnemonic keys; an Irish *ollamh* had to know 350 prose tales as a professional qualification and the Welsh *cyfarwydd* was no less professional though much lower in status than the poets. Many, perhaps the great majority, have been lost. The apparent absence of Madoc before the fifteenth century (at least in Wales, if not in Europe) may suggest that his story was not central or considered important.

In the fifteenth century, there are hints of a recurrence, and possibly a revival, of such stories. If this were in any way connected with the writing of *Inventio Fortunata* at the court of Edward III, with the new British contact with Iceland and perhaps Greenland, or with the quickening of interest in exploration during that century and the peopling of maps with more and more islands marching further and further west after the Portuguese discovery of the Azores, one would expect the kind of story that Maredudd ap Rhys's verse hints at to have had a northern bias, though one could also expect earlier tales of island paradises bathed in sun to confuse the picture.

It is impossible to say when that evocative moral challenge entered the story with its haunting image of Madoc, the man of peace, seeking a new start for an old people as he leads his little ships into the unknown (though one might perhaps guess at the fifteenth-century aftermath of the rebellion of Owain Glyn Dŵr). It certainly proved permanent.

> See them starting, three-and-ten
> Little ships on a brave morning . . .

runs a Welsh verse of the nineteenth century. Madoc came too early, his legend came too late, writes an American poet of the twentieth century, celebrating a Peace-maker.

After the news of Columbus, any Madoc story would have found it difficult *not* to mutate into a 'discovery of America'. It probably happened much as Humphrey Llwyd said it did and in much the same way as it happened with him. By that time, there was a wealth of material to draw on. Madoc's land 'must be . . . by order of Cosmographie . . .' the land the Spaniards had come to . . . a poor second. And however many fables had been fained . . . 'sure it is that there he was . . .' How sure anyone else can be is another matter! We know now that such a journey was technically feasible, but that is all we know. Whether there was a real Madoc, whether he was the Freeman or someone like him, whether he sailed and where he sailed if he did, Heaven only knows and now only Heaven ever will know.

What is abundantly clear is that any story of Madoc *as a discoverer of America* was and is, in itself, essentially *precarious*. After all, even if, by some miracle, it had proved possible (or does prove possible) to verify the story, what would that signify or have signified? It would scarcely rank as an historically operative discovery. Whether proven or not, such a Madoc story would at best serve as an historical curiosity or perhaps as balm to an injured patriot spirit. It was not for such antiquarian or psychiatric reasons that the Madoc story, launched at the world in the 1580s, lived for nearly 400 years and, at two critical moments in its life, itself became an operative historical force, consciousness transformed into act, an idea-that-walks, an idea that moved men to historical action. At those two climaxes, the story acquired memorable power from a complex of causes entirely independent of itself.

One such moment was its very birth as an historic legend. It was the intervention of Dr John Dee, building his 'Brytish Empire' and confronted with his Arthurian survivors in the north, which snatched what had evidently been a marginal, perhaps underground, story and thrust it into the centre of Elizabethan enterprise. Before 1583, English writings usually took the Cabot voyages as title and warrant for expansion into the new world. From 1580 onwards, as relations with Spain spiralled rapidly into open conflict, Madoc moved majestically to the forefront.

'The Queen of England's Title to all the West Indies or at least to as moche as is from Florida to the Circle Articke is more lawfull and right then the Spaniardes' declared Richard Hakluyt the younger in the eighteenth chapter of his *Discourse of Western Planting* in 1584. ' . . . ffor the firste pointe wee of England have to shewe very auncient and auctenticall Chronicles written in the welshe or brittishe tongue . . .' Madock ap Owen Gwyneth, weary of civil wars, had made his two voyages out of Wales and 'discovered and planted large Countries which he founde in the Mayne Ocean south westwarde of Ireland in 1170'. His discoveries were confirmed by the language of 'some of those people that dwell upon the continent between the Bay of Mexico and the graunde Bay of Newfoundlande'. The West Indies had been discovered and inhabited 322 years before Columbus, thanks to Madoc. Furthermore, the Columbus brothers had themselves offered the lands they proposed to 'discover' to Henry VII before they had entered the service of Spain and Madoc's primacy had been re-affirmed by the Cabots.

After the climacteric year which witnessed the defeat of the Spanish Armada, Madoc made what must be counted the most fortunate landfall in his entire career. For he promptly lodged, securely and centrally, in what Froude called the 'prose epic of the English nation' — that massive and magnificent compilation, the very voice of a new and triumphant British empire, Hakluyt's *The Principall Navigations, Voyages, Traffiques and Discoveries of the English Nation*. From the first edition of 1589 through to the massive volumes of 1598-1600, they are all there, bubbling up from the Welsh pre-history of Britain, drawn from David Powel's *History of Cambria* and his annotated *Gerald the Welshman* of 1585, from Geoffrey of Monmouth in the Comelinus Heidelberg edition of 1587, from William Lambard and John Dee and William Camden: the Romano-British Helen, who gave her name to all the Roman roads of Wales and Constantine who 'conquered Rome', hero and heroine of *The Mabinogion;* Pelagius and John Erigen, 'the Welshmen'; the Arthur and the Malgo of Geoffrey; the greater Arthur of Lambard; Cnoyen and the Arthurian priest in Norway; *Inventio Fortunata* and the Nicholas of Lynn of Johr. Dee; Gerald the Welshman and his maelstrom and, heading the list for America and the West, the Madoc of Powel and Peckham and Ingram and Llwyd, and the Maredudd verse supplied by Camden, with his supporters the Cabots and the Columbus brothers of the offer to Henry VII . . .

For one brief generation, the Worthiness of Wales reached its Tudor climax in Madoc as the symbolic spearpoint of the first British thrust into a new world. From Hakluyt, this Madoc swept swiftly into general European discourse and for a generation lodged in the many imperialist tracts produced during the struggle — Purchas, Marriott, Abbott and the rest — all in that cause aptly summarized by a title of later date, *The British Sailor's Discovery or the Spanish Pretensions Confuted*.

Whatever his original provenance and character, Madoc first effectively entered history as an instrument of imperial conflict. His story henceforth was to follow the ebb and flow of imperialism, trade rivalry and colonial settlement with hypnotic precision.

4

Frontier Madoc

In the history of the Madoc legend, the decisive moment was the shift to the North American mainland. As with many such migrations, this effected a profound qualitative change. A tradition of a 'Discovery of America' became a tradition of 'Welsh Indians'. The Welsh Indian myth in turn became perhaps the most powerful and influential, certainly the most persistent, myth of American westward expansion. Its entry into history was explosive; in the last years of the eighteenth century, something like a Madoc fever broke out in America. In its essentials, however, the myth had been created in the seventeenth century.

The century of the English civil war opened with an abrupt demotion of Madoc from his Tudor eminence. With the coming of the Stuarts and the influx of Scots, the execution of Raleigh and the settlement with Spain, the Madoc story went into eclipse. The tradition dwindled rapidly and, outside the obscure deliberations of the uncommonly learned, became as marginal as the people from whom it had sprung. References in the seventeenth century were rare. They were, however, decisive. For they occurred, every single one of them, in books which scored a resonant success in their own day and went on echoing down successive generations. Three in English and one in Welsh, they were all best-sellers; two of them established a new literary genre, and one of them ran to twenty-four editions in forty years. Madoc and his Welsh Indians, though now a footnote and perhaps only a half-remembered one, lodged in the common literary discourse of most reasonably cultivated men.

'Peregrination (well-us'd) is a very profitable school, it is a running Academy', wrote James Howell in his *Epistolae Ho-Eliana* (Familiar Letters), published in three successive volumes between 1645 and 1655 and running to ten editions by 1753. Howell was one of the earliest men to make a living by literature. He had to; imprisoned in the Fleet by Parliament men in 1643, he was kept there by creditors until 1651. He lived by his pen, light, racy and vivid. Much-travelled and an accomplished linguist, he had been born in Builth, the son of a clergyman who held livings in Breconshire and Carmarthen. A graduate of the largely Welsh college of Jesus, Oxford, he had served king, lords and merchants in Italy, France, Holland and especially Spain. Appointed secretary to the Council of the North, he settled in York and became MP for Richmond, though he was a friend of London writers, particularly 'Father' Ben Jonson. Made a Clerk to the Council shortly before his arrest, he blotted his copybook by writing in favour of Cromwell, but remained a king's man in defiance of that 'wavering, windy thing . . . humersome and cross-grained animal . . . the common people', and at the Restoration was made Historiographer-Royal, a post said to have been created especially for him. He wrote a good deal, but was remembered for his *Familiar Letters* which were brilliantly done and started a new fashion. In those *Letters*, during the Commonwealth's campaigns in the West Indies, Howell planted Madoc's men ineradicably on land in a fit of absent-mindedness.

He built on the work of another Welshman of York who, at the same Restoration, was made a baronet even though he had served Parliament. Sir Thomas Herbert had been the last companion of Charles I, appointed his attendant in prison and made groom of his bedchamber. He slept in the same room and went on his last walk with the King, who gave him his silver watch. Born in York into a merchant family which was a collateral branch of the celebrated Herberts of Monmouthshire, he secured a place through the patronage of William Herbert, Earl of Pembroke, in the retinue of Sir Dodmore Cotton, ambassador to Persia. From 1626 to 1629, Herbert travelled extensively in the Middle East and India.

In 1634, he published a *Description of the Persian Monarchy* . . . which was successful enough for him, four years later, to settle down to a considerable revision and expansion, rich in vivid illustration, which he published as *Some Yeares Travels into divers parts of Asia and Afrique* . . . 'My Lord, Having past the pikes, I take new courage to come on againe. One blow more and I have done. Ten to one it lights on my owne pate . . .'

Well might he say so; he had already peppered his work, brimming with eye-witness descriptions, and long historical and topographical disquisitions, with references to 'Welsh remains in several exotique places of the world' in that audacious and blissfully ill-informed linguistic speculation which was common to most 'projectors'. The names of the Isle of Wight, Coney Isle off the Cape of Good Hope (with a suitable drawing of the *Pen-gwyn*) and *Chumro* north of Madagascar were clearly derived from the Welsh, and as for *Digarroys* near Mauritius:

> Digarroys (as Sea-men tell us) was first discovered by the Portuguise: but except some Welsh-man had the honour of naming it, I know not whence call'd *Dygarroys*, for *Digarrod* in the British dialect fitly complies with it, an Ile so desolate . . .

Describing the foundation of Cairo, he noted sagely, 'Caire in Syriac and

69

Brittish signifying a City . . . '.

Accurately observing that 'I have formerly in a line or two vindicated the honour of our Country lost in the greater part by protract of malitious time,' he announced his intention to write more fully on the theme. In the 1638 edition, he was true to his word, developing and expanding a short chapter from the book of 1634. He wrote a sub-title into his frontispiece — 'with a revivall of the first Discoverer of America' — and in the section of his book where he described his return passage past America, he created a special chapter: 'Madoc ap Owen Gwyneth discovered America above three hundred yeeres before Columbus . . .' Vivid, pungent, memorable, it was this chapter of Herbert's, more than the learned and particular Tudor texts, which became the classic popular exposition of the Madoc myth. For nearly two hundred years all other Madoc celebrants built on him.

'In the first place it may be asked,' he began, 'whence Madock's resolution came. I answer. From an innate desire to travell and to avoid domestique broiles, he put that in action which some old prophetique sayings gave him light and encouraged him in. 'Tis very like he had read *Plato* (for what part of the world has ever more affected learning than the *Brittans*)'. He cited the familiar litany of ancient authors 'known' to have written of a New World — Aristotle, Theophrastus, Hanno and in particular Seneca, whom he quoted at length. 'Madoc from these lights discerned it' (in a new edition of 1665, these authors had become 'but dim lights to show the way into the Western World').

Herbert rehearsed the story of the civil wars. Madoc had foreseen the threat of a Norman conquest which these divisions invited, but no one listened: 'he thence-forth studies his owne preservation'. He had remembered a prophecy penned long since by the noble Bard Taliesin who was also quoted at length. So 'he put to Sea without bidding his kindred farewell, least too much love or hate might have withdrawne him' (a useful explanation of contemporary silence on the voyage!).

Herbert had Madoc sailing from Abergwili (probably a corruption of Abergele in north Wales, an area rich in *Gwennan Gorn* stories). He reached land, 'probably New found Land', and then ranged the coast to find settlement. 'Here Madoc planted (in *Florida* or *Canada*, some part of *Mexico*)'. This location, comprehensive enough in all conscience was abandoned in later editions! Madoc raised fortifications and left 120 men behind him on his return — 'I follow the old Copie in this Storie', Herbert added. By Providence (the best compass) and the Pole Star, he regained Wales, loaded his 'Ten good barques' and fortunately re-attained his 'plantation', only to find most of the settlers dead through 'two much eating', the novelty of the climate and the treachery of the natives. 'Madoc digested it with a Christian fortitude' and with the aid of his brothers Eneon and Edwall (Einion and Idwal — unheard of elsewhere) restored the settlement and awaited further migrants. But there was a 'breach of promise of settlers', because the state had been 'turn'd topsie-turvie' by the last struggles of the Welsh princes against Edward I. 'Nevertheless, albeit Madoc and his Cambrian crew be dead and their memory moth-eaten, yet their foot-steps are plainly traced . . . '

In support, Herbert cited the familiar linguistic and cultural evidence: 'How come those Brittish words (not much altred from the dialect used at this day) amongst the Mexicans? whence had they the use of Beads, Crucifixes etc.' He referred to the Spanish sources, noted the Mexican tradition 'that a strange people came thither in Corraughs' and rehearsed the story of Montezuma's speech — 'the people he meant were Welsh rather than Spaniards'. 'Nor is it a Phantasie of yesterday,' he added, marshalling the three poets central to the tradition and the Tudor writers. He quoted and translated the verse of Maredudd ap Rhys, which Hakluyt had printed. The whole argument was 'made more orthodoxall by Welsh names given there to birds, rivers, rocks, beasts etc.', which list Herbert considerably extended.

He ended with the familiar anti-Spanish exhortation. Had all this been known, Columbus would not have carried off the honour. 'Nor had Prince *Madoc* been defrauded of his memory nor our Kings of their just right and Title to the West Indies.' 'Far be it from me to detract from Columbus,' he added, before promptly proceeding to do so, heavily implying that the Genoese had been armed with fore-knowledge of America. 'But this I would withall have also granted; That this his voyage was after the other (of our Country-man) three hundred and two and twenty yeares; and that the Spaniards have not so much right to those Countries (I meane of *America*) as our King has; so long as they arrogate their claime from a primier discovery.'

In later editions of his work, the Madoc story was given rather less prominence; it lost its special chapter. On the other hand, the charge against Columbus was strengthened and the tradition remained essentially unimpaired. In this form, it ran through edition after edition of the *Travels* until the book achieved classic status in a travel-collection of 1785. No one knows the source of Herbert's novel additions to the canon, his *Old Copie*. Gutyn Owain's 'lost manuscript' perhaps? True believers were to assert, quite without warrant, that the author had had access in the Raglan Castle of the Herberts to material which was destroyed during the civil war (Madoc historiography is full of such cruel mischance).

But how extraordinarily reminiscent the whole story is of the actual history of the celebrated *Lost Colonists of Roanoke*, the first and abortive English colony in the Virginia of Sir Walter Raleigh.

After a reconnaissance in 1584, the first party of 108 were landed at Roanoke, north of Cape Hatteras, one of the islands of the long spit off present-day North Carolina which shelters Pamlico Sound. These deserted the island in 1586, missing two relief fleets, the second of which left fifteen men behind as a holding party. In 1587 a new expedition arrived with 117 people under John White (of the famous drawings). They found no survivors. They sent White home to get supplies but he was unable to return until 1590, when he found that these people had vanished as well. Not until the Jamestown settlement in modern Virginia was launched was any news obtained, when John Smith (of Pocahontas fame) learned that most of the settlers had been massacred by the chief Powhatan along with the Chesapeake tribe. There were, however, persistent reports of handfuls of survivors, some said to have gone native or to have been working copper in a region which was, then or later, that of the Tuscarora Indians.

The Roanoke tonality of Herbert's narrative is quite striking. James Howell shifted the emphasis further towards settlement in a letter to John Savage, Earl Rivers (fictitious, as most of them were) which he published in the 1650 edition of his work. He was discussing the fourteen originally independent languages of Europe, of which the 'Cambrian or Cymraecan tongue, commonly call'd Welsh (and Italian also is so call'd by the Dutch)' was one, the 'prime maternal tongue' of Britain. 'But my Lord, you would think it strange, that divers pure *Welsh* words should be found in the new-found World in the *West Indies* . . . ' and he went on to give Herbert's list. He concluded, however, with the sensational assertion, 'Nay, I have read a Welsh *Epitaph*, which was found there upon one *Madoc*, a *British* prince'.

Howell was obviously writing from faulty memory. He antedated the journeys by over a century, and made Madoc a prince of *south* Wales, who sailed from Milford Haven. In the 1655 edition of his book, however, he stuck to his guns and in a probably genuine letter to his cousin Howell Gwyn, who had, understandably, asked about the 'epitaph', quoted a corrupt version of the Maredudd ap Rhys verse, which he specifically said had been 'English'd thus in Mr Herbert's Travels' (though he 'improved' on the translation).

This incredible misreading, accidental or wishful, of Herbert became an accepted truth. It ran with the multiple editions of the *Letters* into the eighteenth century when not to know Howell was 'an ignorance beyond barbarism'. The Maredudd ap Rhys verse, in this, its novel trans-Atlantic *persona*, duly lodged in Hackett's *Collection of Epitaphs*. It so impressed Dr Samuel Johnson that he translated it into Latin.

The shift registered in European writing on the settlement of America. Herbert's *Travels* soon found both a French and a Dutch translation and the Dutch writer Hornius, arguing in 1652 that America had been peopled by all manner of races, cited the Welsh as a major component. In this context, he recalled that Peter Martyr had reported that Indians of Guatemala and Virginia had revered one Matec, whom he identified with

Madoc.

In the margins of European literary discourse, then, the widely-held belief persisted that there had been Indian tribes in the West Indies and the neighbouring mainland, loosely grouped in an original 'Mexico', who had long carried the stigmata of an initial Madocian migration. In 1674, indeed, John Josselyn, in his curious and credulous account of New England and Virginia, spoke of Indian customs which resembled those of the Ancient Britons. These stories remained within the frontiers of 'history'; no one had claimed that the descendants of Madoc's people had survived as a distinct ethnic entity. That shadow line was crossed in the most unexpected and also the most influential work of them all.

The Letters of a Turkish Spy, published in eight volumes in multiple editions over 1687-93, and as a complete set in 1694, were an instant success. A new edition came out every other year for forty years; by 1770 there had been twenty-six. They were singled out for praise by Swift who suggested them as a model; writers as varied as Charles Lamb, Isaac d'Israeli and Cibber were to acknowledge their debt. The *Letters* appear to have initiated that style of comment, satire and polemic which masqueraded as a description of the author's own country by a foreigner. For the *Letters* were alleged to be those of a Turkish Spy, Mahmoud, who had lived undetected in Paris for forty-five years and had commented freely on western life. They had been discovered by an Italian and passed from Arabic through Italian into French. They were a sensation, not least because Mahmoud 'seems to Banter all Religion' and 'in a Word, he appears in all his Letters, a Deist'. Published in England through the crisis of 1689, they struck the resonant frequency of the 1690s with their endless war, social dislocation and intellectual experiment.

Their authorship was, and is, in dispute. The eighteenth century, relying on Dr Johnson and the memoirs of an eccentric bookseller John Dunton, believed them, or at least all volumes after the first, to have been written by William Bradshaw, a Grub Street hack whom Dunton credited with 'genius quite above the common order and . . . style . . . incomparably fine'. Bradshaw himself was said to have operated under the direction of Dr Robert Midgley, a Yorkshireman, Cambridge graduate and physician who served as Licenser of the Press from 1686. Midgley had translated a great deal and, certainly, many of the English prefaces to the *Letters* are very reminiscent, in their hostility to the Christian 'Schools', of his own *New Treatise of Natural Philosophy* of 1687.

The *Letters* themselves, however, were said to have been derived from the Italian. Giovanni Paolo Marana, a Genoese exile, published a small volume, *L'Espion Turc*, in Paris in 1684; two others were prepared by 1686, but trouble with the censorship drove him to Amsterdam, where however the public proved lukewarm. The English publisher Henry Rhodes picked up the material in Holland and there was talk of a dozen more 'little volumes'. Robert Midgley certainly owned the copyright of the English version by 1693, and Bolton Corney, a nineteenth-century critic, suggested that he had advanced the money for Rhodes to buy the Italian's work. Corney thought the entire English version a mere translation. Marana himself withdrew to Italy 'in melancholy' in 1689 and died in 1693. Although Henry Hallam, the historian, put forward the counter-argument that four of the Italian volumes would scarcely make one of the English (it was agreed that the contents of the first English volume were pure Marana) and insisted on an English authorship for seven of the eight volumes, orthodox opinion, in the shape of the *Dictionary of National Biography* and the Catalogue of the British Museum, came down on the side of Corney.

It has been too precipitate; to quote Corney himself, 'Our periodical critics are too frequently compelled to travel with railroad speed'. In the eighth volume of the *Turkish Spy*, there appears a story which Marana could not possibly have known and which could have had only one source — the Welsh and their Madoc myth.

In Letter XII of Book Three in the eighth volume, allegedly dated from Paris on the second day of the eleventh moon, 1686, Mahmoud commented on Charles II of England; 'a Prince of great Wit and Policy, nor of less courage . . . of Humour, Debonaire and Amorous, much addicted to Wine and Women; munificent in his Gifts and Rewards to Persons of Merit, and to those who have the Happiness to please him in his Recreations, especially to his Concubines'. After touching on the Popish Plot, the Spy went on:

> This *Prince*, as I said before, has several *Nations* under his Dominion; and 'tis thought, he scarce knows the just extent of his *Territories* in *America*. There is a region in that *Continent*, inhabited by a *People* whom they call *Tuscaroras* and *Doegs*. Their language is the same as is spoken by the *British* or *Welsh*; a *Nation* that formerly possessed all the *Island* of *Great Britain*, but were by Degrees driven out of it into a Mountainous Corner of the *Island*, where their *Posterity* remain to this Day.
>
> Those *Tuscaroras* and *Doegs* of *America* are thought to descend from them, being the *Posterity* of such as follow'd the Fortune of one *Madoc* a *British Prince* . . .

The Spy then gave a summary but lively account of Madoc, derived entirely from Herbert's *Travels* (he, too, had the founders of Mexico arriving in *curraghs*) but then added that there was a tradition in 'that province' (apparently the Tuscarora country) that Madoc lived to a great age and saw his people multiply by many thousands before he died, because he had brought women with him on his second journey. 'They show his Tomb to this Day; *Beads*, *Crucifixes* and other *Reliques*' (a nice fusion of Howell and Herbert). He followed through the Herbert narrative until he reached the point where Sir Thomas had listed the Welsh words in use in 'Mexico', but then added the shattering comment

> And a certain Inhabitant of *Virginia* (a *place* subject to the *King of Great Britain*) stragling not long ago into the *Wilderness*, by chance, fell among a *People* who according to some *Law* or *Custom* of theirs condemned him to Death when he, in Hearing of them, made his *Prayer* to *God* in the British Tongue; upon which he was Releas'd.

This startling statement, duly transmitted through three generations, could have been derived from one source and one source only, the dramatic narrative of the Rev. Morgan Jones, which, for the Madoc myth, was the very hinge of fate.

The Morgan Jones narrative comes out of the first serious Welsh migration, that of the Quakers who accompanied William Penn after 1681. Though their hopes of creating a *Gwladfa* or National Home for the Welsh in a Welsh Barony were frustrated, the Welsh were very prominent in the first colony. Thomas Lloyd was one of the most powerful figures and served as Penn's deputy. Before the migration, he and his brother Charles had heard the first stories of Welsh-speaking Indians at home in Dolobran, Montgomeryshire, in north-central Wales. Their cousin Thomas Price told them that some time in the 1660s, one Stedman of Breconshire, sailing in a Dutch ship, had conversed in Welsh with Indians at some point between Virginia and Florida. They told him their ancestors had come from a place called Gwynedd in Prydain Fawr. Their sachems must have been veritable Druids, for the land was not called Prydain Fawr or Great Britain until after the accession of James I. At roughly the same time, an English privateer careening his vessel near Florida learned the native tongue only to find, when he encountered Oliver Humphreys, a Welsh merchant in Surinam who reported the affair to Charles Lloyd, that he had learned Welsh.

With these remarkable stories ringing in his head, Thomas Lloyd in New York met Morgan Jones, who had been a contemporary of both brothers at Jesus College Oxford. Morgan Jones, of Bassaleg, Monmouthshire, had become the pastor of a Presbyterian church near Newtown, New York, but had quarrelled with his flock over their non-payment of his stipend and his own 'ill-life and conversation'. He told Thomas Lloyd a story so astounding that the Quaker had him make a signed statement for transmission to his brother at home.

The statement, dated 10 March 1686, declared that in 1660 Jones had been a chaplain to Major or Major-General Bennett in Virginia and had been sent as minister with an expedition of two ships which Sir William Berkeley directed to Port Royal, South Carolina. They sailed in April, reached Port Royal and waited for the 'rest of the fleet' under Mr West, expected from Bermuda and Barbados. When it arrived they went 'up-river' to Oyster Point. But by 10 November, they were nearly starved for want of provisions, so Jones with five companions set out through the wilderness. In Tuscarora country, they were captured by Tuscaroras 'because we told them we were bound for Roanoke'. Thrown prisoner into a hut, they were told the next day by an interpreter that they were to die in the morning:

> whereupon, being something cast-down, and speaking to this effect in the British tongue, 'Have I escaped so many dangers, and must I now be knocked on the head like a dog?' an Indian came to me, who afterwards appeared to be a war-captain belonging to the Sachem of the Doegs (whose original I found must needs be from the Welsh) and took me up by the middle, and told me in the British tongue I should not die; and thereupon went to the Emperor of the Tuscaroras, and agreed for my ransom and the men that were with me, and paid it the next day. Afterwards they carried us to their town, and entertained us civilly for four months, and I did converse with them of many things in the British tongue, and did preach to them three times a week in the British tongue, and they would usually confer with me about anything that was difficult to them; and when we came from them they shewed themselves very civil and courteous.

They were seated upon Pantigo river, not far from Cape Atros . . .
Jones added that he was ready to take any Welshman there who wished.

This is a complete farrago and may have been intended as a hoax. The Barbados planters formed a settlement south of Cape Fear in 1665; Sir William Berkeley, Governor of Virginia, organized settlement in North Carolina in 1666. Oyster Point was settled by an expedition led by Joseph West, which stopped at Bermuda on the way. Jones seems to have combined all three, though the last was clearly meant to be the operative one! The whole story is vividly reminiscent of Captain John Smith's famous Virginia adventure, the first version of which appeared in 1608, and the version with the Pocahontas romance in 1624. George Fox had reported in 1672 that peace between the Emperor of the Tuscaroras and the North Carolina settlers had been effected by one 'loving Indian captain'. There were stories later that the Welsh Quakers, in preparation for their settlement, had circulated reports of Welsh-speaking Indians and had appealed for missionaries. No trace of this document has ever been found and its existence is questionable. Thomas Lloyd made no mention of it and William Penn himself shared a common belief that the Indians were descendants of the Lost Tribes of Israel. Morgan's own apparent ignorance of the Madoc story, which later writers made much of, was, on the part of a Jesus graduate, surely assumed.

The whole story, with its Tuscaroras and Roanoke, the Cape Atros which seems to have been Hatteras, the Pantigo which was Pamlico, also vividly recalls the original 'lost colonist' stories of the first English colonies. Thomas Stephens in fact makes the intriguing suggestion that there might have been Welshmen among Raleigh's lost colonists who created some kind of sub-culture within the Hatteras Indians. Certainly both the Spanish accounts and the English stories of 'Lost Colonists', with their tales of clothed Indian tribes in stone houses, white Indians and so on, first established that tone and style which were to become very familiar in and characteristic of the endless later stories of *Welsh* Indians. This particular area of the continent, with its remains of old fortifications, its mysterious relics, and its Spanish searches, seems to have been rich in such stories. Almost a century earlier, the Spaniard Juan de Ortiz had reported similar experiences to the de Soto expedition in a narrative which might have been the model for all of them.

Conceptually, of course, the Jones narrative transformed the Madoc legend into a myth of Welsh Indians. It certainly served as a model or paradigm for a host of similar tales. This myth was ultimately to burn like a prairie fire across the continent. It took some *seventy years*, however, before that fire started to burn. Nothing illustrates the functional character of the Madoc myth better than this long delay in the shock impact of Morgan Jones.

For, to quote Aneurin Bevan on his maiden speech in the House of Commons, if Morgan Jones thought he'd thrown a stone, he soon found that he'd thrown a sponge. Charles Lloyd does not seem to have responded to his startling intelligence; it was at least seven years before it passed into circulation. The moving force was Edward Lhuyd, son of a Welsh gentry family, who had got to Oxford and made a name for himself as an antiquarian. In 1690, he became the second keeper of the recently-founded Ashmolean Museum in Oxford, in succession to its first keeper, Dr Robert Plot, antiquary and professor of chemistry. Lhuyd, who was a friend of Isaac Newton and Hans Sloane, was very active in Celtic studies, travelling widely in Wales and Cornwall, where he and his friends were arrested as thieves, and in Brittany, where they were arrested as spies. He published an *Archaeologia Britannica* in 1707, which was heavily philological, and he was elected a Fellow of the Royal Society in 1708.

'Honest Lhuyd', a man of 'modesty, good nature and uncommon industry', had planned to go to the West Indies himself in 1692, and in 1693, on a collecting trip in Wales, he met Charles Lloyd. To judge from a letter which Lloyd wrote to him the following August, the Quaker must have told him of the Morgan Jones narrative. It was Lhuyd who became excited, asking for a copy to be sent to 'that great antiquary', William Lloyd, Bishop of St Asaph. It must have been by this word-of-mouth transmission of a half-remembered story that Morgan Jones's narrative, though not his name, reached the authors or editors of the *Letters of a Turkish Spy*, in time to be published in the eighth volume in December

1693.

For Charles Lloyd did not send on his brother's transcript until 14 August 1694. A long absence from home had hindered him, he said, and he was quite extraordinarily confused over the whole Madoc tradition. He evidently used Herbert's *Travels*, which he had left behind in Herefordshire, though he also knew of the Powel and Humphrey Llwyd versions. He did say, however, that he had thought of publishing the story, if no one more worthy than himself could be found. He suggested that Morgan Jones's Doegs were a corruption of Madog's Indians and that Cape Atros might be Cape Hatteras. The river Pantigo 'is perhaps an old name, yet hath a British sound'. He asserted that Tuscaroras and Doegs were placed near Virginia in 'the new maps of the English empire' and he guessed that the adventure had occurred about the time of Bacon's Rebellion (he altered Jones's original date to 1669 to fit).

Edward Lhuyd passed this material to Dr Plot. Plot was an assiduous collector and a genial man, though acquisitive and something of a time-server. An FRS, he had just been re-elected as secretary to the Royal Society, but was counted rather credulous: country gentry used to boast how they had 'humbugged old Plot' over his *Natural History of Staffordshire*. He read Morgan Jones's narrative to the Royal Society some time in 1694 or 1695. To set it in context he simply paraphrased Herbert. He pointed out that it offered 'the most incontestable proof that can be desired' of the whole Madoc tradition. England, not Spain, had the just title to America, which 'should have more justly been called *Madocia* than *America*.' Addressing the Fellows, he asked them to decide: whether all this 'rather deserve your imprimatur, or to be committed to the flames, is humbly left to your judicious decision'. The Fellows evidently came down in favour of the latter course of action, for there is no trace of Morgan Jones in their *Philosophical Transactions*. Except for the brief and anonymous mention in the *Turkish Spy*, the story simply did not register in print, though oral versions without doubt circulated.

Morgan Jones's narrative did not see the light of day, in fact, until 1740. The occasion then was familiar: war with Spain (the War of Jenkins' Ear). In 1739, an anonymous *British Sailor's Discovery* appeared, a blistering attack on Spain's claims in America, in terms of the Black Legend, a dismissal of Columbus and a reaffirmation of Madoc. The author relied on the Tudor history of David Powel and seemed ignorant of more recent acquisitions, repeating, for example, that the Madoc people had been absorbed into Indian culture and had disappeared.

In precisely the same cause, however, a letter appeared in the *Gentleman's Magazine* for March 1740 under the name of Theophilus Evans, who called himself Vicar of St David's in Brecon. This, at long last, launched the Morgan Jones story on the world. Theophilus was erudite, referring to Powel, Herbert and Howell and quoting the Maredudd ap

Rhys verse. The new evidence made it clear that the Madocians had survived. From Elizabeth's time, he cited Dr Heylin's *Geography* to prove that the Queen had been reluctant to use Madoc against Spain — 'But they had only an obscure Tradition *then*, that was thought would not bear proof'. Now, however, all was changed, changed utterly ... 'let not the proud *Dons* any more assume the Glory of this noble Discovery; but let our most Puissant Monarch of *Great Britain* claim his most just Rights ... Britons, strike home!'

Madoc had certainly struck home, for he was once more fortunate in his landfall. Theophilus Evans was the author of a Welsh best-seller which became a classic. A Cardiganshire man by birth, he served for many years as vicar of Llangamarch in Breconshire (where, oddly enough, James Howell's father had also served). He is reputed to have been the discoverer of the curative properties of the spa at Llanwrtyd Wells and became famous in Welsh annals as a resolute enemy of Methodists ('secret Papists') whom he denounced in a celebrated *History of Modern Enthusiasm*, and as a historian dedicated to the defence of the Church of England and the glory of Wales's nobility and antiquity.

While still a young man of twenty-three, he published privately at Shrewsbury his famous *Drych y Prif Oesoedd (Mirror of the Early Ages)*, a history of the early, British years of the Welsh. This was by no means as uncritical as a later generation of too self-consciously critical Welsh scholarship was to assert, but it was, inevitably, steeped in the myths which had clustered around the Dark Ages. In this first edition of 1716, there was no mention of Madoc. By 1740, however, Theophilus had become vicar of Llangamarch and had secured the patronage of men of note, including the celebrated Glamorgan antiquarian and poet John Bradford, the leading lights of Jesus College Oxford, and the Welsh Librarian of the Bodleian. In that year — the very year, paradoxically, in which his new curate appeared, in the person of William Williams Pantycelyn, a founding father of Methodism and the greatest hymn-writer in Welsh, a conjuncture which considerably enlivened parish affairs — a second edition of the *Drych* came from the press. This was the version, full of incisive phrases and striking metaphors, which became a classic of Welsh prose. During the early nineteenth century, it was repeatedly reprinted, particularly at Merthyr and Carmarthen. The only English translation appeared, appropriately, in Ebensburg, Pennsylvania, a settlement originally founded during the Madoc fever of the 1790s. By that time, probably 1834, there had been thirty editions of the *Drych*, according to its hamfisted translator George Roberts.

It was Theophilus Evans's *Drych* which, before the age of modern scholarship, shaped and formed the historical outlook of the Welsh. It was this book, more than any other, which made Madoc into a rooted popular 'tradition' among them.

For in the 1740 edition, in its first chapter, Madoc appeared. 'It is a great and unprofitable task to relate the history of the Welsh people,' said Theophilus' '. . . it is painful and lamentable to relate how ungrateful they were to God . . .'. 'There are no people under the sun,' he went on, 'who have retained their country, their language and their privileges uncorrupted, undiminished and without mixture . . .'. He followed up this sagacious comment with a discussion of the intermixture of early Irish and Welsh and of the coming of Brutus the Trojan to found the great dynasties of the island. They spoke Greek which had left its impress on Welsh, 'because Brutus and his companions associated with the Welsh, in the same manner as *Madog ap Owen Gwynedd* did with the American Indians' ('Canys Brutus a'i Bobl a ymgymmyscodd a'r hen Drigolion yr un ffunyd as y darfu *Madoc* ap *Owen Gwynedd* ymgymmyscu a Phobl America').

Then followed the Madoc story. This was drawn entirely, with specific reference, from David Powel and Thomas Herbert, but it was couched in Theophilus's own dramatic, indeed compulsive, style (he wrote a short speech for Madoc and a good one, too). He added the striking detail that, on his second voyage, when he brought the women, Madoc took eight months and ten days to reach America — intelligence which Theophilus had presumably acquired through direct communication with the Almighty. In the text, however, he followed the older tradition by having the Madocians blend with the natives after a generation 'like milk with water' ('fe ymgyfathrachodd y Tô nessaf a *Thrigolion y wlad* ac aethant yn un Genedl a hwy, fel y gwelwch chwi Dwfr a Llaeth yn ymgymmyscu': his American translator omitted this turn of phrase).

Evidently, the Morgan Jones story had reached Theophilus after his book had been set up. It also reached him independently of Charles Lloyd's version, from which it differs in some particulars, including the date (originally 1660). After he had sent it to the *Gentleman's Magazine*, he included it in his preface to the *Drych* dated 1 May 1740. He made Morgan's Pantigo into *Dyffryn-pant-teg* (vale of the fair valley). The Morgan Jones transformation of the Madoc tradition finally registered in the Welsh consciousness.

And it was from this familiar, indeed by now traditional, anti-Spanish starting-point that the Madoc-Welsh Indian myth entered wholly unfamiliar territory. For it was probably Theophilus Evans's book and letter which enthused the Baptist Association of Philadelphia, at that time very Welsh in composition, into the first organized hunt for Welsh Indians. It failed, but in 1752 an excited letter from Philadelphia, which passed to Wales along the Baptist network, announced that the Welsh Indians had been found — beyond the Mississippi. From this moment stories on the Morgan Jones model began to come in, at first in a trickle, later in a flood, extending further and further west.

There was evidently a sudden upsurge of Welsh Indian stories, for in the summer of 1753, Governor Dinwiddie of Virginia officially asked for a report on them from the famous frontiersman George Croghan, which the latter delivered in August. Croghan had picked up his story from a French friend who had been brought up among the Indians of the west. The first the French had heard of this potent breed was from some Indians 'settled at the back of New Spain', who had fallen in with a strange tribe they took to be French 'by their talking very quick'. The Governor-General of Canada sent out three young priests in Indian dress who were gone sixteen months before they returned. These found the strange tribe to be Welsh (the priests were clearly no mean linguists — Jesuits no doubt) and they brought back 'some old Welsh Bibles' to prove the point. The Welsh had once been settled at the mouth of the Mississippi, had been cut off and almost destroyed by the French, but had escaped up the river, cherishing an understandable hatred of the sons of St Louis. The French in Canada at once prepared an expedition against them, but were distracted by war nearer home. Governor Dinwiddie, in his turn, responded no less promptly to Croghan's letter. He offered £500 to some back-country traders to go to find the Welsh. Cruel mischance, however, forever seems to dog the steps of the Madocians. Dinwiddie was recalled before the expedition could set out.

This story is of far greater significance than even dedicated Madoc men have assumed. It proves that the theme of a Welsh Indian migration from the region of the Mississippi mouth up to the land of the *White Padoucas* was in circulation long before Cherokee legends to this effect and other better-known evidence had passed into the canon. Croghan himself was sceptical, considering the story a 'delusion', but men like him were soon a minority. That Welsh Indian stories had become more common than any other on the frontier, the Rev. Charles Beatty was to learn to his chagrin.

Beatty, an Ulsterman who had migrated to America in 1729, served the Presbyterian church as a minister to the Scotch-Irish of the Pennsylvania back-country and in the cause went on two fund-raising tours of Britain. In 1766 he was commissioned to go on a two month mission to the Indians of western Pennsylvania and, in 1768 when in Scotland to obtain medical treatment for his wife, he published an edited version of his journal to raise funds for Dr Wheelock's Indian charity schools. Beatty was not only a missionary to the Indians, he was a passionate believer in their descent from the Lost Tribes of Israel and, in a letter to an Edinburgh minister in February 1768, made the most of his findings, citing the reports of Mosaic rituals and other Jewish observances made to him by Benjamin Sutton, whom he had met on his travels and who had been an Indian prisoner for many years. He concluded, 'I might have added some peculiarities of less note . . .'. Charles Beatty was whistling in the dark, for those 'peculiarities' fill pages of his published journals in one long footnote.

In August 1767, making his way west through the Pennsylvania wilderness, he had picked up Levi Hicks who had been an Indian captive when young and knew many of their villages. On 2 September they came into the last of the folds of the Appalachians and lodged with John Millar. It was here that Beatty met Benjamin Sutton, who was obsessed not with the Israelites but with the Welsh. Sutton said that at an Indian town west of the Mississippi, and a long way above New Orleans, he had met a tribe who were whiter than other Indians and who spoke Welsh. They also had 'a Welch Bible, he supposes' (in his published text, Beatty demoted this 'Bible' to a 'book') wrapped carefully in skins, which he could not read. His identification of their language as Welsh had probably been a later assumption, because afterwards he had met a captive Welshman called Lewis at another town and heard him talk to some Indians in Welsh. Sutton added that the Welsh Indians had now gone over the Mississippi.

This was not all; Levi Hicks promptly joined in. He had gone on an embassy to an Indian town west of the Mississippi, whose inhabitants spoke Welsh 'as I was told'. Even Joseph Peepy, Beatty's interpreter and a Christian Indian, said he too had met Indians, presumably of the same tribe, who talked Welsh. He repeated some of their words which he 'knew to be Welsh', as he had known some Welsh people. Sutton himself, while giving Beatty his 'Jewish' material on the Delawares reported a tradition among them that they had come from a far distant country because of a civil war between two sons of a great king of theirs. They dated this exodus in the European early fourteenth century by their wampum beads. They, too, had talked of a sacred book. Beatty himself felt constrained to add a clergyman-prisoner-turned-priest story in the Morgan Jones style, throwing in a sacred book for extra weight.

At about the same time as Beatty's mission, according to an account published eighteen years later, Captain Isaac Stewart was going through even more remarkable experiences.

Isaac Stewart said that he had been taken prisoner by Indians about fifty miles west of Fort Pitt (Pittsburgh) around 1764 and carried off to the Wabash where he saw many whites tortured to death. He was saved by 'what is called the good Woman of the Town' who ransomed him with a horse. He remained two years in bondage with a Welshman, John Davey or Davies, but they were redeemed by a Spaniard who had been 'sent from Mexico on Discoveries'. They moved west and crossed the Mississippi near the Rouge or Red river, 'up which we travelled 700 miles'.

Here Captain Stewart's syntax is as confusing as his geography. A later commentator interpreted this story to mean the Red River of the South, which would certainly have brought Stewart out in country not far from *New* Mexico. It is difficult, however, to conceive of reaching this river by going *west* from the Wabash. The Red River of the North, on the other hand, flows north into Lake Winnipeg from the country about the headwaters of the Mississippi, and 700 miles up it, were that possible, would land a traveller in the middle of Hudson's Bay. A run of 700 miles up a *Mississippi* reached from the Wabash, however, would bring a man out in the vicinity of the Red River. Since the Red River of the North rises in the vicinity of a Mississippi which could be 'crossed' near it and since that Red River opens on to *Mandan* country, most interpreters took this as Stewart's meaning.

For he came to a small river called the Post (Mandans and Hidatsa lived along short rivers) where there was an Indian nation 'remarkably white, and whose hair was of a reddish colour, at least, mostly so' (a standard description of the Mandans). 'In the morning of the Day after our Arrival, the Welsh Man informed me that he was determined to remain with them, giving as a Reason, that he understood their language, it being very little different from the Welsh.' Through the Welshman, Stewart learned from the elders of the tribe that their forefathers had come from a foreign country and had landed on the east side of the Mississippi, 'describing particularly the Country now called Florida, and that on the Spaniards taking possession of Mexico, they fled to their then Abode.' As proof they produced 'Rolls of Parchment, which were carefully tied up in Otters' Skins, on which were large Characters written with blue ink.' The Welshman knew no letters, not even his own, and Stewart could not make head or tail of them. 'They are a bold, hardy and intrepid people, very Warlike and the Women beautiful when compared with other Indians.'

It was in those same 1760s that Lord Shelburne, then Colonial Secretary in the Rockingham administration, ordered a copy made of Croghan's letter of 1753. Maurice Morgan, his under-secretary and once secretary to the Governor of Canada, got one from Dr Morton of the British Museum, while another was made for an antiquary. Neither Morgan nor Shelburne could accept the French story, because of those 'old Welsh Bibles', but Maurice, better known in Wales as the essayist Morgan Blaen Bylan, later passed it on to his Baptist kinsfolk and it duly lodged in the Madoc canon.

For by the 1780s a veritable tidal wave of Welsh Indian stories was breaking on English-speaking America. It was in 1782 that Captain Isaac Stewart finally published his experiences. He had waited eighteen years, and much of the material was both familiar and suspicious. On the other hand, it was full of circumstantial detail (the 'blue ink' soon found a satisfactory explanation) and it certainly gave sceptics pause. By 1786 it was appearing in the London press. Stewart had timed his publication well. Welsh Indians had become a staple of tavern talk by this time in Kentucky and all along the frontier. In 1784 John Filson brought out his study of that beautiful but blood-stained land, and devoted a good deal of it to the old relics and ruins of the region. In this context he spoke of Madoc, of the eclipse of his legend and its full-blooded revival in his own

83

day — 'Of late years the Western settlers have received frequent accounts of a nation at a great distance up the Missouri, in manner and appearance resembling other Indians but speaking Welsh and retaining some ceremonies of the Christian worship; and at length, this is universally believed to be a fact.' Indeed, Captain Abraham Chaplain, stationed with the Kentucky militia at the western outpost of Kaskaskia during the War of Independence, had actually heard two Welshmen in his company converse freely with Indians who had come down to the Mississippi.

Few could resist, at least in America. By 1786, Morgan Edwards, Welsh historian of the American Baptists, could tell his fellow historian Joshua Thomas back home that stories of Welsh Indians had become commonplace. So, at long last, Morgan Jones got his posthumous sensation. The legend swept to its second great climax as, through the late eighteenth and into the nineteenth century, a Madoc fever burned through America.

Finding Welsh Indians became a minor industry. John Sevier, founder of Tennessee, knew they had been the first comers to Alabama before other Indians drove them out. Francis Lewis of Llandaff, who was to sign the Declaration of Independence as New York delegate, was captured by Montcalm during the French war and turned over to Indians. He found a chief who conversed with him in Welsh. The frontiersmen knew them well. Daniel Boone had seen their moccasin prints in the trail ahead. The renegade woodsman James Girty knew so many Welsh Indians that he helped compile a Welsh-Indian vocabulary. President Jefferson boasted that his family had come from Wales and instructed Lewis and Clark to find the Welsh Indians (two of their men did so!). There are literally scores of instances of people reporting that they had actually talked to Indians in Welsh. Cherokees said *digon* for enough and *eisiau* for want. One man found the Comanches rather hard to understand. He was a south Walian and they spoke north Wales Welsh. There are several authentic cases of Indian chiefs solemnly swearing to statements that their ancestors had been Welsh, a triumph of good taste over good sense. For by this time, the historiography of the Madocians had swollen to massive proportions. They now had those old Welsh Bibles which they cherished. They were correct to cherish them; they'd had them a couple of centuries before the old folks at home. Those relics which occasionally turn up in field and building-site to tease the mind, and which today at once summon up Leif Ericson and his Norsemen, were in the late-eighteenth and nineteenth centuries equally automatically assimilated into the proud culture of the Madocians. Most of the myths of early America were fitted into this one magnificent folk epic.

Welsh Indians existed; 'everyone' knew they did. Only they were always a little further on, in some place we had not reached yet, perhaps beyond that next blue mountain barred with snow. They were the Dogs or the

Delawares or the Shawnees until we reached the Ohio. When it was clear that they were not the Pawnees, they were the Comanches. Practically anywhere west of the Mississippi they were the Padoucas. At least thirteen real tribes were identified as Welsh Indians; five other imaginary tribes were given names to fit; three others were described but not named. It was by the last decade of the eighteenth century, the dramatic decade, the age of the French Revolution and the struggle for the soul of the new American republic, that people finally realized that the Madocians had gone into the land of mystery up the great and unknown Missouri river, where they enjoyed their golden age as the Mandans.

For central to this outburst of speculation, of course, were precisely those stories filtering back through the French fur traders of white Indians on the Missouri with their superior civilization. It was in the 1780s that the Canadians got through to the Mandans. There were probably contributory factors: the increasing tension with Spain as the American War ended, both over continental frontiers and in the West Indies, and the fact that Herbert's *Travels* reappeared in 1785. The major cause, however, was no doubt the multiplication and increasing plausibility of stories of White Indians on the Missouri, as they ran back into imitators of Morgan Jones in the eastern lands and into the growing interest in ancient forts and ruins that were uncovered as settlers pushed west to encounter more and more tribes and a multiplicity of new languages. It is a fascinating illustration of the relationship between myth and brute reality. All the rival imperialisms of the continent — American, British, Spanish and the ghost of the French — were inexorably coming to a focus on the Upper Missouri, a process which was at once a consequence and a cause of their mythical geography of the Shining Mountains with their 'short portage' to the Pacific, the Volcano, the Great River of the West, and the strait of Juan de Fuca — which the Nootka Sound crisis of 1790 was to focus yet more sharply. Map after map in the eighteenth century blazoned 'White Padoucas' vaguely across the presumed headwaters of the Missouri.

It was almost inevitable that those White Indians become Welsh, because it was the Welsh who had behind them, 'warranted' by those confident and semi-official proclamations of Elizabethan England, a powerful and persistent tradition of a pre-Columban discovery of America. Moreover, among the potent American populations now straining and stretching beyond the Alleghenies, driving into Kentucky and towards the Ohio and the Mississippi, thrusting against Indians, British and Spaniards, the Welsh were well represented. Although Welsh emigration more or less halted for a generation and more after mid-century, there had been two waves of movement around the turn of the seventeenth and eighteenth centuries, and distinctive Welsh settlements in Pennsylvania and the south. Welsh books were being produced in

America and the Welsh themselves had become sufficiently prominent in American life for the people back home firmly to believe that most of the signatures on the Declaration of Independence were Welsh!

Nor was it too difficult to connect those distant Madocians with their presumed landing places 'near Florida'. For running up from the Mobile Bay, which one Spaniard years ago had called *Tierra de los Gales*, were those mysterious relics of forts, burial places and habitations which seemed the work of a race superior to the Indians currently in residence — the fortifications around Mobile, the great hill-forts, Lookout Mountain, the fortress on the Hiwassee river and the Old Stone Fort on Duck River, in what became Tennessee and Kentucky. There were the mounds along the Ohio, those mysterious pillars which men said recorded some great calamity which had befallen an ancient race. Did not those far-off White Padoucas live in cities with streets, ringed by earthworks? Did not they sail the Missouri in those coracles which people had seen on the Alabama river?

A beautiful illustration of the way minds were working in the late eighteenth century — and of the power of suggestion which white minds could exercise over red — is provided by the account which John Sevier — Nolichucky Jack, founder of Tennessee — gave of his talks with Oconostota, a chief of the Cherokee. In a campaign of 1782 against the Cherokee, Sevier had noted the old forts, particularly the one on the Hiwassee river. When the war ended, he questioned Oconostota, who had been a chief for sixty years. The chief reported:

It is handed down by the Forefathers that the works had been made by the White people who had formerly inhabited the country now called Carolina; that a war had existed between the two nations for several years. At length it was discovered that the Whites were making a large number of boats which induced the Cherokee to suppose that they were about to descend the Tennessee river. They then assembled their whole band of warriors and took the shortest and most convenient route to the Muscle Shoals in order to intercept them on their passage down the river. In a few days the boats hove in sight. A warm combat ensued with various success for several days.

At length the Whites proposed to the Indians that if they would exchange prisoners and cease hostilities, they would leave the country and never return, which was acceded to; and after the exchange they parted friendly. That the Whites then descended the Tennessee down to the Ohio, thence down to the Big River (the Mississippi) then they ascended it up to the Muddy River (the Missouri) and thence up that river for a great distance. They were then on some of its branches . . .

An old Cherokee woman Peg had been given some part of an old book by one of those Missouri Whites, but unfortunately it had been lost in a fire

86

(presumably a Cherokee version of Raglan Castle). But, said Oconostota, 'they are no more White people; they are now all become Indians, and look like other red people of the country.' When asked whether the Forefathers had said anything about the nation these Whites belonged to, the chief answered that 'he had heard his grandfather and father say they were a people called Welsh, and that they had crossed the Great Water and landed first near the mouth of the Alabama River near Mobile and had been driven up to the heads of the waters until they arrived at Highwassee River'.

This hypnotic story was admittedly not written up until thirty years later, for Amos Stoddard's history of Louisiana, but thinking of this nature was becoming commonplace in the last years of the eighteenth century. Zealous antiquaries followed up in the nineteenth century, to such effect that in 1953 the Daughters of the American Revolution erected a monument to Madoc at his 'landing-place' near Fort Morgan (and how appropriate *that* name is) on Mobile Bay.

Curiously, while this corpus of knowledge was building up in America, and at accelerating speed, a profound silence brooded over the alleged homeland of this potent people. Nicholas Owen's *British Remains* of 1777 did include the Lloyd correspondence on Morgan Jones but it was not until the 1790s that the Madoc climax registered in Wales. Once more, the occasion was traditional — the war crisis between Britain and Spain over 'lawfull tytle' to America at Nootka Sound in 1790. Dr John Williams, a learned Welsh divine of Sydenham, had been working on the Madoc story for years (he had probably been himself inspired by Theophilus Evans's *Drych* of 1740) and his book, consciously or unconsciously, was as remarkably well timed as those of his more renowned contemporaries, Edmund Burke and Thomas Paine (and no accidental conjuncture either). It was in 1791, after a year which had witnessed a growing Madoc obsession in Wales, that he published his *An enquiry into the Truth of the Tradition concerning the Discovery of America by Prince Madog ab Owen Gwynedd about AD 1170*. Within a year, he had to bring out a second edition with a wealth of new information. The response must have startled the good doctor.

For that response was nothing less than an outbreak of America fever in Wales, particularly among its Dissenters and radicals. Not only was there a serious effort to establish Madoc and his Welsh Indians in Welsh history, and to relate them to that ancient and libertarian tradition of the Druids and the Bards which a new breed of intellectuals was reviving; not only did Wales send a young man in search of Welsh Indians to the outermost limit of European knowledge and penetration of the New World; Madoc became central to a strong thrust of emigration peculiarly Welsh in spirit, which sent another young Welshman exploring all over the USA for a site for a *Gwladfa*, a national home for the Welsh people, an enterprise which

87

in its turn sent the Welsh by the hundred to the America boats. Not only this: Madoc found his place in a new and *revolutionary* pantheon. For the new breed of Welsh intellectuals were steeped in the American and French Revolutions — *Jacobins*, in the current parlance. Madoc was not only to appear in, but to address a call to renaissance to the Welsh from, the pages of the very first political periodical in the Welsh language. This new *Jacobin* Madoc of the 1790s is perhaps the most miraculous of them all.

For the Welsh to whom Madoc returned were no longer those proud and prestigious Tudor Britons who had sent him out into the world in the first place. These Welsh had lived through five generations of what their spokesmen considered Decadence, the years of 'Poor Taffy'. They were now in the throes of their revival. Madoc, in fact, instrumental to the last, was a trigger to a process which was nothing less than the birth of a new Welsh 'nation'. Britons these men no longer called themselves, except when it was expedient; they were 'Cambro-Britons' now. Their spirit and the spirit of this newly resurrected Madoc is caught, briefly but memorably, in the excited letter of June 1791 which William Richards, Welsh Baptist minister of Lynn in Norfolk and a passionate supporter of the American and French Revolutions, addressed to his brother-in-the-cloth, the no less Welsh American, Dr Samuel Jones, minister of Pennepek Baptist church, Lower Dublin, Philadelphia.

'And if such a nationality (as the Welsh Indians) exists,' ran the breathless words, 'and there seems now to be no great room to doubt the fact, it will then appear that a branch of the Welsh Nation has preserved its independence even to this day.'

5

Jacobin Madoc

To All Indigenous Cambro-Britons: Permit me at this juncture to congratulate you on the agreeable intelligence lately received from America, viz., that the colony which *Madog ap Owain Gwynedd* carried over the Atlantic in the twelfth century are at this time a free and distinct people, and have preserved their liberty, language and some traces of their religion to this very day.

So ran a remarkable manuscript assiduously circulated in 1791 at the eisteddfod in Llanrwst, north Wales, sponsored by the vivacious London-Welsh society, the *Gwyneddigion,* and attended by the leading intellectuals of the Welsh revival. The author was passionate and extremely well informed on America; he quoted at length from Dr John Williams's book and both early and late scholarship on the *Madogwys,* as learned antiquarians were beginning to call Madoc's Indians. However, scholarship — and here the *Gwyneddigion* (or most of them) would heartily have agreed with him — must serve the people:

> It is to be hoped that the congenial feelings of some Cambro-Britons will prompt such whose circumstances will allow, to contribute towards the expence of sending a qualified person or persons to settle a correspondence between us and our remote brethren; a mutual benefit may in time arise from such an intercourse, besides the gratifying the curiosity of both parties. Primarily, the resuscitation of the Light of the Christian Religion in a more clear manner than they might have had it, in case they had retained it in the form it was professed by their progenitors; which truth doubtless they will be disposed to cultivate when they shall be circumstantially informed. Secondarily a communication with their country may be beneficial to us by way of trade, though *Europeans* by the existing treaties are precluded from trading beyond the Mississippi in compliance with the exclusive claim of the arrogant Spaniards, peradventure our countrymen whose progenitors had taken so rigorous a stride for the preservation of their

89

liberty have not *bent the knee to Baal,* nor sold their birthright for a mess of pottage and that they are at this time a free people and the complexion of the times may favor them to preserve their independency . . .

After all neither Britain nor the USA could subject them without infringing treaties; the Spaniards had enough on their hands without bringing down 'the northern Indians to fall upon their thin settlement in New Mexico which is their weakest side'. Unfortunately, Britain had reserved no more than the mere right to navigate the Mississippi and held no land below the forty-fifth parallel, 'but if a mart should be formed somewhere about the confluence of the Ohio and proper instructors sent to reside among the Padoucas, they may be taught to bring the produce of their country to barter for European goods, where the avaricious Spaniards could not prevent them'. For it was clear — 'that Madog and his people became possessed of the sovereignty of a great part of the *American* continent'.

But the address had a bite to it and ended with a ferocious blast against oppressors: 'Some modern skeptics have thought proper to deny that Madog never discovered America because (forsooth) they will not acknowledge that a Welshman is capable of performing any brave or generous action. Namely that haughty reviler of our nation, *Lord Lyttleton* and the presumptuous *Scottyn Dr Robertson* . . . it is evident by their belchings that there remains still some latent malignity in the bottom of their stomachs which sometimes affects their brains . . .'. These arrogant louts (their mushroom nobility and gentry descending from 'some bastards, arrant thieves and murderers whether Saxon or Norman') even denied that the Welsh *had* any 'religion, learning and learned men'.

. . . it may not be amiss (in regard of their uncourteous abuse) to remind them of their ancestors' behaviour towards us in that respect. Their predecessors the Romans under the general Seutonius Palinus undertook an expedition to kill the Druids in order to destroy our then *religion, learning and learned men.* Two Saxon kings joined their powers at the instigation of Augustine the Roman *Monk,* to come to *Bangor* to massacre the students, in order to destroy our *religion, learning and learned men.* The tyrant *Edward* the first ordered the Bards (which were our historians) to be slain, gave our bishopricks to strangers and doubt-less caused our books to be burnt in the Tower, with an intent to destroy our *religion, learning and learned men.* The usurper Henry the 4th made a law to prevent any Welshman from attaining to any science nor even to learn to read in order to extinguish our *religion, learning and learned men.* And even unto this day, our Bishopricks and best benefices are too frequently given to Englishmen which is a great discouragement to our *religion, learning and learned men* and the advancement of sectaries . . .

90

The author was in fact composing what he hoped would be a Welsh national anthem, a counter to *The Roast Beef of Old England;* it was one long evocation of the endless struggle against English oppression which had been the history of the Welsh. It was to be sung to the tune of *Toriad y Dydd* (Daybreak). For there was another purpose behind his address. He told William Owen, a leading figure among the London-Welsh and in the Welsh revival, that recreating the Welsh nation out of reach of oppression was more important than resurrecting old Welsh poetry. It was alongside the Old Brethren in America that the future of the Welsh lay. He was badgering the American consuls and calling for an organized Welsh migration; and he sent Owen a petition to be forwarded to influential Americans:

WE, THE POOR REMNANTS OF ANCIENT BRITONS are confined in the mountains of Wales, cultivating an ungrateful soil, whose production is insufficient to support its occupiers. The tendency of our boasted constitution to accumulate property into few hands, and the present wretched mode of taxing the produce of labor and the necessaries of life, has of late increased the number of our poor into an alarming degree, and must sooner or later reduce the laboring class into a servile dependency or absolute slavery, and which the insatiable avarice of the landed gentry has partly effected in our country. These primary planets or blazing stars move eastward (as usually contrary to the heavens) towards the capital in quest of places, preferment, plays or ladies of pleasure, and leave us under the malignant influence of their satellites, the supercilious and insolent agents and bailiffs; these rapacious cormorants not satisfied with open racking, frequently join the fox tail to the bear's claws and make use of base circumventions to fleece us more effectually; and if tenants cannot make prompt paiment on fixt days, a train of Bum Bailiffs and other under-strappers will be let loose upon them, to make a havock of their property and reduce the unhappy defaulters in a few days into the utmost distress of want and poverty: and if we happen to complain of our hardships, we are immediately told in a true Aegyptian phrase 'that we are idle'.

Numbers of the Scotch and Irish when oppressed by petty tyrants have crossed the Atlantic: we presume that our countrymen are not more destitute of feelings, courage and inclinations; but want the means of necessary information and instruction to accomplish such a design. Therefore it is humbly requested that this representation be forwarded into the hands of some Gentlemen concerned in the affairs of the United States of America, in order to solicit the concurrence of some public or private proprietors of unoccupied lands in those parts, to form a scheme for conveying emigrants from our country.

He reported that this Address had been very well received at the

Llanrwst eisteddfod, except for what he called (in Welsh) 'a few anglicized coxcombs who think they can exalt themselves by despising their own people' (still as much a 'Welsh disease' as suicide and homosexuality were once said to be 'English'). And in extreme form, his attitudes are an accurate reflection of the America fever which seized significant numbers of the Welsh after the publication of Dr John Williams's *Enquiry*.

The form, however, *was* extreme, for the author was William Jones of Llangadfan, a tough, tight and bitter parish in Montgomeryshire in north-central Wales, in the cloth country which was going through the travail of modernization, and which was to become a major centre of American emigration.

William Jones, born around 1729, was that rare Welsh bird, a follower of Voltaire. He was said never to have spent more than a fortnight away from his native parish, but that was not his choice. He had yearned to travel, but the desperate circumstances of his family, in that upland core of Wales trapped in the bleak and bony grip of unremitting poverty where the farm-based cloth trade was the vital margin between tolerable existence and intolerable misery, trapped Jones at home. Again in extreme form, he was representative of the new native, rough-hewn and often self-taught Welsh intellectuals who clawed and fought their way up into knowledge and frustrated talent. Local education gave him, according to Walter Davies, another leader of the Welsh revival who became a Fellow of All Souls and rather mandarin in his attitudes, 'a little broken English and an ability of writing his name'. William Jones built himself into an accomplished poet and musician 'among the profoundest critics that Wales ever produced'. He learned enough Latin to translate Horace and Ovid into excellent Welsh verse. Amateur astronomer and physicist (as so many were at the time), and credulous addict of any suitably 'Celtic' and antique-romantic 'anthropology', he was also a skilled antiquarian. He cured himself of scrofula and set up as a country and unofficial healer, with some success. Crippled by the Medicine Act, harassed by landowners and burdened with a poverty-stricken family, his Voltairean temper alienated him from the Establishment and the rising power of Dissent alike. 'I have offended the elect in these parts some time ago; and upon that account I am excluded for ever from the list of saints, which are so regularly kept here, that the book of life is to be but as it were a transcript of the methodistical registers . . .' He fought an endless battle against landlords, even in the school he ran. He was once asked what the evils let loose by the opening of Pandora's box were. He replied — 'with his usual sneering smile' to quote Walter Davies's schizophrenic obituary — 'Why, George Whitfield, John Wesley, Tom Vernon, Fr. Chambre, all the quack-doctors, pettifogging attorneys and others' naming the two leaders of Methodism and two bailiffs of Sir Watkin Williams Wynn. He was a 'red-hot Welshman' ('hot-arsed' as a compatriot called him in discreet Welsh) and a great hater of Saxons.

And from the moment his yearning to travel was stifled, he became a spiritual American. To judge from his correspondence, he must have been one of the best-informed men on popular America in Britain. Wherever it came from, his information on America was invariably accurate, his comments unfailingly cogent. Madoc must have come to him like a messenger from a Voltairean Deity. No one did more to focus Welsh minds, through Madoc, on the idea of a *Gwladfa*, a National Home for the Welsh in the Land of Liberty. William Jones is counted idiosyncratic and eccentric (though most of his eccentricities were such only to the nineteenth century). He nevertheless became an authentic spokesman for an authentically Welsh movement in the revolutionary decade.

This paradox, if it is that (why should not a marginal man become a spokesman for a marginal people?) focuses a major problem of this decade in Welsh history, the relationship between a people and the 'organic intellectuals' who emerge from it. For this Voltairean loner in a nominally Anglican-Tory Wales, amidst a people who still cherished a pre-industrial folk-culture, with the future slipping inexorably towards highly literate, pious, Bible-bound and contentious Dissenting sects, managed also to become a spokesman for a highly distinctive and highly un-Voltairean society within the complex called Wales. For he came from Llangadfan, in the heart of the mid-Wales cloth industry; Llanrwst where he distributed his Address was itself a focus for the remarkable knitting and stocking industry of the north.

The Montgomeryshire cloth trade in flannels was the essential margin for an austere pastoral district; it could not go a week without payment, had been subjected to the Drapers' Company of Shrewsbury and produced neither capitalist clothiers nor a proletariat until the late eighteenth century. The acceleration of industrial growth in England, the intrusion of 'Welsh Drapers' from Liverpool and Lancashire, the quickening of the commercialization of agriculture by 'spirited proprietors', and the appearance of the first factories along the Severn, at Welshpool, Llanidloes and Newtown (birthplace of Robert Owen the socialist) thrust the whole region into a prolonged crisis of modernization which was vastly accelerated by population explosion and the twenty-year war against France. Poor but independent producers were being reduced to proletarians, traditional community disrupted by the intrusion of the annual lease and rack-renting; there was a sharp increase in pauperization.

There was, parallel to this process, an explosive acceleration in the growth of Methodism and Dissent, the former often mushrooming out from the precarious footholds already established by the latter. The Independent weavers of Llanbryn-mair, for example, never rode to Welshpool on a Sunday. Llanbryn-mair, however, also produced the man who fathered the first native-born governor of the state of Ohio in the USA. For one response to the crisis, particularly among people of a little substance and some independence (as most Dissenters and many Methodists were), was emigration. During the 1790s, amid social turmoil, riot, and the marching and counter-marching of red-coats, an emigration fever ran through these districts. It turned the sharp-tongued and quirky Voltairean in Llangadfan, with his nationalist Madoc, into the voice of Calvinist rebellion, a spokesman for rebels who voted with their feet.

So he was for the poorer and intensely Welsh districts further north. In Merioneth, there was the rougher, cheaper cloth, the web, with an established market among British soldiers and American slaves; the busy little port of Barmouth served the region and the Gulf of Mexico was a major outlet. A brief golden age after the American war was brought abruptly to an end by the outbreak of war with revolutionary France in 1793 which virtually paralysed Barmouth.

This transformation also affected the most remarkable district of them all, a stretch of mountain country which ran from just north of Llangadfan north-east along the Berwyn Mountains to Corwen and Owain Glyndŵr (Glendower) country, north-west to the armpit of the Llŷn peninsula and north towards the Conway valley. The market at Bala was its focus, and this, the very heartland of Welsh Wales, a land of harsh and sometimes degrading poverty in which a lively and an imaginative people scratched a living with their bare nails, devoted itself with a kind of desperate passion to the knitting of woollen stockings which, in the 1780s at Bala, could produce sales of nearly 200,000 pairs at £18,000. From September to March, whole families, to save money on candles, would gather at chosen farmhouses and cottages to knit en masse. The local harpists would cheer them on, story-tellers and poets entertain. A celebrated Welsh historian has suggested that it was precisely this pressure which made the district such a nest of singing birds. What the Welsh call country poets flourished, skilled versifiers in the old metres, out of whom some genuine poets emerged; the old culture was revivified. And from the same area, particularly the district around Bala and Llanuwchllyn, came the popular preachers of Nonconformity, the unstoppable disputants on Biblical texts in Sunday schools. Perhaps no area in Wales except Cardiganshire was to be such a stronghold. Bala was to be the Mecca of Welsh Methodism.

But Bala, Corwen and Llanrwst were also the centres of that eisteddfod which violently anti-Methodist London-Welsh patriots revived. Here, above all, those London-Welsh found their point of contact with the homeland. And here, too, William Jones Llangadfan could find *his* point of contact. Bala was the centre for Dissenting conferences on emigration in the middle of the 1790s. For the crisis here produced a reaction similar to that in Montgomeryshire, and to that in the nearby quarrying districts of Caernarvonshire and the isolated Llŷn peninsula where a different challenge — in this case, enclosures — evoked an analogous though independent response; people voted with their feet.

In short, in the social travail of the 1790s, the autonomous development of a nascent Welsh intelligentsia, itself complex and contradictory in composition — the Llangadfan freethinker, bohemian London-Welsh patriots, the multiplying regiments of Methodist and Dissenting ministers — ran into confluence with the responses of a traditional people disorientated by sudden change. One major product of the conjuncture was a 'rage to go to America'. Its mythic symbol — and a perfectly apposite one — was a resurrected Madoc.

In the south-west was a society very similar in many respects to the central-northern belt. Around Tregaron and Llandovery, there was another stocking-trade concentration of Bala-like intensity with the same social and cultural tonality. Cardiganshire, with its lovely sweep of coastline and its rugged hills, the Teifi threading its way into the summer lushness of its coracle-haunted mouth from the bleak plateaux of the central uplands, became an almost legendary place in Welsh experience. Rooted in its Welshness, and one of the most persistent of the old kingdoms, it had been noted from the days of its Saint David (patron saint of the Welsh) for extremes of both piety and excess. In the eighteenth century, its small-scale lead industry was operative, if on a slow decline, and its little ports were lively, but it was essentially a rural community, with its small-holders and cottagers and upland farms encroaching on that two-thirds of its soil which was owned by the Crown. It was hit by the population explosion harder than any county in Wales. It became a community of land-hunger, of deadly struggle against poverty and for inching self-improvement. It was pre-eminently a land of migrants — to the Welsh lowlands, to England, to London (where its people were ultimately to dominate the milk-trade) — but of migrants who frequently and seasonally returned.

For Cardiganshire, too, and the very similar regions of north Pembrokeshire and upland Carmarthenshire nearby, was a nest of singing birds, full of country poets, rich in folklore as it was to be rich in Dissenting preachers, hymn-writers, and craggy polemicists over Biblical texts. It was a county of contrasts: while the great Methodist father Daniel Rowland was throwing crowds into those public ecstasies which earned them the nick-name of Jumpers or Holy Rollers in the south-west, a tight fistful of rock-ribbed Unitarians in the south-east looked on with Enlightened scorn. In the next generation, the claustrophobic crisis of Cardiganshire was to make it the most disturbed county in Wales; it was these people, with their compatriots from upland Carmarthenshire and Pembrokeshire, who were to people the mushrooming industrial complex of Merthyr Tydfil to the east — and to split chapel after chapel there, confounding the stern intellectuals of Old Dissent with their demands for sensuous hymns and 'vital religion'. It was, no doubt, this peculiar conjuncture of forces which shaped that alleged Cardiganshire 'personality' which other Welshmen built into a myth. For this, the Galicia of Wales, earned the reputation which Aragonese enjoyed (if that's the word) in Spain; its inhabitants hammered nails into stone walls with their bare heads. No Jews could survive among the *Cardis*, ran the scurrilous comment. Certainly *Cardis*, and their cousins from Pembrokeshire and Carmarthenshire, were successful as emigrants wherever they went, even if their hearts yearned constantly for those evenings with the harp and the intricate verses, the wordplay and the textual wrestling over the *pwnc* or Biblical thesis.

The whole south-west, particularly the border zone of Carmarthenshire, Pembrokeshire and Cardiganshire, which in the next generation was to launch that classic guerilla struggle of the small-holder, the Rebecca Riots, was a stronghold not only of Welshness, of Methodism and of Dissent (some of the most famous old chapels were there) but of emigration. From the Teifi and its hinterland had gone one of the earliest and most distinctive of the Welsh migrations to America. William Williams of Cardigan was one of the very few Nonconformists to serve as a JP and his Baptist kinsfolk were as numerous in Pennsylvania as in Wales. His friend William Richards was to be one of the most striking figures of the Madoc-migration movement. William Richards became the Baptist minister of Lynn in Norfolk, whose history he wrote, but his heart (and himself, very frequently) was in south-west Wales. A compiler of dictionaries in the style of Horne Tooke's *Diversions of Purley*, an Enlightenment man and a radical, and ardent in every liberal cause, he wrote a defence of the atheism of the French Revolution. A dedicated but caustic friend of America, his copious correspondence with American Baptists was one of the axes of the migration movement. He invested £800 of his money in the USA, tried to organize both Madoc hunts and mass migrations, and bequeathed his library to Rhode Island College (Brown University).

But the south generally and the south-east in particular was more open, more varied and complex in its social structure. Carmarthenshire had not only its upland farms but its rich Vale of Towy, its busy little ports in contact with Bristol, the economic capital of south Wales. Carmarthen itself, with its small-scale industries and its active press, was a lively and often tumultuous little town, a focus for much of south Wales. In Pembrokeshire, there were ports, coal-mines, an influential Baptist nucleus and an English population. Across the whole south, there was a scatter of mines and small forges, a network of improving landlords, and pulses of commerce. In the Vale of Glamorgan was Wales's nearest equivalent to the champion farming lands of the English lowlands.

Copper and tinplate found their British centre around Swansea and Neath, linked to the mines of northern Anglesey. Swansea, a sea-port and a centre for an industrializing hinterland, though only 6000 in population, was a fully-articulated and complex little capital town. On the northern rim of the coalfield, the intruding iron industry was beginning its rapid sweep to hegemony which was to make the district into one of the major industrial concentrations in Britain. Novel communities were shaping in the Glamorgan and Monmouth valleys, and at the matrix of Merthyr Tydfil, nearly 8,000 people were crowding into a single parish in a process which was to turn the place into the strongest concentration of Welsh people on earth.

This south-east was more fully integrated into a *British* culture; many of its major intellects were west-Briton. But Glamorgan, too, had its distinctive Welsh traditions, its poets and hymn-writers, its clusters of devoted patriots; and in the eighteenth century there had been a Welsh revival. At this time, there was such a strong Welshness in the south-east that Glamorgan and Merioneth had more in common than their present-day inhabitants could conceive. One bond which linked Merioneth and Glamorgan was the growing power of Dissent. It was the endless travelling of the essentially peripatetic ministers of Dissent and Methodism which was increasingly to knit the Welsh together. In a sense, Nonconformity was perhaps the only unmistakably all-Welsh power in the country.

And it was in this south that the London-Welsh found another, though rather different, homeland anchorage for their new 'patriotism'. They found it, in particular, in what was at this date the richest and most literate of the Welsh counties, Glamorgan.

> He was apprenticed to a joiner and carpenter, which trades he followed till several years after he was married together with that of glazier, stone-cutter and wire worker; but in the latter part of his life he took a farm and added to that a largish country shop. He was a man of universal genius both for literature and mechanics. He was employed by many in surveying, planning, measuring, calculating, writing all sorts of law instruments . . . He could exercise any trade he had seen better than most of its professors, he could and did build a house, finish and furnish it himself . . .

Thus his son on Lewis Hopkin who died in 1771, the leading figure in a coterie of Glamorgan craftsmen, popular poets, amateur scholars and Welsh patriots, who furnished the county with its remarkable literate artisanry. Descendant of a notable Llantrisant-Llanharan family of poets, and a skilled artisan who frequented gentry houses and made the 'tramp' to Bristol and London, Hopkin carried his craft into the hill-country, the *Blaenau*, and, married to a Quaker, was himself an advanced

97

Independent of the liberal breed coming to be called 'Presbyterian'. His farmhouse was full of books, Welsh, English, Latin and French, the grammars of Welsh poetry and the latest numbers of the *Spectator*.

There were others. William Edward who built the famous and beautiful bridge at Pontypridd was one of his circle. So was John Bradford of Bettws Tir Iarll, one of the hubs of this bilingual world. Versed in the classics and the literature of France and England, Bradford was no less an enthusiast for Welsh poetry and antiquities. A fulling-dyeing business gave him time to read and to pen his contributions to the *Gentleman's Magazine;* Bristol and London saw him often, a tough-minded and obsessive man, who was renowned as the most fearless Deist in south Wales. Perhaps the best poet of them all was Edward Ifan, an Aberdare man apprenticed in wood and verse to Hopkin, on tramp in his day, like most artisans, before he settled to become the first Unitarian minister at Aberdare.

No region in Wales during the Age of Revolution seem quite so distinctive and quite so bi-lingual as Glamorgan and, in particular, its Vale *(Bro)*. This was one of the rare Welsh regions where a cereal culture flourished, and where villages were nucleated, not the usual scattered Welsh hill hamlets. Village life was vigorous; even the humdrum index of clubs and friendly societies testifies to a remarkable social vitality. Bristol in particular, but also London, were within reach. Itinerant craftsmen, booksellers and schoolmasters were commonplace. Social intercourse was easy in the relatively big villages, with their crafts celebrated throughout Wales, their thatchers, stonemasons and clockmakers. Rural life could acquire some urban graces. The Cowbridge Book Society could broadcast seminal works, Bridgend be the focus of a Welsh literary revival. Anglicization had ebbed and flowed in the Vale throughout history; in the eighteenth century there was a renewed thrust of Welshness. Perhaps it was the very friction and interaction of Wales's two cultures which explains the style of the place, in a lively and open and populous society exposed to the trade winds, and feeling the tremors of change rippling through from Swansea and the coalfield. It has the feel of a place like Norwich — or for that matter, Philadelphia. Benjamin Franklin would have felt at home (his books certainly *were* at home). So would Duplay, one imagines, with whom Robespierre lodged, a man who much favoured the freethinker Volney who was to be translated into Welsh by Morgan John Rhys from Llanfabon, on the edge of *Bro* and *Blaenau*.

Morgan John Rhys, a pastor at Pontypool, was to be recognized a hundred years later as one of the major precursors of Welsh democracy. A Baptist minister of unsectarian mind and freethinking spirit, he launched some of the earliest Sunday Schools in Wales. Committed to the abolition of slavery and the defence of the new American republic, he crossed to France after the outbreak of the Revolution in much the same spirit. His crusade for Protestant liberty in Paris cut short by the outbreak of war, he came home to publish the first political periodical in the Welsh language, the *Cylchgrawn Cymraeg* (Welsh Journal) of 1793. In the first issue he announced that its proceeds would go towards finding the Lost Brothers in America, the Madogwys. In 1794, at the height of the revolutionary crisis, he toured the heartlands of dissidence and migration in the west and north, and crossed to America as the self-appointed Moses of the Welsh. After an epic pilgrimage through the new republic which embraced a struggle to establish a black church in Savannah and to defend Indian identity at the peace talks in Greenville, he was to launch the Welsh *Gwladfa*, which William Jones of Llangadfan had called for, at Beula in western Pennsylvania.

If one looks for a nursery of the democratic intellect in the age of revolution in Britain, France and America, it is in societies like this that one finds it; it was an Atlantic phenomenon. Glamorgan society produced two Welsh radicals of European and Atlantic reputation: Richard Price, the sacrificial victim of Edmund Burke's *Reflections on the Revolution in France*, one of the most powerful and effective defenders of the new American republic who was invited over by Congress to be its financial adviser, and David Williams, author of a Deist religion which won praise from both Rousseau and Voltaire, friend of Condorcet and the Girondins, who was invited over to France to advise on its new constitution.

And this was the society which produced Iolo Morganwg.

'Why do you take needless alarms?' Iolo once asked his long-suffering wife Peggy, a high-spirited and independent woman who used to comment in pungent verse on her husband's extravaganzas. 'I do not intend to print my petition for the Abolition of Christianity till long after I have done with this work that I have in hand. . . .'

Iolo Morganwg was born Edward Williams in 1747 in a cottage near Llancarfan in the Vale of Glamorgan, in the heart of the celebrated *mwynder Morgannwg* — the 'suavity of Glamorgan' as he translated it. His own life was anything but suave. His family might have interested the early D.H. Lawrence. His father, while an intelligent and literate man, was an ordinary working stonemason with a little property. His mother had married 'beneath' her. Anne Mathew was a poor and distant kinswoman of the celebrated gentry family of Mathew of Llandaff; she was also descended from an ancient and brilliant family of Welsh poets from famous Tir Iarll, the Welsh jewels in the county's crown. Frail, proud, aloof, and a dreamer, she never let her favourite, young Edward, forget his lineage. For hours she would talk about poetry and music, the twin and ancient traditions of her Glamorgan. Without doubt, something of the demon which was to drive Edward Williams came from her. He was ultimately to create that gorgeous Glamorgan-that-never-was (beneath which, however, one can catch glimpses of the Glamorgan-that-might-have-been) to throw in the teeth of sundry supercilious and superior north Walians and sneering Englishmen, and to charm later generations of addicts.

From the beginning, Edward Williams absorbed the two cultures. He spoke English at home but revelled in the superbly rich folk-culture of Glamorgan (and was to hate the Methodists for destroying it). He was taught the intricacies of Welsh verse by a couple of local country poets and, more seriously, mastered the difficult 'grammars' of the bards from poets in the hill-country, notably Edward Ifan of Aberdare (later on he was to say that he and Ifan were the only true bards left). He was taken up by several of the learned gentlemen steeped in the revival. Thomas Richards of Coychurch, who had produced an excellent Welsh thesaurus in 1753, taught him to handle manuscripts, to learn classical Welsh, but also to respect his Glamorgan dialect. John Walters of nearby Llandough was producing a massive and excellent English-Welsh dictionary. It was he who coined the Welsh words for 'dictionary' and 'subscribe' (words which could have served as presiding Deities for this generation of the Welsh revival!). Iolo helped him and acquired those lexicographical and antiquarian passions he never lost. He kept wandering endlessly all over the *Bro* and the *Blaenau*, locking into the active world of Glamorgan poets and hymn-writers, making contact with similar circles in north Wales, and also open to all the currents of English writing into which romanticism and a yearning for the antique were seeping. Active in the haphazard and beery eisteddfods of the locality, Edward began to publish himself, under the pen-name *Iorwerth*. At some time, too, he acquired a working knowledge of French and Latin, and maybe Greek.

In 1770 his mother died. Shortly afterwards, he began to take notes and to collect, a process which was ultimately to make his little cottage at Flemingston into something approximating the library of Anatole France's historian in *Penguin Island*, packed with manuscripts from floor to ceiling. He also began taking laudanum for his painful asthma. He became, spasmodically, an addict like Chatterton, in contemporary Bristol, whom he so often evoked. About this time, too, he hit the road.

His walking feats were incredible. He had taken up his father's trade, and as a stonemason he tramped for hundreds of miles. He went on long travels through north Wales, raiding libraries, collections and poets' houses for documents. He went to London and worked in Kent. He saw warships leave for the American War — and at once recollected Madoc. His brothers emigrated to Jamaica, but he went on walking England and Wales. He met everyone of note in Welsh letters, was duly snubbed by Dr Johnson and overwhelmed by Stonehenge. He haunted Bristol and Bath, tried Devon and Cornwall.

He went home to marry Peggy Roberts, the daughter of a farmer neighbour. She brought him £1,000, which pretty soon went on the castles in the air she said formed the bulk of his mason's work. They discussed Hume and Deism; she could be sarcastic about his poems. She had good grounds to be sarcastic about much else. Edward set up shop in Llandaff, went bankrupt, ran a sloop along the coast, failed, tried farming at Rumney and spent the time instead with Evan Evans *(Ieuan Fardd)*, a wayward genius of the earlier generation who took him to the ruins of the house of Ifor Hael, patron of the great medieval poet Dafydd ap Gwilym. Edward Williams turned Ifor Hael into such a household name in Wales that the first native Welsh benefit society cum trade union called itself the Ivorites. But in 1785 the family had to flee by night from its creditors. They fled to Somerset, were chased out by yet more creditors; and in 1786 Edward, who was now beginning to call himself Iolo Morganwg, was in Cardiff prison.

There he began to sort out his papers (breaking off to play the flute), and when he emerged he made contact with the London-Welsh and launched on what was, in effect, his life's career. He was in the very forefront of the Welsh revival. In 1791 he achieved his first Druidic perspective on Welsh history and culture, and moved to London, leaving his family in penury for several years. He returned to run a *Jacobin* shop in Cowbridge, to fill his life with writing and, towards the end, to shift his interest to the new town of Merthyr, where his son Taliesin was running a remarkable school (and putting the boys to copying the Iolo manuscripts). By the end of his life in 1826, Iolo had achieved a fame which, despite vicissitudes, was to prove lasting.

At this distance, Iolo stands out as one of the most original geniuses Wales has ever produced. He may not be unique; one can detect similar symptoms in others. Sometimes Iolo can look like a Dr John Dee unburdened by a university education (Iolo worked in Oxford, but he hated it as fiercely as he hated Methodists). In his own day, he was without doubt, and was acknowledged to be, the most learned man in Wales on Welsh literature, history and antiquities, a collector and annotator without peer. He was much cherished by the first generation of English romantics. 'Old Iolo', as the Poet Laureate Robert Southey called him. 'Iolo, Iolo, he who knows . . . Whatever lore of science or of song, Sages and Bards of old have handed down.' His appearance helped, of course. With his walking pack arranged so that he could read while he walked, his sharp nose, Merlin hair, and relentlessly captivating conversation bubbling with wit, erudition and fantasy, he seemed the original Wild Welsh Bard: an image he unscrupulously cultivated. But the achievement was genuine. Repeatedly and without equal, he penetrated directly and cogently to the inner reality of Welsh traditions. He was a poet, scholar and historian who projected a Welsh national library, a national museum, and a national eisteddfod. He was one of the first serious Welsh folklorists. He created an entirely new Welsh institution and bid fair to create a new Welsh national ideology.

But he also created bards, chroniclers and druids by the score. He invented a whole Glamorgan of myth. His myriad forgeries and fabrications he wove so intricately into his masses of authentic documents that Welsh scholars have had to spend years unravelling the truth. For a generation of Welsh historians he became the 'Mad Ned' that he was to a few sceptics in his own day. It has taken the herculean labours of a magisterial and dedicated Welsh scholar of the twentieth century to cut a path through this jungle, and to cut Iolo clean and clear. In the process, however, not only does Iolo, diminished but still decisive, stand out once more as an original and distinctive figure in Welsh tradition. His very fabrications (which were often brilliant: some poems he fathered on Dafydd ap Gwilym — to bring out his connections with the ancient bardic lore of Glamorgan, of course — are gems in their own right) acquire a certain logic, form a pattern and, moreover, embody a perception in depth which nobody else at that time could have achieved. Without a doubt, after a while, Iolo, writing madly away in that cottage, and hitting the laudanum, could himself no longer distinguish between fact and his own inspired fiction. For they were all coming to serve one overriding purpose — to awaken the Welsh to the Truth about their History and their Mission.

To Iolo, one can apply the words which Wallace Stegner once wrote about Bernard de Voto — 'His exaggerations were likely to be extensions of observed truth; and when he was wrong . . . he was often wrong in the right directions'. For example, he seized on the celebrated and enigmatic Triads of Welsh literature, which seem to have been mnemonic devices of bard-remembrancers, and embroidered fantasies around them; but alone among scholars at that time, he accurately perceived the *historical* perspective they were trying to convey — and adapted that perspective to the needs of the Welsh of his own time. The same is true of his huge and elaborate invention of Druidism, the matrix of the bardic and other orders, and exemplar of World Truth from Patriarchal times, of which the Welsh, and in particular their directive intelligentsia, the Bards, were heirs. This fabulous structure, with its grammars and orders and mysteries, is an incredible achievement of which no one else would have been capable. What Iolo had, in his maimed genius, was an apparently intuitive perception of the basic intellectual and spiritual forces at work among the old Welsh, and a grasp of their functional utility to the starved, neglected and often self-despising Welsh of his own day.

It was only to be expected that it would be this man who would seize hold of the revived Madoc, penetrate to the realities of American geography as they were then known, penetrate also to the hidden meanings of the Madoc myth, master its intricacies and correlations and then, in a web of brilliantly logical speculation, present the Welsh of the 1790s with a Madoc who could so well serve their needs.

His central, major perception was of Druidism, Bardism and the Gorsedd. He broke through to it effectively in 1791, which was, significantly enough, the honeymoon year of the French Revolution. He had long perceived that Welsh poets were not 'poets' as the English used the term. They were the rib-cage of the Welsh body politic. They had been remembrancers, historians, keepers of the flame. The bardic eisteddfod had been strict, professional, a guild, far removed from the tavern eisteddfods of recent times. The London-Welsh at that moment were trying to 'revive' and create an eisteddfod which was national, more strict, organized, a kind of national academy. Iolo went much further. Early on, he had argued that Arthur and his knights had regulated Welsh poetry in the days of Aneirin and Taliesin. He used the word *gorsedd* in this connection. Originally it had meant 'mound', and had come to mean an open-air tribunal. At first, Iolo used it simply to indicate a bardic gathering.

But, of course, Druids were coming into fashion in the late eighteenth century. They were Gothic, antique. It was a time given to the remote, a time of the Noble Savage and of Rousseau, of Wordsworth and of the cult of Nature. It was also the time of revolution, of natural religion, and of William Blake. And it was a time of high-minded forgers — Macpherson, Ireland, Chatterton. Iolo read the key work in the Druidic mode, Henry Rowlands's *Mona Antiqua Restaurata* (1723), which identified Anglesey as the heartland of Celtic Druidism. He pored over works which traced the Druids of the ancient (and vast) Celtic lands to the Patriarchs, and noted similarities with the Jewish Cabbala, Brahminism and the eastern religions. This, too, ran into confluence with many of the antique obsessions of the London-Welsh and other revivalists. The foremost Oriental scholar of the day, Sir William Jones, was a Welshman. Welsh writers were brooding over the relationship between Welsh, the survivor of the great Celtic languages, and Sanskrit; was it the survivor of Earth's mother tongue?

Iolo's Druid-Bardic order began to assume the character of Rousseau's natural religion. That religion was the originally pure natural religion of Unitarianism, uncorrupted by priestcraft. Iolo became a Unitarian, wrote a collection of Unitarian hymns and, when the Unitarian Association of south Wales was launched in 1802, held a Druidic *gorsedd* on a nearby hill. These Druids were also *Jacobins* devoted to the principles of truth, liberty and natural law which the French Revolution, like the American revolution before it, was trying to realize. When Iolo and his London friends launched the *gorsedd*, they made 'liberty' its motto. Iolo said he recited his famous poem *The Rights of Man* within the *gorsedd*'s stone circle. In 1798 the Cowbridge Volunteers dispersed a *gorsedd* on Garth mountain as 'democratic', and threatened to wreck the Flemingston cottage for its subversive documents.

This almost cosmic vision of the bardic tradition (which Iolo promised but failed to write up in a *History of the Bards*) was evolved in stages as he settled down to collaboration with the London-Welsh during the 1790s. In 1789, he helped them bring out their edition of *Dafydd ap Gwilym*. From 1791 to 1795 he lived among them. In 1792, his vision found its first expression in William Owen's edition of early Welsh poems, *Llywarch Hen*. This caused a minor sensation among some French intellectuals. In 1794, it found further expression in Iolo's own *Poems*. Material towards it he unloaded into the major achievement of the *Gwyneddigion*, their great collection the *Myvyrian Archaiology*, which started to come out in 1801.

This vision of the Druidic tradition of the bards was never expounded fully and clearly in Iolo's own lifetime, but enough was transmitted to act as a potential focal point for the Welsh revival. 'I am giving you,' he said in 1792, 'the patriarchal religion and theology, the divine revelation given to mankind, and these have been retained in Wales until our own day'. The Welsh, in brief, were the heirs to a human universalism — 'the venerable remains of the theology and economy of the primitive world'. The traditions descending from those ancient Druids and their universal human creed of liberty, natural religion, equality and unitarianism had been transmitted to the Welsh bards, remembrancers of the people who were the survivors of that ancient race, transmitted orally through the bardic order with its rigorous eisteddfod and its controlling *gorsedd*. (The last survivors, naturally, were in Glamorgan.) The *gorsedd*, then, was the essential instrument for the realization of this tradition, for pure theology, genuine morality, the art of the poets (lawgivers to mankind), and for the search for 'rational principles of government . . . truth and universal peace'. The *gorsedd*, therefore, should superintend every aspect of Welsh life. The ancient bardic institutions had to be adapted to the present. To that end, Iolo devised a *gorsedd*, with its robes, its three ranks, and its ceremonies. The first *gorsedd* was held by the London-Welsh on Primrose Hill in 1792. The Londoners had 'revived' the eisteddfod in modern form in 1789. By 1819, a *gorsedd* was associated with the eisteddfod for the first time. Today, a version of that *gorsedd* is an integral element of it. But this is not the *gorsedd* that Iolo had in mind. His *gorsedd* was to be the directive intelligentsia of a Welsh nation which was itself, or rather could be, the exemplar of universal humanity. When Iolo devised a plan for a Welsh liberty settlement in America, which was to make contact with the Lost Brethren the Madogwys, it was to be run by just such an intellectual élite. The Cowbridge Volunteers, in fact, were quite correct to disperse the Druids on the Garth, for those Druids were Jacobins. And though Iolo denied (probably because he had to) that Druid-bards were Freemasons, he had himself said that the ancient religion had been forced to mask itself as Freemasonry, 'the *forbidden* GOD' of one of his poems. The similarities between Iolo's Druidic-Jacobinical *gorsedd* and the radical societies of *Illuminati*, the Jacobin religion of nature and the Masonic conspiracies of the Continent, were sufficiently visible to authority. What Iolo was offering the Welsh was a 'revival' of ancient traditions which in fact constituted a new, and radical, national ideology.

What Iolo's theories further offered was a *focus*, a unifying theme for the scattered and disparate clusters of intellectuals who were busy, each in their own way, about a resuscitation of the Welsh. So many of the themes in Iolo's Druidism would strike so many chords — among antiquarians, speculators in language and anthropology, revivers of the eisteddfod, Dissenters anxious to purge religion of corruption and restore its pristine purity. Freemasonry and Unitarianism ran as underground currents through this first phase of the Welsh revival. Few people wholeheartedly embraced either, just as few people wholeheartedly embraced Iolo's Druidism. But the *instincts* which found expression in Druidism, masonry and Unitarianism could cohere around a half-acceptance of Iolo. Intimations of his creed could begin to shape a half-formed ideology around which a new Welsh intelligentsia could unite in common action. The creed must have been peculiarly attractive to such men. They were not merely antiquarians, poets and lexicographers; they were the moral legislators of a people. They were not merely 'poets', they were 'bards', people's remembrancers.

From 1789 they had an eisteddfod once more, from 1792 a *gorsedd;* all that was needed was a journal to reach the unregenerate. In 1793, it appeared in the *Cylchgrawn* of Morgan John Rhys, a Baptist minister who favoured Freemasonry, translated Volney and did not object to Voltaire. His backer was William Owen of the London-Welsh. Its motto was the one which Iolo had given his bards: *Y Gwir yn erbyn y Byd* (Truth against the World). In its first number, it blazoned the name of Madoc. Its editor was to launch the *Gwladfa*.

Like their counterparts the Czechs, emerging from a 'non-historic' existence in central Europe, these men said they were resurrecting a nation. In fact, they were creating one.

6

The kingdom of Wales

That new Welsh 'nation' of the intellectuals began to emerge in London.

> In Walbrook stands a famous inn
> Near ancient Watling Street,
> Well stored with brandy, beer, gin,
> Where Cambrians nightly meet.
>
> If on the left you leave the bar,
> Where the Welsh landlord sits
> You'll find the room where wordy war
> Is waged by Cambrian wits . . .
>
> Here men from various parts repair
> And different hemispheres;
> Who breathe the dale or mountain air,
> Towns, villages and shires . . .
>
> Their various texts they talk about,
> In arts and taste and learning;
> And often solve historic doubts,
> With classical discerning.
>
> One moon-light night it was decreed,
> To sift the tales that run;
> Concerning Owen Gwynedd's breed,
> Madog, his gallant son.
>
> Who, as our ancient bards explore,
> And histories a few;
> Found out America, before
> Columbus and his crew . . .

See clouds of smoke from pipes ascend,
And, hark! the pint pots rattle;
Let every valiant soul attend,
It is the sign of battle . . .

. . . Here Myfyr shook his head;

And springing with elastic bound
As if to cut a dash,
Kick'd Arthur's table to the ground
With one tremendous crash.

All further reasoning to prevent,
And bring on stormy weather,
He upset candles, argument,
Pint-pots and all together . . .

So seeking out the various holes
Alleys and lanes, of London,
Routed Caradogs ran in shoals,
Like damnèd spirits úndone . . .

So David Samwell, Captain Cook's surgeon (and a great hurler of pots in the cause of Truth himself) in his *Padouca Hunt*, on a famous debate on Madoc in 1792.

The *Gwyneddigion*, of whom the *Caradogion* and other groupings of much the same people were offshoots, had largely displaced the earlier *Cymmrodorion* as the premier London-Welsh society. In a colonial economy with poor internal communications and easy routes to the east, with the north finding its natural outlet in Chester and Liverpool, the centre in Shrewsbury, and the south in Bristol, London had been a focus since Tudor times. The great drove herds sweeping in, the tramping hosiers, often women, the even poorer weeders and the migrant labourers were seasonal features of the London scene, followed by more permanent residents. The early carpetbagger Tudor migrations had established an upper-class movement, but as the eighteenth century moved on, a more distinctive middle-class and lower-middle-class pattern of settlement emerged. The majority of the Welsh vanished into the London population, except for periodical outbreaks of sentiment and nostalgia. Those who actively cherished their Welshness tended to be a minority, to be north Walians and to people the societies. The celebrated Morris brothers of Anglesey, particularly Lewis Morris, played an active and distinguished role in revivifying Welsh letters, recapturing traditions, and establishing a classicism. But Lewis Morris was an incorrigible snob and a rather bilious literary-linguistic sectarian; the *Cymmrodorion* society he helped to create had a handful of hard workers, plenty of aristocratic ornaments and a crowd of piously Welsh and socially climbing philistines. The shift from *Cymmrodorion* to *Gwyneddigion* in the 1770s in some senses parallels the shift from *academies* to *sociétés de pensée* in Europe. The new men were, many of them, less substantial and more populist, but they were all committed; many inhabited the shadow-land between respectable middle-class or lower-middle-class professions and Grub Street, odd teaching jobs, and literary taverns; from the beginning the printing trade attracted a surprising number of Welshmen. Towards the end of the century, there was a steady inflow of young men who had talent, or thought they had, to be articled or apprenticed while they looked for their big break.

The *Gwyneddigion*, as the name implied, were mostly northerners; a high proportion of the leading figures came from Denbighshire; that county, which was varied, populous and relatively affluent, was to north Wales what Glamorgan was to the south, and it was growing. One suspects that, besides the natural propensity of the men of the north to take the old traditions with them to London, the accelerated modernization of the northern economy may have had something to do with it. They were in no sense exclusive, however; Iolo Morganwg was madly popular with them for a long time and they welcomed newcomers provided they weren't Methodists, though even there Dafydd Thomas, *Dafydd Ddu Eryri* (Black David of Snowdon), could be excused; he was a good enough poet to win one of their eisteddfod medals! They were an extraordinarily congenial crew. For the historian, working through the records of the period, the impact of these London-Welsh is like a sunburst. Meeting constantly in pubs, they were often riotous; the police were called in several times — for they were radicals as well. At their worst, there was a splendid, raucous, vulgar vitality about them. At their best, they recall the famous correspondence between John Adams and Thomas Jefferson; to quote the former on the latter, their style was 'felicitous'.

Much of that felicity was due to William Owen. *Gwilym Dawel* was his nickname — Quiet Will, Will Friendly, a reputation which his correspondence fully endorses — a 'lovely man', to quote standard Anglo-Welsh vernacular. William Owen, born in 1759 in the heartland of Merioneth, lived his youth near Barmouth, the outlet for that remarkable Welsh society inland. The family sent him to Altrincham near Manchester to get his English. He went up to London in 1776, worked at a number of jobs, but mainly teaching, and did some freelance writing. He did an enormous amount of copying for the patron Owen Jones. Something of a polymath in eighteenth-century style, he was widely read, and skilled with both pen and brush. He was probably the most considerable scholar of them all. He became a Fellow of the Society of Antiquaries. He edited his *Llywarch Hen* poems in 1792, produced a Welsh dictionary between 1793 and 1803, strongly supported the *Cylchgrawn* of 1793–4, published a *Cambrian Register* and a *Cambrian Biography*, translated *Paradise Lost* and was the pillar of the massive *Myvyrian Archaiology*. His occasional writings are numberless; he was no mean poet himself and he was the hub of a circle of Welsh intellectuals which began to form around the *Gwyneddigion*. He often wrote moonshine, but it always sparkled.

The key figure in a more material sense was Owen Jones, called *Owain Myfyr* (the Scholar). Eighteen years older than William Owen, he came up to London from Denbighshire and joined a furrier's business; he worked for years as a currier, but ended up owning the business and a wealthy man. That wealth he poured out in the service of Welsh history and literature. The *Dafydd ap Gwilym* cost him £180 to print; he paid for the eisteddfod medals. He spent over £1,000 on the *Myvyrian Archaiology* (named after him despite his protests). He helped send the brilliant Walter Davies (*Gwallter Mechain*) up to Oxford, paid for transcriptions, and baled out Iolo and William Owen on innumerable occasions. In truth, he had more enthusiasm than taste, though his son was to supervise the decoration of the Crystal Palace. He tended to throw his weight about, intervening in the award of prizes often with dismal consequences. A big, heavy man with a stubborn chin, his temper was as bad as David Samwell's; arguments frequently did end with the table crashing to the floor.

A contemporary has left a vivid picture of his evening entry, after a curt and unapproachable day spent 'scraping skins'. A loud clearing of the throat at the door of The Bull in Walbrook announced his presence. Chairs were hastily cleared for him. Three chairs were reserved for him, two for his arms, one for his behind. There, for hours, he dictated the course of Welsh letters, consuming Welsh rarebits, pipes and porter among 'a heterogenous company of harpers, fiddlers and fifers', talking of 'the Welch language and customs and the poet whose works he had last paid for transcribing . . .'. At the end of the evening, he 'discounted a few bills . . . for friendly and deserving Welshmen . . .'. He was made a figure of fun, understandably, not least by Iolo after that Bard of Liberty had quarrelled with the Londoners (as he did in the end with practically everybody), but it is difficult to see how there could have been much of a revival without him. The jobs he paid for fill a hundred volumes in the British Museum. He went up to London a populist Welsh radical from Denbighshire. And he stuck with it, too, come hell or high water. In 1797, the political-debating section, the *Caradogion*, debated Pitt's Two Acts which suspended English liberties during the crisis of war and revolution. Two-thirds, losing their high and fine *Jacobin* spirit, voted in favour. Owen Jones voted with the minority. He was a radical to the day he died in 1814, when many of his friends, including Iolo, were scuttling for cover, like a different species of Welsh rabbit.

Another and more celebrated Denbighshire *Jacobin* was *Jac Glan-y-Gors*, the very voice of a minority populist radicalism which would ultimately become a Welsh national style. Straight out of Cerrig-y-Drudion, he coined the celebrated expression *Dic Sion Dafydd*, for the kind of Welshman who, on crossing the Severn, begins to be so English that the English feel foreign. Keeper of the King's Head, Ludgate, Jac (John Jones was his actual name) wrote two pamphlets which were pure Tom Paine in Welsh, and he was a biting wit. The wit of the *Gwyneddigion* was a tradition inherited from a founder-member, John Edwards *(Sion Ceiriog)*, who used mercilessly to tease the irascible Owen Jones and David Samwell, as well as the skippers of Welsh sloops in the Seven Stars near London Bridge. It was he who denied Madoc in 1792 and sent Owen Myfyr crashing over the pots. Perhaps he was lucky to die in that year before Pitt's curtain came down; he loved not only music but astronomy, which, along with botany, seems to have been the 'democratic' science *par excellence* at this time.

David Samwell admired him greatly. Samwell was the wittiest of them all. He was Iolo Morganwg's great crony, big, pockmarked, 'wondrous friendly' and fond of his glass. He was forever challenging people to duels (especially eisteddfod adjudicators). Once, when he and Iolo 'waited upon' Ned Môn, an Anglesey poet, they got kicked downstairs for their pains; duelling after all was an *aristocratic* pretension.

Not all these men were radicals, however. There was Edward Jones, *Bardd y Brenin* (king's bard), a brilliant harpist, who collected and published Welsh music, was harper to the Prince of Wales and lived for a while in St James's Palace. Fanney Burney liked his playing but thought him a 'silly young man'. Iolo had harsher words for 'Jones, Reeves and all those sons of bitches . . .'; he thought Edward Jones had denounced him to the Privy Council during the witch-hunt against *Jacobins* in 1794 . . .

All the whores and thieves of London are assembled about the fellow called *Reeves* and his *fiddlers* and *faddlers* in a mighty band, *bawling* and *squawling* like the Songs of Caterwauling, *God-save-the-king — Church and King for ever!* They press every one that passes by into this infernal service, crying to him — *Blast your eyes! Cry Church and King! Church and King, damn your soul!* I jabber'd Welsh, squeaked *Church SANS King* in as broken a manner as I could and passed for a *Dutchman* . . .

For these London-Welsh lived in the heart of the London of John Wilkes and Thomas Hardy, the London Corresponding Society, the *sans-culotte* society of the John Thelwall who lectured on liberty in a cudgel-proof hat. William Owen and his friends knew most of the literary figures who responded to the French Revolution as they did to the antique-romantic in matters Welsh. They first stirred Robert Southey's interest in Madoc. They moved on the edge of William Blake's circle, and

110

knew the millenarians Richard Brothers and Joanna Southcott, whose prophecies punctuated the revolutionary decade even as millenarianism of a less disconcerting kind touched Dissent. William Owen, a follower of Joanna, who shared to the full the lust for a renewed purity and a primitive integrity, credulously accepted bizarre linguistic theories in his search for a basic, human 'language'. In Welsh, it led him to advocate spelling reform and a new orthography, which dislocated his readers back home. In this, he did not differ much from the American Noah Webster who wanted to turn old Gothic English into the Esperanto of Liberty. Men like these responded promptly to the Revolution *and* to Iolo's cosmology. Their eisteddfod was consciously designed to be an instrument of this new, Welsh, rational but also millenarian, enlightenment. They had the engraver to the French National Assembly strike their eisteddfod medals.

They responded no less promptly to a resurrected Madoc. He had, after all, taken his people to start life all over again, out of ignorance and brutal conflict. As the Conspiracy of Kings mobilized to strangle infant liberty, what better to lead the people, guided by their remembrancers, out of an old world into a new than the memory of Madoc and the quest for his noble savages? In his *Cylchgrawn*, Morgan John Rhys printed an Exhortation from Madoc to the renaissant Welsh: *Dyma ni yn awr ar daith ein gobaith* (Here we are now on the journey of our hope).

Their journey did not get far at home. By 1799 Iolo Morganwg was writing an angry letter from north Wales to William Owen: 'North Wales is now as methodistical as South Wales, and South Wales as Hell.'

For this new *Jacobin* nation was in the 1790s a pugnacious little minority. Scattered over the parishes of Wales, it existed in small groups and isolated individuals, infinite in their variety; a clutch of bookish gentlemen, a minority of liberal and rationalist Dissenters, Independents and Unitarians, a handful of Methodists, and above all Baptists writhing in a contradictory crisis of explosive growth. Political society, an oligarchy of forty parliamentary families, sometimes of longer pedigrees than purses, entrenched among 600,000 people most of whom were poor, proved impenetrable, and, during the social crises which ravaged rural Wales to west and north in the 1790s, turned nasty. The remorselessly rising tide of Methodism and the 'methodized' modes of 'vital religion' which were sweeping into the west and north from the east and south, and swirling back again, submerging much of Old Dissent in the process, left little room for it. In a Wales in which all such groups were minorities, in which a colonial economy was yielding to a more modern form of capitalism, and in which political life was blanketed by the violent conservative reaction to the French Revolution, it is perhaps not surprising that the most visible response was a surge of emigration to America under the banner of Madoc.

For politics in Wales begin with the American Revolution. The first purely political publication in the Welsh language was a pamphlet on the conflict with the colonies; even the ballad-mongers were momentarily disturbed in their customary jingoism. By the 1790s the number of political texts in Welsh had multiplied sixfold. Welsh migration to America, while not large-scale in terms of quantity, had been striking in quality and significance. In America, Welshmen were substantially over-represented. The Republic, in any event, was largely a radical and Dissenting Britain made flesh; the struggle was, in some significant spiritual senses, a British civil war in which Welsh combatants, and particularly Welsh Dissenters, were much more visible than they were at home. David Williams who, with Richard Price (another Glamorgan man), was present at the birth of this trans-Atlantic democracy, dated Jacobinism from 1782 and located its birthplace in Britain.

Through and out of this post-colonial crisis, radical and reform movements took shape in Britain in campaign after campaign — against the Test Act, against slavery, for parliamentary reform, and for equal citizenship for Dissenters. In 1776 Major Cartwright wrote the first effective democratic text in the English of England and, as the campaigns reached something of a climax at the centenary of the Glorious Revolution, the French Revolution charged political life with a whole new dimension of universalism, while novel popular movements budded out and, in the crises of war, dearth and accelerating social change of the 1790s precipitated violent reaction, an establishment witch-hunt and government repression.

Within Wales, the scattered handfuls of men who were caught up in this movement were a small and incoherent minority. In terms of that wider Atlantic perspective (of which Tom Paine himself was a living symbol) they were markedly more significant and strategically placed. For, of all the trans-Atlantic internationals which sprang to life in this dramatic conjuncture, the most active and effective was the Baptist connection. To that Baptist international, Welshmen and Welsh-Americans were central.

Baptists had been prominent in Welsh emigration from the beginning. John Miles, founder of the sect in Wales, took his church over at the Restoration to found Swanzey, in New England, in the vicinity of that Rhode Island whose originator, Roger Williams, was in Wales universally and erroneously believed to have been Welsh. Welsh Quakers had gone later, at the end of the seventeenth century, to that promised Welsh Barony of theirs north-east of Philadelphia which never materialized, and Welshmen were very prominent in the early history of Pennsylvania, their compatriots overflowing into the nearby Welsh Tract in Delaware. There was a cluster of settlements bearing Welsh names from Meirion in a great arc round to Pencader. Individual Welshmen settled in all the colonies, but several important Baptist congregations moved as groups. It was the Arminian Baptists from mid-Wales who moved with the Quakers to

112

Pennsylvania. In 1700-1701, there was an influx from west Wales, on the Pembrokeshire-Carmarthenshire border where the mother church of Rhydwilym had its roots. These were Calvinists, and they quit the Arminians to people the Welsh Tract and Pencader. From these nuclei, the Welsh grew in considerable strength, planting offshoots in the Carolinas, particularly at the Welsh Neck on the Peedee river in South Carolina. Pennsylvania remained the Welsh-American heartland; Welsh books were printed early in America, including the first Welsh Biblical concordance. A St David's Society was launched in Philadelphia in 1729.

And while Welsh emigration faded out around mid-century, the American Baptists in particular multiplied and were for long notably Welsh in character. The oldest church was Pennepek in Lower Dublin township, north-east of Philadelphia; it was served by a succession of Welshmen; Jenkin Jones of this church opened Philadelphia First Baptist as a daughter cause. The churches in the Great Valley and Pencader were equally Welsh, and were served particularly by ministers from Cardiganshire. Abel Morgan ran a celebrated academy and, from the middle of the eighteenth century, the Baptists entered another phase of growth. A prime mover was Morgan Edwards, a Monmouthshire man who settled in Philadelphia in 1761, rode 3,000 miles collecting material towards a twelve-volume history of the American Baptists, and rallied them from 1762 to the founding of their own college in Rhode Island. Two young graduates of the college of Philadelphia were key men in this enterprise: James Manning who became Rhode Island College's first principal, and Samuel Jones who was offered the headship after Manning's death in 1791. Dr Samuel Jones was born in Betws near Bridgend, Glamorgan, into a family with strong roots in south Cardiganshire and nearby Pembrokeshire (a highly suitable set of roots). Brought to Philadelphia when a boy, he graduated from its College and served Pennepek from 1762 to 1814. It was he who was the real author of the Rhode Island College charter, and who sponsored its first student, William Rogers, who was in turn to become principal of Philadelphia. Samuel Jones, a man of magnificent physique and a lively, liberal mind, came in the end to be ' a sort of bishop among the Baptists'. He presided over a buoyant denomination. In 1770, there were said to be 300 Baptist churches in America; by 1786, Samuel Jones was claiming that the number had tripled. Particuar conquests were Kentucky, where a new Baptist college was projected, and the new settlements in the south. There were twelve Associations; and the mother organization in Philadelphia embraced fifty churches. Welshmen and Welsh-Americans remained prominent in the leadership.

The contact with Wales was re-activated when two historians, Morgan Edwards in America and Joshua Thomas of Leominster at home, began to exchange material, and particularly when the former returned to

Wales to solicit funds for Rhode Island College. There were more practical reasons. The American Baptists clamoured for preachers and many of their leaders favoured the Welsh. This was in fact to be one motor force of the Welsh migrations. In 1793, for example, the celebrated American geographer Jedidiah Morse wrote from Charleston in response to a query from George Lewis, Independent minister at Caernarvon; he named the members of a society formed to assist immigrants in Boston and indicated the areas of the USA where ministers were badly needed. During the late 1780s, Samuel Jones Pennepek began to act as a kind of corresponding secretary and clearing house for a flow of letters from Welshmen on migration, denominational affairs and politics, with William Rogers as ardent lieutenant. By 1789, William Richards of Lynn was starting a massive correspondence with him, followed by Morgan Jones, who ran an academy in Hammersmith. The circle of Samuel Jones's correspondents steadily widened; by the mid 1790s, this 'bishop' of the American Baptists was in fact acting as an unofficial Welsh consul in America.

His correspondence brings to light a fascinating and vivacious little trans-Atlantic world. There was a constant two-way traffic in books, letters, pamphlets and information. This Baptist international had its own ships — three or four favoured vessels, notably the *Pigou* of Captain Benjamin Loxley of Philadelphia, who had married a kinswoman of Morgan Jones and belonged to a celebrated revolutionary family which was a pillar of Philadelphia First Baptist. The correspondence from Wales was strongly *Jacobin* in tone, full of the prices, the rents, the poverty, the landlords, the Church — and full of irritation, too, at the continuous anti-American propaganda in British newspapers and pulpits. There was a recognized Baptist network in the USA for the reception of immigrants; Rhode Island College became its focus. And during the 1790s Samuel Jones had to deal with a flow of letters of dismission, appeals for help or information, and warnings of the arrival of 'another seven score' from Pontypool or Newcastle Emlyn or Llanbryn-mair. George Lewis, from Caernarvon, seriously discussed the wholesale transfer of the Independents of north Wales to the Ohio; men as old as Morgan Jones yearned for Kentucky. It was the Philadelphia Baptist Association which initiated the revival of the Welsh society in the city and the formation of an immigrants' aid committee precisely to deal with a sudden inflow of people from Wales. It was this alert, living, constantly renewed connection which made the Baptist network the prime channel of entry at that critical moment in the mid 1790s when it looked for a while as if half the Welsh nation was ready to transplant itself.

For this strengthening American connection ran into the crisis of confidence which followed 1789. That year was a new climax for Welsh Dissenters and radicals. A bill to repeal the Test Act was only narrowly defeated in Parliament; George Washington took the new presidency of the USA, to the discomfiture of the many English who hourly awaited the disintegration of the rebel state; and the Bastille fell. The celebration of the centenary of the Glorious Revolution was an affirmation of faith in the future. As the *Gwyneddigion* held the first of their eisteddfods on themes drawn from Iolo's Druidism and French Declarations, and had their medals struck by liberated Monsieur Dupré, William Owen broke into ecstatic and British verse *On the Revolution:*

> Hail sons of Cambria, bards of ancient lore,
> Met on Snowdon's brow, to attune your lay,
> This holy hill where freedom loves to stay,
> The chains of galling bondage never bore . . .

> Once druids sang our laws
> Who were th'oppressor's foes
> Oh! let me approach, give my *Awen* fire . . .

Even at the high-point of that blissful dawn, however, there were ominous signs. In 1790 Burke published his *Reflections* and, in reaction to the new threat, a proposal to repeal the Test Act was decisively defeated; in the following year, even as the liberty eisteddfod marched on at Llanrwst and Morgan John Rhys made his way across the Channel, the Church and King crowd in Birmingham smashed Joseph Priestley's society. In 1792 came the dramatic second part of Tom Paine's *Rights of Man;* unprecedented artisan societies sprang to life in Sheffield, Norwich and elsewhere and, in the autumn when news came through of the overthrow of the French monarchy and the September Massacres, grew into a movement looking for leadership to the London Corresponding Society. Authority struck back, in proclamations against seditious literature and, in that same autumn, in a massive growth of loyalist associations, a ferocious blast of traditional patriotism and a witch-hunt. In February 1793 Britain went to war with revolutionary France. In 1794 there were the treason trials; in 1795, the Two Acts, which suspended British liberties. And war brought an abrupt acceleration of those processes of change and dislocation which had already begun to disturb rural Wales; it brought inflation, taxes, militia levies, the press gang, and the virtual closure of Barmouth. It was at this point that Morgan John Rhys, his journal the *Cylchgrawn* going down fighting against the reaction, appointed himself Moses to the Nation and set off to Llanbryn-mair and William Jones's country, through the troubled north and west, to cross along the Baptist network and create the *Gwladfa* of Beula in the Land of Liberty. After him, in two great waves during the terrible years of 1793-7 and 1799-1801, hundreds of Welsh families made their way to the America boats, Dissenters most of them, people of a little substance and substantial spirit, while behind them, thousands trapped in poverty clamoured to get away.

In this Wales of the 1790s, locked away in a corner of a Britain swept by gales of loyalism, disciplined by suspensions of habeas corpus, patrolled by the Volunteers, deafened by *God Save Great George our King* sung five times over in the playhouses to drown *God Save Great Thomas Paine*, where could its minority of radical intellectuals, its disaffected small-holders, look but to that America which claimed to be the physical realization of the principles of enlightened liberty, where even a Joseph Priestley could breathe? It was in these years that Dr Samuel Jones's correspondence begins to be obsessed with migration. In these years, the celebrated emigrants' guides and handbooks came out, as 'the rage to go to America' as Mrs Lindsay called it, gripped minority Britain: Brissot's *Travels* and Jedidiah Morse's *American Geography* in 1792, the topographical description of the American west by Mary Wollstonecraft's husband Gilbert Imley in 1793, Thomas Cooper's *Information* in 1794. Christmas Evans, the Baptist apostle of Anglesey and a master of the new evangelical style, raised his organ voice in protest —'*Ysbryd America yn trallodi yr Eglwys* . . . (The spirit of America afflicts the Church)'. He denounced the two clever talkers who were corrupting the godly in Wales — *Mr Gwladaethwr* and *Mr Mynd i America* (Mr Politician and Mr Go-to-America).

It was in these years, too, that the *Gwyneddigion* organized clubs for political debate: the *Caradogion*, which was open to non-Welshmen, and the equally uproarious, Welsh and *Jacobin Cymreigyddion*. The latter's initiation song, written by the Welsh Paine, *Jac Glan y Gors*, was a hymn to Madoc.

For two years earlier than Morgan John Rhys, another Welshman had crossed along that same Baptist network, also on a Mission for the Nation. It was the Lost Brothers he was looking for, the men of Madoc.

It was precisely at this tense moment, as the Nootka Sound crisis broke across the excited Britain of 1790, that a resurrected Madoc could work his magic. The new radical and populist movements sought historical precedents to buttress what was in reality an unheard-of innovation. The 'mere mechanics and tradesmen' of the unprecedented British popular societies, with their revolutionary creed of democracy, loudly asserted that they were 'restoring' ancient Saxon freedom and throwing off the Norman yoke. One artisan derived the right of armed resistance from Saxon precedent. How much stronger would this impulse be among a minority of radicals in a people who were themselves a minority lacking parity of esteem? At that moment, the Madoc myth was serving these Welshmen as the myth of the Freeborn Saxons was serving their English colleagues. Welsh Indians were Welsh freedom. The Welsh myth was more universal, almost cosmic, as was to be expected from a small and marginal people, but the role it played was analogous. The Welshman of the 1790s who stood before the clerk in Philadelphia's federal court with his citizenship papers hardly ever gave his birthplace in the standard form prescribed for subjects of the King of England; more often than not he called it the 'Kingdom of Wales'.

Such a sequel to thirty or forty years' dry-as-dust rummaging among ancient texts must have surprised that learned divine in Sydenham, Dr John Williams. For this America fever, focusing so many Welsh aspirations on the Ohio and the Missouri, began in the spring of 1791, when he published his *Enquiry into the Truth of the Tradition concerning the Discovery of America by Prince Madog ab Owen Gwynedd about the Year 1170*.

7

Padouca hunt

'This is a new affair or rather a subject long and deeply buried in oblivion and of late thus raised up,' wrote Joshua Thomas of Leominster, the celebrated historian of the Welsh Baptists, on 30 July 1791. He was talking about Welsh Indians and writing to Iolo Morganwg. He did recall hearing 'some hints of Welch people being about the Mississippi about forty years ago'. So he should have done; thirteen years earlier, he had himself cited the exultant 1752 letter from Philadelphia announcing the discovery of Welsh Indians west of that great river.

Five years earlier, Morgan Edwards, the no less celebrated Welsh historian of the American Baptists, had been telling Joshua that stories about Welsh Indians were by then commonplace in America. He had drawn attention to John Filson's new study of Kentucky. In 1791, Joshua Thomas, who was not sure whether to address Iolo as 'Reverend', did not know whether there was a copy of Filson in Britain. (In fact, as early as the autumn of 1790, Filson was known to that hammer of the Saxons, William Jones Llangadfan, the Voltaire of mid-Wales; William Richards of Lynn was able to send Joshua an extract.)

Even more remarkable than the sensational testimony of Charles Beatty, Isaac Stewart, George Croghan and the rest, is the fact that it apparently passed entirely without comment among the Welsh at home. Nothing of the Madoc fever in America seems to have penetrated their consciousness. Not until Dr John Williams published his *Enquiry* in the spring of 1791 did this whole continent of folklore rise from oblivion like some long-lost Cymric Atlantis.

What resurrected Atlantis was an ancient, indeed in terms of the Madoc legend, a traditional obsession: struggle with Spain. Dr Williams was at pains to indicate that he had intended to publish 'had the late misunderstanding with Spain never happened'; he had been working on the subject for thirty years (William Owen said it had been hatching for forty). It is true that Williams's text was clearly written without benefit of Nootka. Nevertheless, the author made his purpose clear: 'My design in the above Extracts and Observations, I presume, hath been answered, which was to shew that the Spaniards have not an unquestionable right to the Continent of America.' The concluding section of the essay was an indictment of Spanish pride and cruelty, and here he was even more specific: 'The Bay of Honduras and the parts of the adjoining Continent, in which the English have a right "to load and carry away logwood" by the 17th article of the Peace of 1762 and by the 6th article of the Peace of 1783, we are told are already dangerous to the British traders . . .'. But 'the close of the 18th century seems teeming with great Events'; Spain's power would soon be broken as its slave people rebelled with the help of freedom-loving Americans.

The British cutters of Honduras logwood and of that mahogany which was coming to command Georgian taste, were in fact the spearhead of British commercial penetration of Spanish America. They had to fight a running guerrilla, which was peculiarly sharp during 1785-6, and which rumbled on to the outbreak of European war. In April 1789 the Spaniards started to expel British whalers from Patagonia — and whaling was to be one link with the Nootka trade. Spain opened the island of Trinidad to settlement, an action which sent ripples of disturbance through the West Indies, which were already feeling the first effects of the French Revolution and the campaign of the English opponents of the slave trade. Dr Williams's book got a cutting edge from this conjuncture.

And from that same cockpit, earlier than any Welshman and quite without warning, there suddenly came crashing into the world of Madoc an intruder who injected into the Anglo-Spanish tension the most startling evidence of all.

Island of Trinidada,
City of St Joseph, 20th of Maye,
1595

I, Sir Walter Raleigh, commander in chief by land and sea etc. etc. etc. — for the most high and Pusiant [sic] Princess Elizabeth Queen of England, Wales, France and Irland — and of the Dominions and seas there unto belonging and of all lands, continents, islands and *seas*, in and beyond the Atlantic ocean round the great continent called America and unto the South Seas — in and over All Lands and Estates heretofore had and discovered for and on the behalf of the most Excellent, high and renowned *Prince Owen Guyeneth or Guyneth prince and Sovereign of North Wales*, next unto the Nation of the Scotch or *Northern Britions*, discoveries and conquests first made in the year of our Redemption and Salvation *1164* (or their about) by the great and valliant Prince *Madock ap Owen* Guyneth the youngest son of the said *Prince Owen* Guyneth, he being provided with a powerfull *fleete* and Men of War, and arms famous for valour by Land and Sea takeing with him Many Noble Brittons both of *Wales* and of the *Northern race* besides Valliant Men from Irland and other adventurers for new and great discoveries, did first come into these Seas in the year of Salvation aforesaid named and set down *1164* and the second time in *1170* and did Make notable discovery conquest and settlements of all the Parts of the said great Continent of America and of all the Islands round that Mighty tract of Land and in all the seas, from the Latitude of 36 degrees North all along and round the saide Continente Unto this said Island of *Trinidada* passing Unto *Guyeneth, Guyneth* or *Guyannah,* to which Vast Space of Country, he, the said prince *Madock ap Owen Guyneth* gave his own *Name, Gueneth, Guyenth, Guyneth,* now Corrupted and calld *Guyannah,* from thence passing on To the degree and Latitude of *five North* and to Mouth of the Amazonia Great River or *Rio Aragona* and round the vast coast of *Brazilia* Unto the south Sea or Pacific Ocean.

All which lands, Continents, and Islands, from that of the great, wealthy and vast Empire of *Mexico* (otherwise the Empire of Madock) which he, the said *Madock ap Owen Guyneth* did first conquer and People with his *Welshmen* and his *Brittons* and his tribes of brave adventurers, from whence he did carry into *Wales* three Several times Mighty store of massey silver and gold, precious stones, diamonds and emeralds etc. etc. And his race, thereafter reigned Emperors of Mexico untill *Montazuma*, which the Reccords of North *Wales* and Brittons and *Mexico* are the noblest testimonials, proofs and the Most Effectual truths and genealogies of right — the speech and confession of the Emperor *Montazuma* before the Captain of the Spainish robers *Hernand Cortez* in 1520 when the spainard usurped Mexico — Are undeniable truths besides the Proofs of reccord History and the assertions of confessions of many Noble Spainards particularly *Francis Lopez de Gomara, Don Alonzo de Maquira* and *Don Juan de Gallowania* and also *Don Carlos d'Owena Madoxus*, all Noble Native Mexicans owning and challenging their descent from the *Brittons* — these being Princes of the Blood of *Montazuma* by Marriage and Descent, besides these, *The Mexican Tongue*, their habits, manners and various British Customs still remain amongst the Descendants of the first Welsh Settlers in Mexico at this day, 431 since the Royal Race of *Prince Owen Gwyneth* possessed the *Mexican* empire . . .

And on Sir Walter went, in high rhetoric, formally to take possession of Trinidad in the name of Madoc, in this hypnotic proclamation, which Captain John Drummond enclosed in a letter he addressed to Lord Walsingham of the Post Office in August 1789.

There were more 'valuable documents' in his letter. Edward Thurlow, troop commander of Sir John Hawkins in the famous fight at San Juan d'Uloa on his third voyage in 1568, had hanged Spanish gentlemen as a reprisal for the execution of some Englishmen 'not because they were Spainards — and Men — but because they were Traitors to England, usurpers of the Territorys of her Crown and Sovereignty, Murderers and Robbers of Mexicans, the Descendants of the *Ancient Brittons* whom we are come to Rescue from the yoke of Spanish tyrany and usurping slavery . . .'. Thurlow and Captain Joseph Manningham had gone inland to Mexico City to take the surrender. 'The native Mexicans,' they proclaimed, 'are our flesh and blood.'

As if this were not enough, Thurlow went on to comment, after having described the city as a Garden of Eden:

> Women of Mexico are perfect Beautys, *fashioned as one may truly say for Love.* The Men, ugly black and malignant in their looks, especially all the old Spainards. In the natives, we still behold the traits of their *Antient British Beauty* and indeed in the Country Wenches we could trace the *Welsh Pedegree* in their fine, round apple smooth countenances and fat, plump, cheeks and bodys. *These were a perfect treat to Myself and Manningham* . . . God forbid old England should ever be forced to abandon Mexico . . .

A sentiment in which Lord Walsingham, once he had recovered, could surely be expected to concur.

Of all the rich and varied tapestry of fabrication woven around Madoc, these concoctions of John Drummond are surely the most gorgeous. They were done with panache and style, historical names mingling easily with that Don Carlos d'Owena Madoxus, who was presumably born in Vera Cruz on St David's Day. The Hawkins story was deftly lifted from a French account of genuine massacre and counter-massacre in 1568. The 'unprejudiced investigator', to employ the favourite expression of dedicated Madoc scholars, cannot withhold his mede of admiration.

The documents come straight out of the rich, dramatic and implausible half-world inhabited by those international adventurers who entered the service of Spain, sometimes to fight for her, sometimes to intrigue against her, always to make their own fortunes. John Drummond was a Scotsman (as even a cursory reader of the Raleigh 'proclamation' might be driven to suspect). He had gone to Mexico in 1748 and served the Spanish crown as a military engineer and surveyor. In a statement which rivals the Raleigh proclamation itself, he claimed that a kinsman of his had served as a Portuguese bishop in Brazil and had acquired twelve chests of valuable documents from the Jesuits of Guiana when the order had been expelled. On the bishop's death in 1780, the chests had passed to Drummond. He had promised them to the Royal Society of Paris, but he was saving those touching the British nation ('Mine in point of Profit with Notarial copies of the whole') because of the great weight of tradition and interest they brought to bear in the service of the Crown.

For Drummond was anxious to alert government to the threat to the West Indies posed by the Spanish opening of Trinidad, the activities of French revolutionaries, and the Jacobin-inspired schemes of Wilberforce and the abolitionists at home — 'Is it possible that the British ministers can be the dupes of this wicked and ruinous plan of leaving the British people here as a sacrifice to so abandoned a race of monsters as negroes let loose are?' Drummond, with his companions Count O'Reilly, son of the celebrated Irish Governor of Louisiana in 1770, and a Colonel Brown, had devised a new saltpetre manufactory for gunpowder, and they were urging Walsingham to intercede on their behalf with the Master of the Ordnance. Drummond had acquired an estate on a small island off the coast of Grenada and had been close to the previous administration, he claimed, devising plans to capture the enemy Windward Islands during the war. In 1788 he had returned to Britain, and during the summer of 1789 had been in France on business. He said he had joined the entourage of the Duke of Orleans and much of his correspondence with Walsingham between August and October 1789 was about the first crisis of the French Revolution, of which he took a cataclysmic and conspiratorial view.

At that moment, his correspondence with Walsingham was private (except, one imagines, for a small army of wide-eyed eavesdroppers). The first reference to him in the Welsh correspondence comes in November 1790; not until his second edition did Dr John Williams include some of the Drummond material. In fact Williams, Iolo, William Owen and the other Welsh stalwarts eliminated most of it. They were, if anything, more disconcerted by this sudden irruption from the West Indies than the Spaniards had been in Drummond's own dream-world. The abrupt incursion of those heretic Scots must have been hard to assimilate (the Irish were more easily absorbed), particularly since there were plenty of documents still to come from the 'twelve chests'. In a sense, the renewed emphasis on Mexico marked a return to the pristine purity of the Madoc myth in its original form, but it came at the very moment when attention was relentlessly closing in on the Upper Missouri. Nevertheless, Drummond took the searchers directly into the world of the international freemasonry which served Spain — and it was precisely in this world that the Welsh enterprise of the 1790s was to live and move.

Drummond was writing his letters in August 1789. He had moved to Bath, which was a social capital for the Welsh gentry, the prime market for Welsh heiresses and one of Iolo's hunting grounds. It is possible that some tremor from Drummond country penetrated Welsh circles, for it was in October 1789 that the Madocians began to write to the *Gentleman's Magazine*. First in the field was the doughty William Richards of Lynn. He wrote to the magazine on 14 October. He had seen in the *Bury Post* some reference not only to the Madoc story but to a Welsh gentleman in

London who planned to go in search of Welsh Indians. Richards's letter rehearsed the familiar story, and cited Herbert and the Stedman-Humphreys anecdotes from Nicholas Owen's *British Remains* of 1777. He knew of the 1752 letter from America and he introduced a novel element in reports from a 'respectable inhabitant of Kentucky' (in fact the Rev. John Corbly, who doubled as an agent on the Monongahela). Corbly referred to Welsh Indians far to the westward on the Missouri 'called the White Panis or bearded Indians' (a nice fusion of multiple myths here). The Kentucky archaeology of Filson was cited and there was talk of missionaries. William Richards himself was hunting up the Panis or Pawnees on maps supplied by Morgan Jones's academy in Hammersmith.

This letter the editor did not publish. Another, dated 24 October and signed 'M.F.', which simply listed many of the Elizabethan references to Madoc, he did. The Madoc legend crept back into print, then, before the end of 1789; for the moment its presence was ephemeral, though William Richards addressed his first letter to Samuel Jones Pennepek in November of that year. On 7 May 1790, he wrote his first letter to William Owen and did not mention Welsh Indians. In that same month, however, the Nootka Sound crisis burst on the public in a war fever which did not subside until the Spanish surrender in October.

It was this which propelled William Owen and the *Gwyneddigion* into action. Hugh Jones, a schoolmaster out on the Georgia frontier on the edge of Creek (and Spanish) country, had been pressing a G. Revely in Virginia for news of Welsh-speaking Indians whom Richard Lloyd had claimed once lodged in Revely's house. Revely denied the report, but confirmed that Welsh Indians had been reported on the Missouri, a river which ran into the Mississippi 'from the south west' (thus pressing it back, in the current geography, near to New Mexico). The man to contact was Colonel Evan (in reality Moses) Shelby, a north Walian now on the banks of the Ohio. Hugh passed this information to Owen Jones, and William Owen began to bombard the distant Ohio with unanswered letters. Revely had placed the Welsh 150-200 miles up the Missouri; Owen judiciously extended this to 400 miles. By the autumn he was telling Iolo Morganwg that Captain Drummond's testimony 'confirmed' the story (a difficult logical exercise).

It was once again Drummond who was the first into public action. In the *Public Advertizer* for 23 September, he addressed an open letter to the prime minister under the pseudonym *Columbus*. This asserted that Sebastian Cabot, in discovering Florida and Mexico a couple of years after Columbus, had encountered survivors of Madoc's colony. Moreover, Drummond printed a version of Montezuma's celebrated speech before Cortes (which he claimed to have found in Mexico in 1748) in which the Children of the Sun who had founded Mexico were placed in a 'distant Northern nation, whose tongue and manners we have yet partly preserved', inhabitants of a small island which the ravagers of all the earth had failed to subdue. Dr John Williams was not the only thinker to deduce that this must be Britain, in which Caesar 'was rather unsuccessful, or at least not so brilliant as he cautiously endeavours to represent it': Scots, of course, could be less tortuous on this point.

The reviving Madoc enterprise was developing a marked Mexican and southern list. William Jones Llangadfan confirmed the trend in a remarkably well-informed letter to William Owen in October. 'Our good neighbours the English,' he began in characteristic style, 'will but reluctantly allow that a Welshman is capable of performing any noble action or exploit.' The English, after all, had suppressed Wales's own university at Bangor in the early middle ages, even though they had then been forced to send for Welshmen like Asser to run their own. Rather than see America discovered by a Welshman, they'd bend the knee to a Genoese.

William Jones suggested, very sensibly in the circumstances, that Alexander McGillivray, chief of the Creeks, be asked to check the truth of Filson's story (which Jones evidently knew), 'he being a Scotchman.' The writer added, 'I am, as I suppose, the first who took notice of the probability of the Incas being descended from our Britons by the similitude of Mango Copac, Mama Ocha, Inca etc. to the Welsh language and the Abbe Raynall's supposing Mango to be a European who might have travelled through Brazil . . .'. The Incas, after all, regulated the calendar in the European manner.

Jones had evidently read another John Williams's *The Natural History of the Mineral Kingdom* of 1789, which argued that Madoc had discovered not only Mexico but Peru. The two peoples were similar; both had struck the Spaniards as civilized. Both had legends of Founders from the East who would return; the Inca year had 365 days. The progenitors of the Incas were called Manco Capac and Mama Ocello. Williams suggested that the latter was a corruption of *Mama Uchel* (High Mother); would she perhaps be Madoc's wife? The Welsh prince, having reached Mexico on his first voyage, was blown off course on his second and shipwrecked probably near the Amazon. He had, in all likelihood, sailed up that river 'and at last arrived at Cuzco'. William Jones was impressed, but crippled by his ignorance of Peruvian history. He urged William Owen to search the records.

The drift towards Mexico and the south was in fact running counter to the trend of the evidence which Dr John Williams had spent so many years assembling. He ignored it in his first edition and it gave him a lot of trouble in the second (he rejected a direct voyage to Peru, but admitted that Madogwys might have reached the place from the Pacific coast of their Mexico). Fortunately, the sensational testimony of Captain Isaac Stewart offered some hope of linking Mexico and the Missouri and it was

124

duly given prominent notice in his book.

Granted the initial commitment to the Madoc tradition, John Williams's *Enquiry* of 1791 makes impressive reading. With massive scholarship and a calm, open, tentative manner, he moved solidly through the material, handled opponents with some skill and avoided the worst abysses of fantasy. He constructed an effective argument in favour of a measured and tentative acceptance of both the Madoc discovery and the existence of Welsh Indians, perhaps more than one tribe of them. The book was an immediate success; the world of Welsh, and not only Welsh, letters was fascinated. It mobilized opinion and directed it towards action. Once it had appeared, in the spring of 1791, things began to happen.

The first thing that happened was 'General' Bowles. His impact on the Welsh-Indian project was immediate and, for one moment, threatened to be decisive. He had persuaded the Governor of Canada to pay for the passage of his party of Creeks in October 1790, hoping to exploit the Nootka Sound crisis. Government had played with some of his schemes but gave him little support. Bowles stayed on, recruiting allies for a yet more grandiose project: the creation of a Creek state called Muskogee, the core of a larger unit to be carved out of both the American and the Spanish south-east, based on the Mississippi navigation and buttressed by British merchants. In the autumn of 1791, he launched the enterprise, supported not only by Lord Dunmore and his parent firm of Miller and Bonnamy in Nassau, but by such hardened Spanish-frontier conspirators as William Blount and John Sevier of Tennessee.

The *Gwyneddigion* were very nearly swallowed up in this empire-building (which the Spaniards managed to nip in the bud). Bowles, in full Indian regalia, had caused a sensation in London, exhibiting his Indians at Vauxhall, and appearing all charm, good looks and splendour at all the right places. He bedded a distinguished lady and fathered a new dish: 'fricassée des Cherokys — qui fit beaucoup de bruit, alors!' according to the French traveller Milfort. Armed with Dr Williams's evidence, William Owen and David Samwell approached him on behalf of the *Gwyneddigion* and the Madocians. They could hardly have done better. The sceptical David Samwell was so excited after the second 'audience' with the General that he wrote off a report to the *Gwyneddigion* immediately. Not only did the General convince the Welsh patriots that the Welsh Indians existed; he offered them the means to get to them. Serious plans were devised to establish a Welsh base in Bowles's country. William Owen's brother John, a printer (who did actually migrate to Nassau), was to set up a newspaper in Bowles's capital. Iolo Morganwg, after his self-selection as the chosen emissary to the Madogwys, got letters of introduction to Lord Dunmore and his circle and passports for New Orleans. A group of Bristol merchants and their Bath friends gave him letters and other material to take to Bowles. As a result of the Bowles interviews, the mission to the

Madogwys began to figure as yet another Nassau speculation for Miller, Bonnamy and Company.

For Bowles gave the Welsh Indians a location and a name. He knew the white Indians well, he said, having travelled the whole southern frontier of their country. Back home among the Creeks was a Welshman who had escaped from the Spanish mines and had made his way through these people, talking Welsh all the way. One of Bowles's companions was called Price. His father was a Welsh-speaking Welshman who had frequently conversed with them. Bowles said the Welsh Indians were 'the same complexion as we are, some having sandy, some red and some black hair. They are very numerous and one of the most warlike nations on the continent' (Price had said this, too). William Owen, in his breathless letters to friends, was now able to pin them down with some precision:

> The centre of their country is about lat. 39 north and long. 103 from London. Their northern extremity is put down in some maps *The Black Padoucas*, in consequence of their having mixed with the native Indians and are therefore of a deeper colour than the pure Padoucas. Their eastern extremity comes within about 300 miles of the Mississippi or rather less, in lat. 37½ and their length from that point westward (inclining a little northerly) is upwards of 700 miles, but not of proportionate breadth.

This was brilliantly done — 'or rather less . . . a little northerly . . . not of proportionate breadth.' Purists may care to know that this located the heartland of the Welsh Indians in Big Sandy Creek, Colorado, south-east of Denver, with their eastern border on the Kansas-Missouri line east of Wichita, the *Cymry* extending a little northerly from that point through Kansas, Colorado, into Wyoming, possibly touching Nebraska and even Utah and Idaho, depending on that proportionality of breadth. In his report to the *Gentleman's Magazine*, Owen was even more precise and, drawing on material supplied by Iolo Morganwg from his researches, placed the Madogwys on the continental divide, communicating to the east by the Missouri and to the west by a great salt lake (which they navigated in big pirogues) through the Oregon or Great River of the West, to the Pacific by the strait of Juan de Fuca. This, said Bowles, was 'a very easy journey from where he resides' (about 700 miles across two international frontiers).

And he gave them a name. They were the celebrated 'Padoucas'. True enough, on many a map, located vaguely on the Upper Missouri or rather south of it, there were Padoucas, indeed frequently 'White Padoucas'. William Richards of Lynn had spotted them the previous winter, on the maps in Morgan Jones's academy in Hammersmith. The name struck him: could it not have been derived from Madoc? In May he wrote to William Owen to make the point, but he was preaching to the converted.

126

William Owen had recognized them at once. 'These people are found in maps under the name of the White Padoucas, *evidently* [my italics] Madawgwys or the People of Madawg'. As usual in such matters it was left to Iolo Morganwg to put some bone into this argument. 'Madoucwys in modern Welsh is litterally the *Men of Madoc*. In the *Silurian* Dialect, spoken in Monmouthshire, Glamorgan etc. etc. the *M* is changed into *B* and there they would say *Badoucwys* (the *Silurian* dialect is the least changed from what the *Ancient Welsh* was, of any of our dialects . . .'

Bowles's testimony, coming so hard on the heels of Dr Williams's book and the flood of recent information, was decisive. 'Well, Iorwerth!' wrote William Owen to Iolo Morganwg, 'the world *must* believe at last.' Some still did not, or pretended not to, and by May 1792 the *Caradogion* were holding a great debate, with the believers William Owen and David Samwell ranged against the infidels (or those who assumed the role for the occasion) *Siôn Ceiriog* (John Edwards) and *Ned Môn* (Edward Jones). It was an uproarious affair, even by *Gwyneddigion* standards, with pots, fists and chairs flying immortalized in Samwell's splendid mock-heroic poem *Padouca Hunt*.

But in fact the affair had become serious; it had been transferred into actuality. Men must be sent. William Owen fired off letters to friends and supporters, notably the major patrons Paul Panton of Anglesey and Thomas Pennant of Flintshire. The latter was dubious, the former enthusiastic. Owen was ready to go himself, but for family and other commitments. He was sure there would be volunteers. He was perfectly correct. William Jones Llangadfan was first in the field and he linked the project at once with a plan for a Welsh settlement in the New World.

In May, William Richards wrote two letters within a week. In the first he cited Corbly, the Croghan letter and the word Padouca. The second he wrote as soon as he had received his reply from Samuel Jones in Philadelphia. Samuel sent detailed plans of the Indian burial tombs found in Kentucky and noted their similarity to old Welsh burial chambers. Everyone in America knew Welsh Indians existed; if they were found, old though he was, he'd go to preach among them himself. Samuel Jones, calling on his countrymen to come over, directed Welsh minds to what was to prove a key text, *Carver's Travels*. The Reverend Rankin of Kentucky, then in London, was interviewed by Owen and Samwell and supplied more proofs.

The *Gwyneddigion* launched a serious campaign to raise funds and find volunteers. They opened a correspondence with the *Gentleman's Magazine* which lodged a Madoc letter in that journal month after month. They energized the Welsh at home, among whom some were already beginning to catch America fever. It was in June that William Jones Llangadfan circulated his remarkable manifesto among the crowd at the Llanrwst meeting: *To all indigenous Cambro-Britons*. The fellow *Cymry* who had crossed the ocean so long ago 'are at this time a free and distinct people, and have preserved their liberty, language and some traces of their religion, to this very day . . .'

And in July, the first letter from Iolo Morganwg appeared in the *Gentleman's Magazine*. With Iolo, an original mind of genuine distinction bent itself to the service of the Madogwys. This July piece was a classic demonstration. The 'hard evidence' in the letter was yet another anecdote in the Morgan Jones style. About twenty years ago, Iolo had talked with a Mr Binon (Beynon) of Coyty, Glamorgan, in the presence of the respected Methodist John Williams of St Athan. Binon, as a youth, had spent many years as an Indian trader out of Philadelphia. With a small party he had once penetrated 'much further than usual' beyond the Mississippi and had come across a tribe who spoke Welsh 'with a much greater purity than we speak it in Wales'. They had taken to Binon but were deeply suspicious of his English companions whom they took to be Spaniards, with whom they were at war. These Indians had iron; they were better clothed than other Indians; their villages were built of stone and there were stone ruins which looked like Welsh castles and churches. They had a manuscript book which they could not read but which they cherished, believing it contained the mysteries of religion. A man had been among them who could read The Book. He had told them that a people would come who would explain The Book to them and make them completely happy. They were disappointed when Binon confessed he could not read it, but they escorted him and his companions back through vast deserts, begging Binon to send them someone who could read The Book. The Coyty man then found that people in the Welsh Tract knew of this tribe; Welshmen had been among them.

The development of this Binon rigmarole at the hands of Iolo and others is itself interesting. John Williams of St Athan wrote to Dr John Williams to confirm Iolo's story, adding the confusing detail that parties of the tribe sometimes visited the Welsh Tract [and found no one who could read The Book?] and asserting that when Binon said he had come 'from Wales', the Indians replied, 'It was from thence that our Ancestors came, but we do not know what part of the world Wales is'.

A year later, however, Iolo was preparing a paper for the Royal Society, and as part of his preparations he 'developed' the Binon story, in his familiar manner, along the lines it 'ought' to grow. In this newer version, Binon now 'perfectly understood' Welsh; it was from *Cymru*, not Wales that he came. The story of The Book acquired that sonorousness appropriate to the Welsh people in an age when Iolo was rediscovering their Druidic heritage: 'They have a tradition amongst them that they were a *great and happy people* whilst they were able to understand their book and when one comes amongst them that will teach them to read it, they shall become *great and happy* again . . .' More Welshmen than Druids would appreciate that sentiment.

This is Iolo the magician. But even in this very process of 'development', Iolo the scientist is at work. For, in 1792, to supplement the Binon story, Iolo told of Captain Forest of Bristol, a greatly respected man of the utmost veracity who, in the presence of John Williams of St Athan, had asserted his total confidence in Binon's story but added that, of late, the Welsh Indians were much reduced in number through their wars with the Spaniards. This 'truth' entered the canon and it is almost certainly a reflection in myth of the smallpox epidemic which in reality had decimated the Mandans of the Upper Missouri in the 1780s. Furthermore in his second version of the Binon story, Iolo has the Welshman 'going up a large river' entirely absent in the original. For by that time, Iolo knew that Binon *must* have gone up the Missouri.

The seeds of that knowledge were in fact present in that very letter of July 1791, for Iolo supported the first Binon story with a series of 'Remarks'. Those remarks represented honest and extremely perceptive research. Behind them lay the reams of notes, extracts and scribbles which choked that little cottage in Flemingston. In preparing his letter, Iolo took copious notes from Meares's account of his adventures at Nootka; the stonemason bard did a full-scale analysis of Meares's material. He plunged into the writers who were then the major geographical authorities — Charlevoix, Coxe and Bossu (Carver he did not yet have). In the process, in that direct penetration characteristic of him, he took possession of the fundamentals of the speculative American geography of his day — the Oregon or Great River of the West, the Strait of Juan de Fuca, the Inland Sea. That we now know those fundamentals to have been false is irrelevant: these were the truths of American geography as Iolo's contemporaries knew them. In that Glamorgan cottage, Iolo Morganwg, in quest of his Welsh Indians, was beginning to think and write in exactly the manner of the harassed but visionary frontier statesmen of St Louis and Montreal, of Washington and New Orleans; his mind was moving along precisely the same tracks as those cool but passionate brains which were to create the imperialist manifestoes of Alexander McKenzie and Merriwether Lewis.

What Iolo seized on in Binon were the clothed Indians and the stone buildings and the iron. Captain Cook, he noted (and David Samwell could have confirmed it), saw iron at Nootka, which was 125° west according to Meares. The Padoucas on most maps were 110° west. Meares's 'discoveries' suggested a link via Juan de Fuca and the great river Oregon. Iolo cited the worthless Coxe, but only to quote Baron La Hontan who erected an imaginary world on real foundations, to create a great lake with civilized Indians and a river flowing out of it into the Pacific. Was not this 'the Oregan of Captain Meares'? He quoted a greater man, the Jesuit Charlevoix, who also had a lake up the Missouri, with Indians in clothes

129

living in cities, and referred to Bossu who had been told by the Sioux of the Plains of clothed Indians who lived far west of the Mississippi, in great villages built of white stone and who navigated in big pirogues on broad salt water lakes. On the mythical foundations of Binon, Iolo was in fact creating, in brilliant isolation, that structure and pattern of America which were coming to govern the best exploring minds of the continent.

There was still a great deal to do before the jumble of anecdote could be drilled into intelligibility and system; it took him a year to do it. But it was a happy beginning, that London of the summer of 1791, when he finally broke through to his Druidic vision, when David Samwell went everywhere with him, wrote him a poem on his firm stand against treacherous patrons in Bath, and another to celebrate their visit to Sterne's grave; when there was such congenial company in the *Gwyneddigion*, and George Dyer and the *Jacobins*. His favourite patron, Miss Bowdler of Bath, whom he teased about her descent from the Welsh princes (she always referred to the hero as 'Uncle Madoc') was busy transcribing Welsh Indian material for him, pushing his *Poems Lyrical and Pastoral*, and crying that 'her Welsh blood was up!' whenever someone questioned the 'Uncle'. And things were at last moving in Wales; every parish, of Dissent at least, was sprouting its own William Jones.

In that same summer, the summer which seemed the dawn of the New Age to the Friends of Freedom, Morgan John Rhys set out on his Messianic mission to Paris. The following year, under the first jarring impact of recalcitrant old realities, he was driven home by the threat of war. A renewal of hope awaited him, however, for in the meantime the quest for the Madogwys had acquired a whole new dimension of reality.

This was the work of Iolo Morganwg. To the horror of his wife Peggy, the Bard of Liberty had decided that the mission to the Madogwys was his. To prepare himself, he practised living rough in the woods and fields, sleeping in the open in the rain and living off berries. The intellectual preparation was no less arduous. He went back to Flemingston and scoured Glamorgan for information. By the end of December he was in Bristol and Bath, closely questioning the quality and consulting maps and books. By the time he was back in London in the spring of 1792 and preparing to address the Royal Society and the Society of Antiquarians, he had solved most of the conceptual problems, though he was still uncertain about his route.

During these few weeks and in constant communication with William Owen, Dr John Williams and the *Gwyneddigion*, Iolo was preparing what he called his *Padouca Gazette Extraordinary*. He unearthed a mass of information. Many of the Glamorgan stories bore a strong family resemblance to each other. John and Kate Evans, descendants of a man from *Tref y Rhŷg* who'd gone over with William Penn, had told a strange story forty years earlier. An Indian from a party they had entertained in

1 Queen Elizabeth I, her imperial ship and British maritime
empire. Frontispiece to Dr John Dee's *General and Rare Memorials
pertayning to the Perfecte Arte of Navigation* (London, 1577)

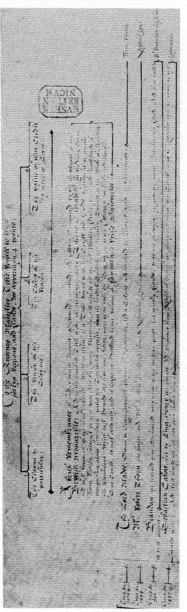

2 The first appearance of Madoc in the historical record.
The *Title Royal* presented to Queen Elizabeth I by Dr John Dee,
October 1580

3 Mandan village. Karl Bodmer watercolour

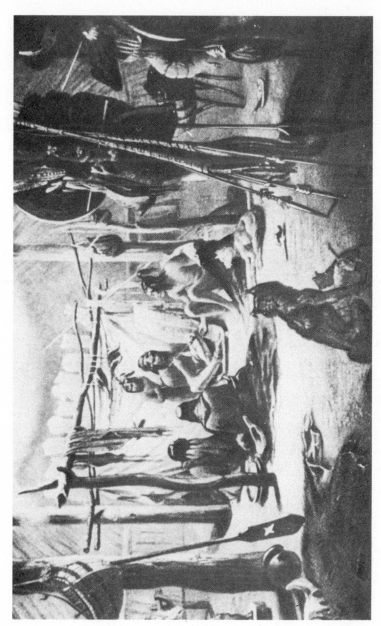

4 Interior of a Mandan lodge. Karl Bodmer watercolour

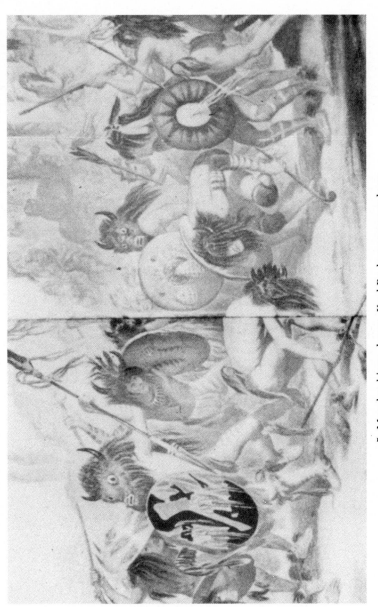

5 Mandan bison dance. Karl Bodmer watercolour

6 Iolo Morganwg

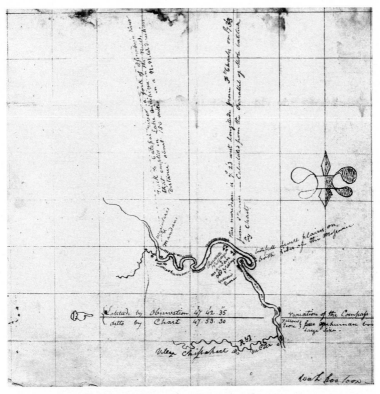

7 John Evans's map of the Missouri 1796–97; the final section
running north from Heart River (R. du Coeur), showing the
Mandan villages at the junction of Knife River and the Missouri
and the track of the Canadian fur-traders from the north

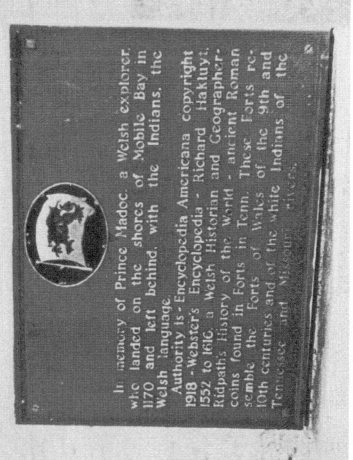

In memory of Prince Madoc, a Welsh explorer, who landed on the shores of Mobile Bay in 1170 and left behind, with the Indians, the Welsh language.

Authority is - Encyclopedia Americana copyright 1918 - Webster's Encyclopedia - Richard Hakluyt, 1552 to 1616, a Welsh Historian and Geographer - Ridpath's History of the World - ancient Roman coins found in Forts in Tenn. These Forts resemble the Forts of Wales of the 9th and 10th centuries and of the white Indians of the Tennessee and Missouri rivers.

8 Plaque at Fort Morgan, Mobile, Alabama recording Madoc's landing, raised in 1953 by the Daughters of the American Revolution

their house near Philadelphia had stayed behind when the others left. Every day he would shoot them some game and leave it without saying a word. In the end, John Evans said, '*Druan ohono, rhowch fwyd iddo* (Poor fellow, give him some food)'. Whereupon the Indian went mad with joy. He had heard Welsh on his first day and had been waiting to see whether he'd been mistaken, for he could scarcely believe that white men could speak his own language.

Forty-five years ago, Thomas Thomas of Coychurch had been one of a party of traders far up country on a very large river. At one landing, they were surrounded by a party of Indians. One of them grabbed a white man, shouting, '*Herc y fwyall, mi a dorraf ei wddwg e'nawr!* (Give me the axe, I'll cut his throat now)'. Thomas was naturally able to save everybody's life [particularly since the progenitors of these Indians, to judge from their language, must have been south Walians]. Evan Williams of Colcoed, however, out hunting beyond the Blue Ridge mountains, came across Indians 'gabbling Welsh' which he thought was north Walian and he painted a vivid (and rather appealing) picture of himself and the Indians earnestly addressing each other, understanding each other's words but unable to grasp their meaning.

These had been but 'wild Indians'. John Phillips of Cardiganshire however, years ago, had told Iolo of a letter which had come from America to his minister Jenkin Thomas. Welshmen from Pennsylvania, going far into the interior, had come across Welsh-speaking Indians at a town called *Capel Seiniau* (Chapel of Saints). The letter was circulated among Dissenters in the hope of recruiting missionaries, and the Indians were 'widely known' in Wales as *Cymry Capel Seiniau* (the Welsh of the Chapel of Saints). Iolo duly cited Lopez de Gomara and Antonio de Espejo in Spanish accounts of the 'country where the Welsh Indians are now said to exist' to the effect that Indians there were more civilized, had some notion of Christianity and built stone chapels.

More interesting than even the local colour of these narratives is the fact that Iolo felt able to cite early *Spanish* authors on Madogwys living somewhere on the *Missouri*. It is an indication that he was now fully possessed of the most advanced geographical thinking, in particular *Carver's Travels*. For, as the information came in, problems multiplied. In Bath and Bristol, for example, while General Conway and the merchant Kennedy could simply confirm stories of Welsh Indians in the most general terms, Sir John Caldwell in Mrs Bowdler's house was rather disconcerting. Stationed once among the Chippewas, he was told by Welshmen in his company that Indians of the tribe of Panis, or Pawnees as the English pronounced it (imitating the French, as Iolo sagely and accurately noted), spoke Welsh, and were relatively civilized. Sir John could quote the great Indian trader Peter Pond himself, the man who began to open up the north-west wilderness of Canada and had no less a person than Alexander McKenzie as assistant. Pond knew both White and Black Panis. Much more civilized than the others, they built stone houses and were willing to work. For that reason, other tribes made slaves of them and even sold them to the English. These Panis were less ferocious and warlike than other Indians. They lived so far up the Missouri, said Pond, a dry old Yankee, that 'from one of the highest of a chain of mountains in their country, he could see the *Pacific Ocean* very plain'.

This geography was pure Carver (except for the ocean view, of course, which was impure Pond), but these slave Panis were worrying. Iolo's notes fill with etymological analyses — Pannwys? People of the plain? Governor Pownall of Canada and his nephew, a secretary in Quebec, confirmed the slave status of the Panis, but Mr Rimington in Bristol was more reassuring. He knew the white Indians west of the Mississippi as Padoucas; Panis, he thought, was not a tribal name, but a generic name for 'slaves'; hence the great variety of the 'Panis'. He thought the white, civilized Padoucas called themselves *Ka Anziou* or *Ka Anjou*, meaning First Men or First of Men (this was certainly an echo of Mandan cosmology). Rimington knew all this, he said, before he'd ever heard of *Welsh* Indians, but once at an Indian mart at the Forks of the Ohio, he'd seen an Indian tribe come in from the far west, 'tolerably white', wearing semi-European dress — trousers, coats with sleeves, and caps made of very small and beautiful feathers curiously wrought. They had fine copper utensils. A Shawnee had expected Rimington to interpret for them. The Englishman had been amused, since he could not understand a word the newcomers said and he assumed that Indians took it for granted that white men could speak every language. But when he told his companions of this, the general cry went up, 'Oh! they are the Welsh Indians. Send for Jack Hughes!'

By now, a pattern of settlement was emerging fairly clearly and even the shape of the possible migrations which had brought the Madogwys to the Missouri, but the Mexican pressure was still heavy, since Drummond kept on turning up fresh evidence. The Captain's servant, a Highlander, had heard an Indian mother in north-eastern Mexico singing to her baby in *Gaelic*. He quoted the Spaniard Juan de Grijalva to the effect that the leading fighters of Mexico wore kilts. Iolo knew of the Spanish accounts of semi-civilized Indians on the northern frontiers of Mexico, where Drummond also disconcertingly placed the Madogwys.

Iolo had little difficulty with Drummond's Celtic Confederation from the European end. Madoc's brother Rhiryd, after all, had been lord of Clochran in Ireland. The Pownalls (who did not believe in Welsh Indians at all) had also cited Highlanders who understood some Indians, and Iolo came across an account of the Scottish settlement of Darien which made the same point. However, half the words of this account cited as Erse turned out to be Welsh, though, as Iolo noted, 'this is no more than what is really the case between Irish and Welsh.' He saw no reason why Gaelic speakers might not have deviated from the main penetration route of the Madogwys.

It was when he finally got a sight of Carver at Bath, however, that his mind was eased. Jonathan Carver travelled into the interior in 1766-7 and published his *Travels* in 1778. The first English report on the far west, it was better than anything the French had produced. The work of an intelligent, observant man who could analyse rumour, it expressed in a crystal clear fashion the notions about North American geography which were becoming determinant in men's thinking. Carver had the great rivers flowing eastwards, the Mississippi, Minnesota and Missouri among them, rising in a north-south belt of Shining Mountains, with their headwaters not far from each other. The Oregon, great river of the west, and the Bourbon flowing north into Hudson Bay, together with the Colorado, took their rise from the same mountains. The focus, then, was on the Upper Missouri. Here was that 'short portage' across the watershed mountains which led from that river over to the Pacific. Here was that foreshortening which rammed New Mexico much closer to the Missouri than the Almighty had actually placed it — and which gave those harassed Spanish officials in St Louis such sleepless nights. For Carver had the Rio Grande, too, running *east* of the Shining Mountains and curving sharply northwards.

The impact of Carver on Iolo is immediately visible. On New Year's Day 1792 at Bath, he first read him and he was writing to William Owen at ten o'clock that night. Early the next morning, he sent a postscript longer than the original letter:

Captain Carver says that the finest furs of North America come down Bourbon river to Hudson's Bay from near the upper part of the Missouri. I can not help (amongst other hopes) wishing that I may, one day or another, be able to procure those articles for my good friend Mr Owen Jones, at a cheaper rate than he has them at present. *Castles in the Air*, you cry — but the idea gives me pleasure . . .

There were more cogent reasons. Through Carver, the Spanish evidence could be brought more closely into line with the by now massive material on the Upper Missouri. Moreover, Iolo found three references in Carver himself which strengthened the case. Indians had told Carver that 'a little to the northwest of the Missouri' there were Indians who were smaller and whiter than other tribes, and who cultivated the ground and the arts. They were supposed to be some of the tribes which had been tributary to the Mexican kings and which had fled when the Spaniards came to Mexico. The Jesuits had also claimed that these people had some confused idea of Christianity. This, and Carver's map, seemed to clinch the business. Distances were still rather great however, and Iolo finally solved the problem by a creative intervention in history. In his notes, Iolo took the bold Captain Drummond, lifted him bodily from Mexico and put him down in *New* Mexico! It made more sense.

It was probably the evidence of Richard Burnell which settled his mind in the practical sense; he frequently returned to it. Burnell had lived for fifteen years near Philadelphia but had lost everything during the War of Independence, since he had been a Loyalist. When Iolo met him, he was living at Swansea, as a steward to Herbert Evans. Burnell had known the missionary Charles Beatty and his informants, and was a close friend of Samuel Jones. He was knowledgeable on Welsh Indians. They lived west of the Mississippi in great numbers, stretching along the Great River of the West. Traders, however, kept information about them a close secret, partly to defeat competitors, but mainly out of fear of the Spaniards within whose realms they lay.

But Burnell pointed to another fruitful area. He knew that the brother of James Willing, the great Philadelphia merchant, had speculated in land at Natchez, on the southern Mississippi, which was disputed between Americans and Spaniards. Two of Willing's carpenters who were Welsh frequently conversed in their own language with Indians who came across the Mississippi. These Indians, allies of the Chickasaws and Creeks, were a party detached from their main body who lived high up the Arkansas river. Burnell's son Cradock, who spoke Welsh, lived near Augusta in the backcountry of Georgia, but he was one of the Yazoo speculators in this district and he had met these Welsh Indians repeatedly as far south as latitude 33°.

This resolved a problem which had been nagging at Iolo's mind for some time — how could there be Padoucas cited on maps as far south as latitude 33° ? It was this concept of 'detached parties' of migrant clans separated from their main body, together with Carver's geography, which fixed his thinking. It also fixed his route. Quebec, Canada and a wholly British route to the far west certainly returned from time to time to tease his mind, but until the March of 1792 he was in fact settled on a southern route. By February, he was once more in London and there he met Griffith Williams, the US consul, who was Welsh and a fervent Madocian. On 11 February, Iolo wrote to Peggy to announce that he had turned down the offer of a job in Canada which would have brought in £300 a year (which must have pleased her!). Griffith Williams had suggested instead a way of getting to the Madogwys which would make the enterprise 'very safe, very comfortable and very expeditious'. Iolo's intention was to make his way to Georgia and then to Natchez. With the help of Bowles and his Creeks, he would then go up the Arkansas until he reached the 'lower tribes' of the Padoucas. To this end, he was equipping himself with letters and testimonials to Bowles, to Lord Dunmore in Nassau, and to the leading figures among the American Welsh. He was getting passports to New Orleans and, presumably as a final insurance, an introduction to George Washington.

In the month of March, however, this scheme was abruptly abandoned. March 1792 was a good month for Madoc. Dr John Williams brought out the second edition of his book, *Further Observations*, packed with new information from Iolo, William Owen, William Richards and John Drummond (the latter's Raleigh-Hawkins material, however, while mentioned, was nowhere quoted). Iolo prepared a paper for the Royal and Antiquarian Societies. He evidently meant to publish it some time, though secrecy, because of the danger from the Spaniards, had now become a preoccupation of his. He drafted a title page:

> Some account of an Ancient Welsh colony in America, humbly addressed to the Royal and Antiquarian Societies, by E.W. Bardd wrth fraint a defod Beirdd Ynys Prydain, Bard according to the Rights and Institutions of the Bards of the Island of Britian. 'Facts are stubborn things' Prov. Y Gwir yn Erbyn y Byd, Truth against the World — Motto of the Ancient Welsh Bards.

In its final draft, it was a very skilful and subtle piece of work, weaving the material together effectively and nudging the sceptical mind towards at least a suspension of disbelief. It ended with a persuasive peroration:

> It may be asked of what use would it be to Ascertain whether there are such tribes of *Indians* speaking *Welsh* and where they are precisely situated? We might answer thus:
> Those who believe in the *Christian Revelation* believe that it is our duty to propagate the knowledge of it amongst those who still remain ignorant of it. With such this is the first and greatest consideration. In a Political view, it would extend our Dominions at a cheap rate, by restoring to us a congenial nation, our own children, who probably would be glad to find themselves protected by their Parent Country, and a hundred well-disposed *Welshmen* there (being of the same language with them) would do more towards acquiring a considerable accession of Territory to *Great Britain*, than a hundred thousand scoundrels in *Botany Bay*, and that in a very short time. It would open a resource of considerable wealth to the nation, would be the means of greatly extending the inland trade of *America* and take off our hands very great quantities of *British Manufactures*. It would enable us to establish very strong posts in the heart of that Continent which, being done with caution and with a view to National Good rather than the enriching of individuals, would soon be a blessing to the Natives, and be a means of protecting them against their savage neighbours who enslave them, if they are really the *Panis*. If Nootka Sound is worth colonising, it would be the means of establishing invaluable overland communications from Quebec or

Montreal with the settlement there.

Many other advantages might be pointed out. National Honour is not to be despised. *Great Britain* would be entitled to the honour of *prior discovery* and the *right* derived from that which the *Spaniards* so much insist upon. It is worthy the notice of the *Historian*, the *Philosopher*, the *Politician*, and the *Man of Commerce*. It is in every sense worthy the notice of a *Briton* and of *Britain's King and Parliament*, much more than a few insignificant islands in the *South Seas*.

Not Alexander McKenzie or Thomas Jefferson himself could have put it better.

Those 'hundred well-disposed Welshmen' turn up in another context at this time. For by the spring of 1792, what had been a personal obsession of William Jones of Llagadfan was becoming a subject of common discourse among 'enlightened Welshmen'. Concurrent with the Welsh Indian preoccupation and the missionary impulse it engendered, ran a growing and parallel dedication to the establishment of a *Gwladfa*, a National Home for the Welsh people. At about this time, Iolo drafted a plan for just such a settlement, which represents the first attempt to translate William Jones's dreams into a practical proposal. The proposal, in fact, followed the lines already established by some bold New World projectors for the creation of such settlements on the American frontier.

Plan of a Welsh Colony
1. To petition Congress for their interfering assistance in purchasing, on peaceful and equitable terms, of the Indians, a portion of land near the Mississippi between the Ohio and the Illinois.

2. As soon as 100 Welsh emigrants exclusive of Women and Children are obtained, to engage a vessel to carry them over.

3. As there are none rich, it is requisite that each person or family should be able to pay the proper quota towards defraying the expence of passage and land travelling.

4. Those who are able to purchase land, to give freely for ever as many acres as necessary for raising provisions for their families or otherwise to require no other payment than X months' labour for every acre to the donor.

5. That plans of Government and religious polity on the purest principles of Justice, Peace and Liberty shall be assented to by solemn affirmation and manual signature by every emigrant before he can be admitted of the party.

6. That such mechanics as appear to be remarkably skilful and of good character shall with consent of the majority be taken over at the

expence of the Association provided such mechanics shall engage to follow their profession for seven years.

7. The mechanics deemed necessary and to be taken over at the common expence are Masons, Carpenters, Smiths, Miners, Weavers, Fullers, Potters, Braziers etc., schoolmasters.

8. Every one that can pay £5 towards the Land-Purchase money, exclusive of passage and travelling expences, to be admitted of the company of Colonists, all others to be admitted of another company of Mechanics, who are to be endowed with proper privileges during the time which they shall follow their several occupations.

9. That none be admitted of the Company who cannot speak Welsh or have at least a wife that can.

10. That the legal language of the Colony shall be Welsh and all pleadings in Law, all Religious worship etc. shall be in it, the English also to be taught as a learned language and source of knowledge.

11. To purchase a common Library, 2 copies of Chambers' Cyclopedia, 1 of the Scotch Cyclopedia, Pryde's Mineralogy, Watson's Chemistry, 5 copies Owen's Dictionary for a select society.

required from Congress

1. some pieces of cannon
2. a garrison to be paid by the Colonists.

This splendid exercise in Welsh Enlightenment, with specific provision for a *Jacobin* élite of Druids to direct his Free Cambria (in which, however, 'schoolmasters' were apparently an afterthought), did not merely gather dust in the Flemingston cottage. Thinking of precisely this order governed the attempt to establish a *Gwladfa* in America three years later, when Morgan John Rhys, fresh from his crusades among the French and the unregenerate home Welsh, adopted it as the last and most splendid of his missions. From the beginning, the project ran in harness with the quest for the Madoc Indians. Each mission interpenetrated with and informed the other.

This project, of course, was sited in the Land of Freedom; there was nothing here about the extension of *British* authority. But note where Cambria is to be sited — on that American frontier closest to Spanish Louisiana, within striking distance of the presumed homeland of the Madogwys. There is another dimension to this location. That site, in the Illinois, close to the junction of the Mississippi and Missouri, was precisely the locale for several schemes, potential and actual, to settle people within the orbit of Spanish power, now in collusion with, now in opposition to, Spanish authority. Within a couple of years, it was to produce another grandiose western dream — a new independent state of western

Americans and Louisiana French, linking up with friendly Indians and maintained by British commerce. It is difficult to avoid the inference that this particular plan for a Welsh *Gwladfa* sprang from an encounter of Iolo's which, in this March, changed his whole perspective on the Madoc mission.

In the summer of 1791, Iolo and William Owen had interviewed the Philadelphia bookseller William Pritchard (who promised to propagate Iolo's poems in the USA). He had been the first to warn them that Indian traders, the prime source of information on the Madogwys, might conceal and distort information from interest or fear. Those traders had flitted ghost-like through the evidence since. By March 1792, Iolo and the *Gwyneddigion* had actually met a couple in the flesh. The encounter proved decisive.

The key figure was old, white-haired James Jones, on a visit to London. The son of a Welshman, he was a merchant in Spanish New Orleans where he owned much property. In January 1792, Griffith Williams the American consul had passed him Dr Williams's book. In a letter to Griffith Williams dated 28 January, Jones said he was quite convinced of the existence of Welsh Indians on the Missouri, who had migrated there as so many other tribes had done. He had just met an Illinois merchant come to London who knew of Indians west of the Mississippi whom the French called White Bearded Indians. They lived in thirty-two towns or villages, were vastly attached to certain religious ceremonies, and had actually been visited by a 'Mr Ch.', a merchant of reputation in the Illinois. When he sent this letter to the *Gentleman's Magazine*, Griffith Williams added that he had encountered this Illinois merchant whom Jones referred to. 'Mr Ch.', a kinsman of his, had met the chief of the Padoucas, who ceremonially washed the merchant's feet because he was white. Williams introduced a practical note into the discussion. These Indians were more civilized because the whites were encroaching on them. The river trip from New Orleans to the junction of the Mississippi and Missouri was arduous, but a light boat could get to the Missouri tribes in six weeks and the land was a goldmine.

The merchant from the Illinois was Charles Gratiot, one of a pioneer merchant family of St Louis, who lived in St Genevieve, *La Miseria*, and who was in London that summer. His kinsman, the 'Mr Ch.', can only be one of the celebrated Chouteau family, the founder merchant dynasty of St Louis. Griffith Williams had introduced Iolo to James Jones and, through him, the Welshman met Gratiot. Williams had still been pressing the New Orleans route on Iolo, but the American consul suddenly and shockingly died and, quite clearly, it was the advice of Gratiot and Jones which induced the poet to change his plans. By early March, he had decided to leave for Philadelphia in August, strike inland to the Ohio and take a flatboat to St Louis.

He revealed his thinking in two extraordinarily sycophantic but amusing letters he addressed to Miss Bowdler and another lady in Bath on 28-29 March, begging an entry into polite society for James Jones. 'Who knows,' he said, 'but that at *New Orleans, New Madrid*, or some other part of the *New World*, I shall sometime in future be so happy as to meet with one who knows Mrs and Miss Bowdler?' New Madrid was in truth the new focus. Telling Miss Bowdler of Gratiot's account of 'her Cousin', the Prince of the Padoucas, he reported that Jones and Gratiot would supply him with commendatory letters and he stressed the need for secrecy. James Jones 'strongly recommends silence and secrecy to those who intend going in quest of these people, as they are in the Spanish territories'. In consequence, Iolo was going to *suppress* the publication of his material. 'My papers are to be laid before the Antiquarian and Royal Societies tomorrow, but with Mr Jones's caution, not to be publicly read.'

Gratiot's influence was decisive. Thomas Pennant, prime patron of the *Gwyneddigion*, had overcome his diffidence to the point of promising to support 'any rational undertaking' and William Owen had been busy trying to whip up support. He organized a *Madogeion* Society, a group limited in the first instance to twenty; members were to pay a small quarterly subscription, meet quarterly and vest executive authority in a committee of five. Their prime purpose was to collect information, both on the Madogwys and on the means of reaching them. In his search for funds, he approached the missionaries of the African Association (Bowles had also been associated with the Sierra Leone project). It was Charles Gratiot who provided him with Pennant's 'rational undertaking'. At a vital meeting of the *Madogeion* on 22 April 1792 in the Prince of Wales Coffee House in Conduit Street, they decided to 'follow the instructions and embrace the aid promised by a French Gentleman, Mr G., a merchant of St Louis'. Thomas Pennant agreed, at last, to act as director and trustee.

Gratiot's advice was soundly based on his knowledge of the Indian trade:

> Mr G. proposed that a sum of money should be placed in the hands of a Banker, to create a security for his Correspondents in London, Messrs Sneider and Co., Merchants, to induce them to give a Letter of Credit with the persons going on the expedition, addressed to him at St Louis. That on the arrival of such persons there, Mr G. would introduce them, or one more properly as principal, to the commanding officer of St Louis, and represent them as persons come to settle there, to trade with the Indians. That on obtaining such permission, Mr G. would direct the equipment of a boat and furnish all the articles necessary for Trade, and the contingencies of the voyages, which would amount to from a thousand to fifteen hundred pounds. That when ready in the spring the expedition should commence and proceed up the Missouri River,

trading with, and procuring interpreters from the different Nations they passed, to those farther on and thus would safely arrive at the Country of the Padoucas . . .

He went on to warn that the Padoucas did not kill beaver and that the chief material return would be buffalo robes. Losses could be expected. It had happened to his brother. Whatever goods they brought back could be disposed of in St Louis and losses covered by a payment into Schneider's from the subscription money raised by the *Madogeion*, who chose to deposit it in the Bond Street Bank of Sir Humphrey Mackworth with its Welsh connections.

By April 1792, then, the quest for the Madogwys had taken shape in a hard, practical plan geared to the realities of the Missouri. Gratiot had used the plural in talking of the explorers and it had become perfectly clear that Iolo would need a companion. By May, he had appeared in the person of a 'young man from Caernarvonshire'. At that time, some leading *Madogeion* thought they could bypass the tedious process of raising funds with a direct approach for government help. But Iolo and his companion were now hell-bent on leaving before the end of the year, whether they got any help or not.

And with the appearance of this young man, the story of the Welsh and their Indians begins to assume the character of an odyssey. He was John Thomas Evans, a Methodist from Waun-fawr, near Caernarvon. After all the talk and the debate, the speculation and the theorizing, this was the man who would ultimately set his foot on the outermost rim and take The Language and The Book to that empty place on the map at which Iolo's magic finger insistently stabbed.

8

Off to Louisiana in the morning

John Evans belonged to a family which was distinctive in north-west Wales in that, at a time when Methodism (with Dissent some way behind) was beginning its inexorable advance towards hegemony in the area and precipitating local crises of authority during a period of economic strain, it represented the earliest Methodist penetration of what had been a recalcitrant region. The first Methodist *seiat* or society in the district was at the farmhouse of Hafod y Rhug in the village of Waun-fawr near Caernarvon town. Evan Dafydd, its tenant, had assumed the leadership of the group which after his death passed to Thomas Evans of the *tyddyn* of Tai'r Ffynnon, near Bangor. Thomas Evans built up a reputation as a preacher before his death in 1788 and was followed by a son Evan, three years younger than his brother John.

John therefore came from a pious family and was certainly Methodist in his writing style, at least in his early years. Those early days, however, lacked the Calvinist brutalism and narrowness which became dominant modes in the next generation. The emollient preacher Evan Richardson was a friend of the family and used to annotate their letters to John in America. He evidently exercised that softening influence he was to exert on a later Welsh hero, Hugh Owen the educational pioneer. Congregations terrorized by Christmas Evans used to cry aloud for Evan Richardson to come and comfort them. The family seems to have mixed easily with Dissenters of a liberal turn of mind and to have been open to the world. David Thomas the poet, *Dafydd Ddu Eryri* (Black David of Snowdon), with his *Gwyneddigion* connections, was a Methodist friend and may have been John Evans's teacher. The young man grew close to Iolo Morganwg. Once out in the world, he moved as easily from Methodism into the Baptists and Freemasonry as any Morgan John Rhys.

Twenty-two in the summer of 1792, John Evans was an able young man who earned the respect of such diverse individuals as Thomas Charles the Methodist leader, Iolo Morganwg, James McKay the Scottish fur trader, the Spanish Governor of Louisiana and Black Cat, chief of the Mandan

Indians. Events were to prove that he had the makings of a great explorer and geographer: he talked his way through the Arikara. But there was an impulsiveness in him, an uncontrollable passion. He was given to bold rhetoric and high-minded boasting, tended to refer to himself in the third person and wrote a florid, flamboyant hand (much reduced after his experiences on the Missouri). He yielded to impulse and could launch himself into implausible enterprises with near-lunatic insouciance.

In the summer of 1792, perhaps he needed to. For by July, William Jones Llangadfan was alarmed. The Spanish capture of General Bowles — 'colled afrifed imi (an immeasurable loss)' — had riveted their grip still harder on the Missouri and the Madogwys. It had to be prised loose. The Canadian route was too far north. William Owen, said the old Voltairean, must get in touch with American landowners and put a migration project to them. The Republic of Despots which was at that moment crushing France would soon turn on America. Conditions in Wales were becoming dreadful; soon Voltaire's prophecies would be fulfilled, and there would be nobody left but tyrants and slaves. On the other hand, news of the Madogwys was spreading rapidly. The only hope for the Welsh was migration to join their Lost Brothers. Already a young man from Llanbryn-mair was on his way to Liverpool to organize a vanguard party.

What had frightened William Jones was the abrupt withdrawal of the Bard of Liberty himself. Iolo Morganwg slithered into some kind of emasculating personal crisis during this summer. The *Madogeion* suspended their subscription in the hope of getting government support; this could hardly have encouraged Iolo, who was a man of forty-six with a family. His letters to his wife chronicle a hair-raising descent into a kind of purgatory. He had been so ill, he told Peggy, that for two weeks he'd been unable to say a single word (certainly the worst catastrophe which could befall such a man). He was ashamed of the necessity of begging patronage from the Prince of Wales, the unofficial head of the opposition. His poems were held up in the press; London was a horrible place. He suffered some of his periodic lapses into enervation and for weeks had been unable to work. In mid-summer, he became convinced that all his children had died and that Peggy was keeping the news from him. Whole weeks went by without a proper meal and he was hitting the laudanum hard. By the autumn he was talking wildly about Chatterton's suicide and calling his life 'HELL, HELL, HELL'.

It is difficult to know what to make of this, for in the same period, he was getting jaunty *Jacobin* notes from David Samwell and William Owen, working on the latter's dictionary and preparing his own exposition of Druidism and the Bards which was to create a minor sensation in France. Iolo was up to his eyes in the fervour of *Jacobinism* and millenarianism, which was mounting in some quarters in London from the bubbling fraternity around William Blake to the strongholds of Old Dissent and the

142

debating clubs of earnest artisans.

The sudden shift in the political spectrum was certainly one major factor. The second part of Paine's *Rights of Man*, which really launched that seminal book on its populist career, came out in April; so did the first proclamation against seditious writings and the first anti-*Jacobin* witch-hunt, a minatory foretaste of the years of iron ahead. Church and King had already mobilized against dissent — and Dissent — in many localities; the Priestley Riots of July 1791 had been a warning. A new popular movement began to take shape alongside the respectable reform campaigns, to drive forward against the nascent conservative reaction. Eyes focused on the desperate struggle in France as tension built up towards the explosion of the Revolution of the Tenth August and the bloody advent of democracy in Europe.

In these circumstances, more and more men thought of the Apocalypse, listened to Prophets, and read the signs of the times. Morgan John Rhys's campaign for French Bibles lost all impetus as he and William Richards entered into liaison with the *Gwyneddigion*, and read Iolo on the Bards. During this summer and autumn something like an embryonic Welsh intelligentsia began to shuffle into shape, national at least in aspiration. *Codi'r hen wlad* (to raise up the old homeland) demanded concerted effort and something more than scholarship. What the people needed was the Word: *Y Gwir yn erbyn y byd* (Truth against the World). William Owen, Morgan John and Iolo began to talk of journals and printing presses.

The Madoc legend and the *Gwladfa* were in fact integral to this rapidly forming collective mentality, but with the increase in political tension and the withdrawal of Iolo, Gratiot's project that had been launched with such eclat at the April meeting of the *Madogeion* threatened to come to a stop.

There was one man, however, whom nothing and no one could stop. John Evans's name had first been mentioned in correspondence as a companion for Iolo in May 1792. All the evidence (including his later performances) suggests that Evans moved abruptly out of Waun-fawr to London and out of London across the Atlantic. By early October 1792 he was in America; he must have been established in London during the summer. We do not know when he left Waun-fawr, but it seems reasonable to suggest a date between June 1791 and May 1792. For it was in June 1791 that his friend and tutor *Dafydd Ddu Eryri* won a prize at the Llanrwst eisteddfod for an ode on the conversion of the Madogwys. John Evans was to quote the ode to Samuel Jones in Philadelphia, and he may well have attended the gathering. It was there that William Jones had published his address *To all Indigenous Cambro-Britons* which ignited the first outbreak of America fever in north Wales.

John Evans's response was at once more individual, more exalted and more rhetorical. The young man was evidently seized with a sense of

143

mission, that *penchwibandod* (giddiness) which the Voltairean William Jones found so repulsive in Methodists. 'You know that every Welshman is possessed of intrepidity of mind,' John wrote to Iolo Morganwg after his arrival in America:

> it would have been easier with your humble servant had he been born without this quality, but as the Almighty saw it good to endow me with it, I will manage it to the glory of his Name! Is there one thing in the possession of Ieuan ab Ivan that he would not sacrifice to the cause of the Madogion? No, not one: even my precious life would I lay down for their sake.

To Dr Samuel Jones in Philadelphia, he announced his readiness to appear before Congress, declared that the quest for the Madogwys which God had lain upon him was driving his mind and quoted from the ode of *Dafydd Ddu Eryri*.

His most ventripotent letter from America, however, was reserved for his brother Evan. In highly-coloured Welsh, laced with the pious evocation which punctuated the discourse of his fraternity — 'Blessed, Blessed be His Name for Ever that is my Help and Stay through the Thousand Tribulations which now confront me . . .' [*ac felly yn ymlaen* and so forth, to use a standard form of the Welsh pulpit] — he made the distance from Baltimore to Philadelphia into 300 miles, promoted Dr Jones into a Senator and had that worthy gentleman offer him a bodyguard of twenty armed men! The major thrust of his comment was more earthy. Far from crabbed old Waun-fawr or pinched old London, he was now earning £50 among troops of friends. The poor in America lived better than farmers back home. If Evan sold the home *tyddyn* at Tai'r Ffynnon, the money would buy an estate in America even bigger than Glyn Llifon!

The tone is understandable, because Evan Evans had evidently been disconcerted by his brother's decision to tear up his roots and make for London. The exhorter blamed it on John's *'chwant am gyfoeth'* (lust for wealth) and muttered about Balaam's Ass. *'A chofia, fy anwyl frawd'*, he wrote in reply to his America letter, *'fod r arglwydd megis wedi rhoi iâs ar dy grochan di pan aethost gynta i Lundain* (Remember, dear brother, how the Lord tempered your pot when you first went to London)', leaving him without place and shelter. For without doubt, John Evans was driven no less by hunger for a better life and sheer adventure, as were so many young men like him.

It was into such a London fraternity that he moved in the summer of 1792. We catch glimpses of it in the letter his closest friend John Williams wrote to him after he'd crossed. They were all young, all articled or apprenticed to some trade or profession, all impatient and all full of America and its 'brave citizens'. They were all *Jacobins*, too. The French had overcome the 'allied tyrants', John Williams told *Ieuan ab Ifan* in February 1793, but now Britain was joining the pack in its liberticide war, 'to our great discredit and disadvantage'. How much nobler was the attitude of the *sans-culottes*. 'They say they do not want to fight us — if we must, we will, though we respect you as our brethren.' A few months later, he was denouncing to Samuel Jones the traitor General Dumouriez — that perfidious general who had betrayed poor, distressed France — 'but still I think I may safely say they will rise like a *Phoenix* out of their ashes and strike their enemies with terror in the Infancy of their Constitution, while surrounded with External enemies and the *Masked* and internal ones, too . . .'. This was powerful stuff in that August of 1793, in a Britain at war with France, when the guillotine was working in Paris and Botany Bay judges in Edinburgh.

In 1792 John Evans had lodged with Hugh Beauchamp, Hugh Roberts and their friends and shared with them their threadbare city days and nights loud with talk; hungry young men whose heads were full of dreams. A bunch of them crossed the Atlantic after him in 1793, hoping to buy land from Samuel Jones. The young man from Waun-fawr must have talked big. Everyone knew about his mission. 'Thousands would emigrate to their old Brethren in your Climes,' John Williams told Samuel Jones, as soon as Evans had completed his task — a sentiment echoed by every single Welshman who wrote to America in these years. 'It would be better for you not to have so many connections in London,' he told John Evans. Everyone was simply waiting for the word from him. Write close to pack more information in, he said, 'as you did the chart of St Michael.'

John Williams, *Madoc Bach Meillionen,* a neighbour of John Evans, was in the 'last year of his time' with Strafford and Smith, Holborn Bridge. He had squared things with his parents — 'I have wrote my Parents about coming, they have no objections provided I should do well' — but it was essential that John should continue to send good reports back. Williams would take them to Lord Bulkeley in Anglesey when he went home to say goodbye. They might get some help from that quarter. There were other possibilities . . . 'I may bring a Nice Girl with me over for what I know, for I will have one . . . I can almost say to a certainty she will pay the expence of bringing her. What do you think of *dau fill o Bunnau?* (£2,000) Would it not do there better than none? I must leave off wishing . . .'. But he would certainly bring 'a Capital Sum and Brace of Pistols and sabre, same for myself and a few other things as you may direct me being most useful.' John Evans, Williams urged, was to be careful not to go among the tribes until a peace was signed. Could he not approach Congress and George Washington and offer to serve as a government agent? What about buying some land in the back country, so that the pair of them could get a good settlement before doing some good for their fellow citizens? It was a

145

good idea to learn surveying, but John Evans, with his 'honest face', must be more careful. 'I am afraid of you being too venturesome.'

His fears were well grounded. John Evans seems to have stormed through London like a clipper under full sail. Although John Williams told Samuel Jones in the following year that he had become the official reporter of the new journal the *Cylchgrawn* — 'It is through me the Society gains the Intelligence to Publish in the Welch Magazeens' — he had to report in February 1793 that he had not seen William Owen for five months. The Madocian subscription had been suspended in favour of an approach to the government. On 15 August 1792, however, in a letter written for John Evans, Iolo Morganwg explicitly stated that the British government knew nothing of the affair; the Welsh were going to approach the American minister. John Evans seems to have got no financial help from the Madocians. In fact, he borrowed his passage money.

'I have lent him the sum of £20 to pay his passage,' wrote Hugh Roberts to Samuel Jones in August 1793, 'and would do as much more for him had he use me well, but I think he has used me very ill in not giveing me any account of America and that time he well knowed that I had no Setlment but now I do not know whether I shall never come over or not.' If he did come, however, he informed the good doctor in slightly ominous terms, 'I am bound to say that I shall make my residence with you.'

Despite (or perhaps because of?) his largesse, both John Williams and John Evans detested Roberts. Williams kept John's letters secret from him. 'The best way for you,' he advised John, 'is still to continue telling him how bad things are in general so as to sicken him on the thought of comeing over.' Williams would clear the debt as soon as he had crossed. In the meantime, 'I admire your *witt* in telling him you have friends in London that will pay him and not mentioning the *names*.' John Williams added, 'Had it in my power, my Dearest Friend, you should not have gone as you did in the steerage'.

John Evans clearly lost patience. He had become a close friend of Iolo Morganwg. Months later he was still hoping, in Welsh and in the familiar *thou* form, that his 'dear friend' Iolo would join him. But by mid-summer 1792, he could wait no longer. On 28 July, the leader of his denomination, Thomas Charles of Bala, reached London. John secured from him a letter to Lewis Richards, once a Methodist in Georgia, now a Baptist minister in Baltimore. Iolo climbed out of his personal hell long enough to write to a Philadelphia bookseller on his behalf on 15 August. John Evans borrowed his £20 and immediately found a ship. Madoc catapulted him into a hideous steerage passage and the missionary to the Madogwys, like a thief in the night, slipped out of an England plunging into its first convulsive crisis of the revolutionary decade.

John Evans arrived in Baltimore on 10 October 1792, a Methodist and committed to the plan recommended by Gratiot: to strike inland for the Ohio and make for Spanish St Louis. Trans-Atlantic reality began to work its erosion at once. 'With regard to his religious tenets,' wrote Lewis Richards the Baptist minister with whom he lodged, to his brother in the cloth, Samuel Jones, 'they are much the same as our own, Baptism only excepted.' By 10 November, John Evans himself was telling the same Dr Jones — 'My conscience tells me I must be a Baptist.' Small wonder. It was with a Baptist minister he first stayed. Samuel Jones was the first man he consulted. Within a week, he walked through Philadelphia out to Lower Dublin and, from there, explored the Welsh Tract and the Welsh churches in the Great Valley. He moved along that Baptist network which was to serve as the major channel for the Welsh migrations a few years later. Dr William Rogers, the celebrated Baptist principal of its College, offered him house-room in Philadelphia.

His Welshness proved more durable than his Methodism. He found only six Welshmen in Baltimore who spoke Welsh (three years later, such were the migrations, Morgan John Rhys preached in Welsh to a large congregation there). The younger people in the Welsh Tract and the Great Valley had lost the language, too. Ieuan ab Ifan resolved to speak Welsh constantly, if necessary to himself, and always to sing in Welsh. He sang one of Dafydd Thomas's carols on Christmas Day.

His very mission was soon under siege. 'He comes to see you for information and direction on a very particular business,' wrote Lewis Richards to Samuel Jones on 16 October, but the doctor was appalled to hear that John Evans blithely meant to set off alone (perhaps Samuel told him he should not go *without* twenty armed men?). He urged Evans to stay put for a while, to learn surveying and to make Kentucky his objective the following year. The Pennsylvania Welsh were gloomy about his prospects; they reminded him of the failure of their own mission fifty years earlier. Back in Baltimore, a chorus of voices warned him off. The Indian War was still raging on the Ohio; there were the Spaniards. Two merchants of the place told him to go back to England, fetch goods and set up in business. Confused, he 'took another walk up the country' to a Mr Davies, who warned him that if he went back to England, he'd never return. By 10 November, he had made up his mind. He took a job as a clerk in the counting-house of his two merchant patrons, who paid him a salary of £50, offered him facilities to trade on his own account and arranged for him to learn surveying. At that point, as his letters to John Williams and Samuel Jones make clear, he was hoping that an approach to Congress would bring official American support and his mind was fixed on Kentucky.

Within a fortnight, he had changed his mind. He wrote a dramatic and peremptory letter to Iolo Morganwg on 22 November. 'Mr Edward Williams Jnr, Bard and Mason', ran the address, 'in Glamorganshire. If he

147

is not in Wales, to be forwarded with all possible speed to Mr William Owen, 17 Great Russell Street, Bloomsbury, London'. As the old Roman said 'Either death or liberty', he proclaimed to Iolo, quoting what was in fact the official oath of the French Republic, 'so it is with me — Either the Madogion or death.' One thing he still lacked, the company of Iolo, 'but if the Providence of God should refuse me that favour, then I shall be obliged to venture alone, without one friend of a Welshman to give an account of me should I fall before my enemies . . .'. He meant to leave as soon as possible in the spring and to reach Quebec by April. Could Iolo get a letter to Mr Williams the solicitor-general there? Failing that, one to Mr Pownall would do, even if he did not believe in the Madogwys. Best of all would be a letter to Governor Simcoe of Upper Canada, because by May, John Evans would be in Detroit. There, in the British heart of the war-torn Indian country, he would spend some time curing diseases, because 'you must understand that I prosper in this Art in America.' (Shades of William Jones Llangadfan!) Dr Williams's books on Madoc had to be sent over at once and in bulk, and John Evans would not fail to let Iolo know 'that I am still without *losing my hair*.'

It is impossible to say what prompted this rush of Canada to the head, but it did not last long. When he wrote to his brother in Boxing Day bombast, he was back on the Pittsburgh-Ohio track. But by the time his letters were coming into London and Waun-fawr and Flemingston in January and February 1793, he had again lost patience. David Jones, minister of the Great Valley Baptist church and a celebrated Welsh-American frontiersman himself, reported that Evans had obtained letters of recommendation from George Washington, but feared he would never make it, what with the Spaniards and the Indians. Back home, William Jones Llangadfan, always *au fait* with matters American, was agonizing over possible Spanish treachery at New Madrid — the very name seemed ominous to the embattled old freethinker in his tormented parish.

But once more, nothing and no one could stop John Evans. As soon as the first shoots of spring were out, he was off, to a chorus of despair from his friends in Baltimore. His last stop was Dr Samuel Jones's friendly house. Samuel begged him to wait. Could he not at least find one companion? The distance . . . the wilderness . . . the Indians . . . the war . . . the Spaniards . . . 'God is my shield and my recompense in a just cause,' replied John Evans, in what must have been a kind of lunatic ecstasy. Shortly after St David's Day, the young man from Waun-Fawr started to walk towards the Wilderness. For company, he had that well-known Welsh intrepidity. In his pocket he had one dollar and seventy-five cents.

And on this, his first venture, he walked straight out of history. The only record of this first incredible journey is a letter he wrote to Dr Samuel Jones over four years later, after a remarkable sequence of adventures. The letter fell to Morgan John Rhys, or Rhees as he spelled his name then.

Rhees found it 'a crude chaos of composition' and rewrote it for publication. In the process, he wrote John Evans's first journey out of history. All we know of it is narrated in Evans's spare prose, sometimes all the more dramatic for its very brevity.

From Samuel Jones's house, he went to Pittsburgh, where he was kindly treated by Dr C. Wheeler. He had to wait a month there 'for the high waters'. Then, by water, he was carried 'in a few days' to Limestone, the Ohio station in Kentucky. John Evans then struck inland into Kentucky at this, one of the critical moments in its history, with the settlers flooding in and the Indians harassing the frontier villages and the Wilderness Trail. Two years later, his fellow-Welshman Morgan John Rhys was to pass through and, a disgruntled Moses come down from the mountain, make the place the theme of sermon and soul-searching soliloquy. John Evans is bare and prosaic: 'I travelled by land to Bourbon and from there through the wilderness to Cincinatta.'

At Cincinatti, frontier base for the war against the Ohio Indians which was still raging, Evans was greeted warmly by Brigadier-General Wilkinson, who was deep in his conspiracy with the Spaniards. John, like Morgan Rhys after him, found the old charmer friendly and helpful. He may have given the Welshman some useful advice, for when he left, after a few days, he made not for St Louis but for New Madrid, a good deal further south. Jefferson warned André Michaux, on his expedition in this same year, to avoid St Louis and Spanish authority. Perhaps John Evans was doing the same, heading for that New Madrid which Colonel George Morgan had planted, in Spanish territory, but full of Americans. He came down the Ohio, past Louisville and out into the great Mississippi, cutting south to New Madrid. At last, the Welshman was to set foot on that sparse and savage territory he and Iolo had brooded over so long back home.

He was not permitted to land in Spanish Louisiana, however, until he had taken the oath of allegiance which Commandant Thomas Portell enforced on all newcomers: 'We, the undersigned, swear, on the Holy Gospels, complete faith, homage and loyalty to His Majesty. We wish voluntarily to live under his laws and promise not to violate directly or indirectly, His royal interests, to give immediate advice to our Commandants of whatever comes to our knowledge and which can in any way prejudice the general welfare of Spain and the special welfare of this province, in whose defence we are ready to take up arms on the first requisition of our leaders, especially in favour of this district, whenever forces should come by way of the upper part of the river or overland to invade it.'

Thus committed to the defence of Spanish interests, John Evans stepped ashore (the ferry was run by a man called Jones) to find the chosen race well represented even on this remote and perpetually harassed frontier. 'Here I was kindly received by Mr and Mrs Rees my countrypeople.' This was Azor Rees and his wife. An Ebenezer Rees had been speculating in land around Natchez in 1790. Azor Rees was a large slave-holder at New Madrid and a prominent figure in the local community. In the May of this year, just about the time of John Evans's arrival, he was granted a lieutenant's commission in the second company of the New Madrid militia, given to 'Don Azor Rees for his courage, zeal and good conduct'. His son Aron was a regular witness at the taking of oaths of allegiance. Azor's wife was a remarkable woman and became a famous frontier character. She was Dinah Martin, born of a Welsh mother and a German father in Pennsylvania. After Rees's death, she married the Scottish-American David Gray, who acted as interpreter in French and Spanish to the officials of the district, but divorced him for cruelty. Dinah Rees was renowned as 'a woman of rare culture and learning'.

It was lucky for John Evans that she was there, for ten days after his arrival in the little frontier settlement, he went down with 'a violent and intermiting fever succeeded by a delirium'. He was laid out for two months. 'Thank God for friends, for I was paid the greatest attention to in my sickness by my kind land lady and all the Great People of the place, otherwise I should have died in the greatest poverty.'

By early July, however, he was recovering and the Madoc passion gripped him again. 'My resolution and anxiety for proceeding on my voyage being hightened to such a pitch that I was determined to risk my life, feeble as I was, and start for the Illinois in Company with one man only.' He does not give his companion's name, nor does he give any hint of the sheer bravado of this expedition. For the Osage troubles were at their height. In January, the Osages had carried off horses from St Genevieve to the north; in March the friendly Indians had tried to massacre Osage emissaries in St Louis itself and Trudeau had had to protect them in person for ten days. It was in April and May that Lorimier at Cap Girardeau, north of Portell's New Madrid and in deadly rivalry with it, had been given his licence to trade with the Lobos and the Shawnees and to mobilize them against the Osages, who had already depopulated the settlements along the Maramec, as Jacques Clamorgan bitterly complained. News of the decision for war on the Osages had leaked out and there was deadly fear of an onslaught. By September, Trudeau was at his wits' end, since the Chouteau family seemed to be losing control over them.

It was through this appalling menace and across the most exposed territory that John Evans and his companion made their way, cutting north behind Cap Girardeau (ironically in the very place where, a decade later, the first Baptist church was to rise west of the Mississippi). The expedition was a disaster.

Neither of us knew the road, if it could be called a road, for it was so overgrown with grass that in several places not the least trace was left. However, such as it was, we had the bad fortune to loose it altogether in the Evening of the first day. Now lost in the infinite wilderness of America. Oh unsufferable Thirst and hunger is an amusement in comparison to this. The parent sun who is so much courted in the northern nations has in this distressing moment turned my Enemy and threatens to beak my brains like a cake and withdraw from me my Pressuous Eye Sight. 3rd day, here my fever returned and my Eye Sight recovering. Came to a country overflowed with water. Travelled several miles in water from the hip to the Arm Pitt amongst a numerous crowd of the biggest water reptiles I ever saw. The 7th day arrived at Virgen a Spanish post in the Illinois. The night before we slepd within 5 miles of this village, but on account of my weakness which kept me unable of Travelling above a hundred yards without rest, it took us all day nearly to get to the Village. In a miserable situation, I arrived bear foot, bear legged and bear headed . . .

'Virgen' is a mystery. It may have been part of Lorimier's settlement at Cap Girardeau, conceivably even St Genevieve itself. But it was more probably the post Lorimier called Rivière-Fort Clark when he occupied it against a French-American threat in the following January. It lay directly opposite Kaskaskia on the American side. For, after resting for a day, John Evans tottered over to the American side to find shelter, and it was in the frontier outpost of Kaskaskia that he found it. The luck of the Welsh stayed with him. In Kaskaskia there was a John Rice Jones, Esq.

John Rice Jones had been born in Merioneth in 1759. His son Rice by his first wife was also born there (to die violently in Kaskaskia in 1808). John Rice Jones crossed to America during the War of Independence itself — a sufficient testimony to his politics. He had fought with George Rogers Clark on the frontier and settled in Vincennes before moving to Kaskaskia. He was a lawyer and well known on the frontier. After the Louisiana Purchase, he moved to St Genevieve and then Potosi and became a judge of the supreme court of the state of Missouri. One of his sons became a general, another a state senator in Iowa. He was very well thought of in later life: 'A man of indefatigable industry, extensive experience and tact for business, in private life a friend of the indigent, the ignorant and distressed . . . he had an active mind, constantly engaged; was a living chronicle of passing events and a student until the day of his death . . . knew much of men and things . . .'

When John Evans met him, however, he was not universally popular. In October 1795, Lieutenant-Governor Trudeau of St Louis had the opportunity to talk over matters of moment with Judge Turner of the US north-western circuit:

I profited by the moment to speak to him and make known to him the sarcastic character of the lawyer Jones whom you have seen, aside from his wranglings, has a talent destined to trouble us. He (Judge Turner) assured me that he knew him and for this reason, he did not wish (even though he was educated) to employ him at any *place* in the administration, for which he preferred honest men with good sense.

Jones was clearly of an anti-Spanish disposition. In October 1793, Trudeau had seized up-river on the Mississippi over 7,000 pesos' worth of goods belonging to the great house of Todd in Canada. Since Clamorgan's Missouri Company was arranging a partnership with the Todds, it was hoped the Canadian firm would not fight this seizure. But they did, and John Rice Jones was the chief mover.

This Todd connection was probably significant for John Evans. After his arrival in Kaskaskia in late July 1793, he drops out of sight for eighteen months, months of a political tension as intolerable on this frontier as it had become for many of the Welsh back home. When Evans re-emerges into the light of evidence, he appears as a close friend of William Arundel, a prominent frontier merchant of Cahokia nearby. A letter which Arundel wrote to John Evans in August 1795 — 'My level and your Square must strike the Necessary Ballance and Best Rules in the World be the Guide amongst friends' — strongly suggests not only friendship but fraternity in Freemasonry — which ran as a continuous descant to this generation of the Welsh revival from Iolo's Druid-Bards to the high command of Morgan John Rhys's *Gwladfa* in Beula, Pennsylvania.

Arundel was a favoured client of Todd and McGill. When the massive and imperial Clamorgan-Todd consortium was finally launched in 1796, special provision was made for Arundel. It was directly to Arundel's house that John Evans went after his return from his journey up the Missouri. John Rice Jones had been the Todds' attorney. It seems likely that Arundel and Jones found some employment for Evans, perhaps as a surveyor or general agent. He might well have operated on the fringes of the Todd fur-trade empire.

His own testimony is suggestive. 'Stayed here 2 years to wait for a passage up the Missurie,' he says, 'but that Country being under Spanish government and Engrossed by a Sett of Indian traders, I had no prospect till Christmass 1794, when I was informed of a gent. at St Louis who was engaged to go up the aforesaid River for three years . . .'.

This is puzzling. Truteau, leader of the first expedition, had formally engaged for three years but had left in June 1794; his back-up man Lecuyer was to leave in April 1795; Breda's emergency boat went out a little later. However, in July 1795 when news of the disasters reached St Louis, Jacques Clamorgan immediately sprang his shock of the proposed third expedition, led by James McKay, which was twice as large as the others. This clearly surprised Lieutenant-Governor Trudeau and most of the share-holders in the Missouri Company, who resigned *en masse*.

Nevertheless, it is perfectly clear that the McKay expedition had been long germinating. Evidence from 1796, when Clamorgan's vast plans, centred on the Todd connection, became public knowledge and were officially taken up by the Spanish Council of State, explicitly singles out the McKay venture as the first phase of a three-year programme of imperial expansion. It set out a bare six weeks after St Louis first heard of the disasters suffered by the earlier expeditions and it was equipped by the Todds. Moreover, James McKay, returning from a trip to New York, reached Cincinatti in July 1795 and there encountered Morgan John Rhys, then on the last stage of his epic tour of the American republic in search of the Promised Land of the Welsh. Rhys told McKay about John Evans and his mission and the Scotsman informed Morgan John that he was engaged to go up the Missouri for three or four years. At that time, his appointment had not even been officially ratified and announced by Trudeau in St Louis.

It was almost certainly through this Todd network that John Evans heard some news or rumour of the proposed expedition in the last week of 1794. Though it was Christmas and the depth of an Upper Mississippi winter, he decided to try his luck in St Louis. 'Now or never, as I thought, it was time to make aplication . . .' He knew he had chosen a bad time: 'I thought within myself that it was rather a ridiculous busyness as it was a Critical time on Spanish side on account of the report of Clark's armie and I not able to speak one word with any body, they speaking French. However I went' . . . and his fears proved all too correct . . . 'and was taken for a Spy, Imprisoned, loaded with iron and put in the Stoks besides, in the dead of winter'.

9

Across the wide Missouri

John Evans did not suffer long. In a few days John Rice Jones and others crossed the river and managed to persuade Trudeau that the Welshman was not a British spy. The Lieutenant-Governor released Evans, but was still suspicious. He held him in St Louis until he could find out more about him. It was when the US Judge Turner, who had heard of Evans's mission, came up river on his circuit that Trudeau was finally convinced. The consequence would have surprised William Jones Llangadfan back home in Wales. At a stroke, John Evans's mission became an official Spanish enterprise.

By this time, Morgan John Rhys on his grand tour was within a few days' journey of his compatriot. When in May he first reached the Miami lands west of the Ohio (which on Bastille Day 1795 he was to claim as the Canaan of the Welsh people) he ran into Judge Turner returning from Kaskaskia-Cahokia. According to Rhys, Turner had pointed out to Trudeau that even if Evans failed to find Welsh Indians, he might find a great deal more. Trudeau, in response, issued John Evans with letters-patent in Spanish, French and English and equipped him with some presents for the Indians. It was evidently to the Mandans that John was directed, because he was to explore d'Eglise's 'Volcano', penetrate the sources of the Missouri and get to the Pacific, bringing back the necessary proofs in Russian to win Carondelet's prize of 2,000 pesos.

A letter from Judge Turner to Evans survives. It was written in Kaskaskia on 10 March 1795. Since a letter from Evans written the same day reached the judge in time to be mentioned in a postscript, the Welshman must have been but a short distance away, probably in Cahokia, where he certainly was in August just before his departure up the Missouri. When he got Turner's letter, he was about to visit Trudeau. Turner told him that he had put in a good word for him with the Lieutenant-Governor and had stressed his need for a companion. The judge was encouraging. Auguste Chouteau, the merchant *patron* of St Louis, had claimed to have gone 500 leagues up the Missouri and could assure the Waun-fawr man 'that the Pacific Ocean can lie at no great distance from the Missouri's source.'

Evans, said the judge, would find exotic beasts on his journey, a creature the size of an elk with two large horns curving backwards in a circle and then forward to two horizontal points in front of the head, and a red-haired goat. Turner asked John to get a couple of skins of the former, male and female, so that they could be stuffed for exhibition. 'I should be glad to receive half a dozen of the horns also . . . Two *complete* skins of *both* sexes' of the goat 'would be very desirable.' The judge told John Evans to keep a journal (he did).

Morgan John Rhys, when he heard all this, was rather envious; the Madoc missionary would make his fortune whether he found the Lost Brothers or not. For Judge Turner, leaving the Kaskaskia area about the beginning of May, did not escape the chosen race so easily. A couple of days later, in the middle of a thunderstorm, he ran into Morgan John about a hundred miles south-west of Cincinatti, just after he'd finished inspecting what looked like the ruins of an old Welsh castle on the Ohio bank.

The problem of John Evans's companion remained. Evans did not meet the Charles Gratiot who had enthused the *Madogeion* in 1792. The merchant may not have been in St Louis; he was certainly absent when the trade of the lower Missouri tribes was allocated in April 1794. It is not inconceivable that Trudeau, deeply suspicious of Clamorgan, had in mind his favourite Jacques d'Eglise, discoverer of the Mandans, who was disgusted with his own brawling *engagé* Garreau. It is far more likely that, some time during this period, someone from the Clamorgan team contacted John Evans. There is nothing in Clamorgan's correspondence to suggest that he had previously met the Welshman, but after his return from the Missouri, John Evans lived for a while in Clamorgan's household and the Director of the Missouri Company was always warm in his references to John's services.

Most remarkable, however, was the speed with which James McKay enlisted John in his expedition. Returning from his trip to New York, the Scotsman ran into Morgan John Rhys at Cincinatti iin July 1795. Rhys explained Evans's mission and gave McKay a Welsh dictionary. The two got on famously. The Scotsman had met no trace of Welsh Indians but 'I believed the Possibility of their existance and considering the light such a discovery might throw on the History of America was determined to use all the means in my Power to unveil the mystery.' A few days after his arrival in St Louis he 'sent for and engaged for my assistant Mr Evans who spoke and wrote the Welch language with facility'.

Knowledge of Welsh was clearly essential for the Madogwys, but hardly for that imperial march to the Pacific which Clamorgan projected and which McKay in fact chose none other than John Evans to make. After two years on the frontier the Welshman was no longer a tenderfoot; the men he had worked with and befriended were agents of the Todds. It is symptomatic that a disgruntled Trudeau (who, in later years and in sharp contrast with his superiors down in New Orleans, tended to play down John Evans's achievements) was to complain to Judge Turner that Evans had left with McKay without complying 'with some Spanish etiquette'. However controversial those proceedings, they could hardly have been more controversial than the very expedition itself.

For Clamorgan had carefully kept secret the scale of the new expedition and his association with Todd and McGill. Jacques d'Eglise had brought news of the collapse of the first two ventures on the night of 4 July. A shattered Trudeau demanded a report from the Missouri Company on 6 July. Within two days he received in return a dramatic plan, imperial in vision and scale, in which Clamorgan called for his third expedition. Trudeau, resigning in anger with most of the shareholders, told Carondelet that Clamorgan was 'playing double or quits'. Jacques quite openly informed New Orleans that the expedition was being supplied by Andrew Todd, 'the young and robust Irishman, Don Andrés Todd' to the Spaniards.

The full measure of Clamorgan's ambition, however, did not become clear until the autumn, a couple of months after McKay had set out. Andrew Todd moved to St Louis and on 18-21 December 1795, he and Jacques Clamorgan presented to Carondelet in New Orleans a project so breath-taking that the Governor immediately forwarded it to Spain.

The crux was the Jay Treaty of 1794 between Britain and America and its provision that the British-held posts in the Illinois were to be handed over to the Americans by June 1796. The great house of Todd was menaced in its very base at Michilimackinac. Andrew Todd made the Spaniards an offer. He would transfer his house to New Orleans and, with his powerful British and Canadian sources pump supplies up the Mississippi to sustain the starved Spanish enterprises on the Missouri. With him, he would bring the allegiance of the tribes already his along the upper reaches of the Mississippi and north of the Missouri. These included the dreaded Sioux. At a stroke, that British threat would be eliminated. Todd offered his support to Clamorgan's other visionary schemes; two forts on the Des Moines and Minnesota rivers to hold the north, and a string of forts and agencies running through the barrier tribes along the Lower Missouri right up to the Mandans, the base for the final leap to the Pacific. These were to be garrisoned by 100 soldiers, which the Missouri Company would maintain, provided the Spanish government paid a subsidy of 10,000 pesos annually, and sent armed vessels up the rivers in support. In return, the Company asked for a ten years' monopoly of the trade, that of the barrier tribes in particular; Todd asked for compensation for the goods which Trudeau had seized in 1793 and for a reduction in tolls at New Orleans. He promised to bring 4,000 bales of peltries down river every year, starting at once.

The whole plan was presented in terms of a final elimination of the British threat to the Missouri which was now menacing Santa Fe and even Mexico. The Jay Treaty would dispossess the Canadians north and west of the Ohio and hand over those tribes of the northern Spanish sector, already lost to the British, to the even more alarming Americans.

The Todd riposte would clear the north, enormously strengthen the thrust up the Missouri and create a line of forts and agencies stretching from the Otos, through the Mandans to the very shores of the South Sea and Nootka Sound, where a Spanish naval squadron was reported to be heading. Todd specifically compared the concessions he requested with those long granted to Panton, Leslie and Company to hold the Floridas and the southern Mississippi. He and Clamorgan would be the Panton and Leslie of the west, but he insisted that he must have a prompt reply. Otherwise he would have to transfer his allegiance to the Americans.

The plan, had it gone into effect, would have shifted the axis of western penetration decisively into the Spanish realms. Carondelet responded eagerly. On 8 January 1796, the Governor forwarded masses of documentation and passionate argument, couched in splendidly imperial terms, to Godoy in Spain. On 17 May 1796, the Spanish Council of State ratified the plan in its totality, though the wording of its resolution on the 10,000 pesos subsidy was critically ambiguous. During 1796, in fact, it began to go into operation, since Carondelet unilaterally reduced the Mississippi tariff for one year. Todd, with his New Orleans agent Daniel Clark, brought the *Antelope* in from England (surreptitiously, since war was now looming between Britain and Spain) and several cargoes went up river to St Louis. Drafts of young Canadian traders were organized to move down in support of the Spanish effort.

In the process, the Missouri Company was transformed. The resignations in the summer of 1795 left only four shareholders beside Clamorgan himself. During 1796, three of them were bought out by Régis Loisel, acting on behalf of Todd; the company of Clamorgan and Loisel was formed, in close liaison with and virtually as a subsidiary of, Todd and McGill, to force its policies on the Missouri Company, resisted only by Jean Robidoux, the last of the shareholders, the growling dissidence of most St Louis merchants buttressed by the pained dissociation of the Chouteaus, and by the gloomy irritation of Trudeau — 'suitable to bridle Morgan'.

This process began with the McKay expedition. In the December submissions, it was expressly singled out as the fort-building mission. Unlike the earlier ventures which had sought to avoid the barrier tribes, McKay's was to confront them head on. The Company was 'perfectly well arranged this year' for the Oto, Maha and Ponca, said Trudeau in

September 1795; all the assigned traders had withdrawn leaving the monopoly to the Company. McKay had presents, banners and medals galore and planned to impose order on all the southern nations. A regular plan had been worked out, which was finally to project John Evans to the Pacific. The choice of John Evans may well have been, at least in part, one element in those plans; in his friendship with Arundel and John Rice Jones, he might well have figured as a marginal member of the Todd connection. In this curious and indirect manner, he did after all follow the plan which Charles Gratiot had recommended to a crowded London coffee-house in April 1792.

The thinking behind the McKay expedition was sound. Its four pirogues carried merchandise worth 50,000 pesos, more than all the previous expeditions combined. One was designed to buy off the Sioux, another was for the Arikara and a third for the Mandans; the final pirogue was to service the party crossing to the Pacific. Presents were carried for the barrier tribes and provision was made for men who were to be away for two years. Wages for the thirty-three men totalled 36,000 pesos; their arms alone cost 15,000. Only a sustained effort could drive such an enterprise through and the Company specifically stated that it did not expect to hear any hard news before July 1797.

What unhinged this whole enterprise was the sudden and shocking death of Andrew Todd in the yellow fever epidemic in New Orleans at the end of 1796. By that time, the Missouri Company, though locked in endless wrangles with the lower Missouri tribes, had actually thrust the human spearpoint of its campaign through to the Mandans. That spearpoint was 'Don Juan Evans'. Three years later, a Spanish Governor in New Orleans, writing to Spain, was to refer to 'the two most famous travellers of the northern countries of this continent, Don Jayme McCay and Don Juan Evans'; he was quite correct. The meeting of McKay and Evans in St Louis in 1795 saw the beginning of one of the most notable (though forgotten) partnerships in the history of western exploration.

McKay and Evans nosed their boats out into the great river at the end of August 1795. It took them forty-four days to reach the Otos. McKay complained of delays caused by bad weather and a leaky boat, but in fact they had made good time; it was normally a fifty-day run. McKay's eyes were fixed on the Omahas beyond as the key to the whole venture, but he was quick to realize that the Otos had to be pacified first. He found them in a kind of anarchy. 'You can not conceive of the difficulties one has in passing through this nation, in spite of the presents we must give them. The chiefs have no command and this nation is so rough that one has trouble to move them, even in their own interest.' From them, he learned the details of the Poncas' pillaging of Lecuyer and it was quite clear that the Otos meant to do the same to him. Their senior chief *Sac de Médécine* had ordered Truteau stopped only a few months earlier and, under the all-pervading control of the formidable Black Bird of the Omahas, they were determined to prevent supplies getting through to the Upper Missouri.

In these circumstances, McKay scored a notable success. He reached the Otos on 14 October a couple of miles below the mouth of the Platte, took in some provisions, but then moved on to a site half a league above the river, where he built a house for the traders he meant to leave among them over the winter. Sixty of the leading men trailed after him and, in a decisive harangue, he denounced them for their evil conduct towards their Spanish Father. His firmness and the sheer size of the expedition overawed them. They did not dare go near the pirogues and accepted only the gifts McKay offered. The Scotsman, however, was equally firm in his report to Clamorgan. This tribe had been debauched by irresponsible traders sent out from St Louis and was exposed to the English along the Minnesota. It was absolutely essential that the Company secure their trade in permanence and exclude all unauthorized agents. He had won them over with two promises. A fort was to be built for them, ostensibly to protect them from their enemies. They had chosen a site at the mouth of the Platte and would move their village to it. That fort was entrusted to an agent they liked but it needed two swivel-guns which should be sent immediately. A hundred rifles were wanted, too, since three-quarters of the tribe were idle all winter. To hold the Otos, these promises had to be promptly fulfilled; at the slightest sign of misconduct, however, all supplies should be cut off, to bring home their dependence on the Spanish Father. When McKay moved on after eleven days, word had already gone ahead to the Omaha that men who knew their business were on the river.

On 27 October the party ran into some of the Company's men returning from the disaster among the Ponca. They told McKay that the Poncas had killed an Arikara who was coming down as a messenger. The total loss of the original stock and the prospect of war on the Upper Missouri darkened their minds. Ice, snow and bitter cold were now plaguing them, but on 3 November they met the son of *Pájaro Negro* (Black Bird) bringing his band to escort them. It was 11 November before they arrived below the central village of the Omahas which was set back from the river in a broad prairie. The chief set a guard over the pirogues at once, but for two days they were holed up against the ferocious gales. On the 14th, McKay was able to unload his boats and store the supplies in safety. On the 15th, he braced himself for a council and for what he knew would be the critical moment of the entire venture, the encounter with Black Bird. The harassed Truteau, milked of half his goods, has left a memorable portrait of Black Bird:

This great chief of the Omahas is the most shrewd, the most deceitful and the greatest rascal of all the nations who inhabit the Missouri. He is feared and respected and is in great renown among all strange nations, none of whom dare contradict him openly or to move against his wishes. They do not set out for war or for the hunt unless he has given his consent to it. His name is recited in all assemblies and speeches are made in his absence in the most distant places to which they go. All the neighbouring tribes hear his word and crown him with presents when he goes to visit them. If any of his men acquire beautiful merchandise or beautiful horses and he appears to desire them, they instantly give them to him. He never goes about on foot, but always mounted on the most beautiful horse in the village. He has slaves for his work, better to say, they are all his slaves, for should he wish to sleep, he has one or two hired attendants who gently rub his legs and feet while he sleeps. If these ordinary valets are absent, he presses into that service even the greatest and bravest of the tribe. When it is time to awaken him, it is necessary to do it with caution, being careful not to cry in his ears nor to stroke him with the hand, but they use a feather which they pass lightly over the face or tickle gently certain parts of his body. Finally, he is a man who by his wit and cunning has raised himself to the highest place of authority in his nation and who has no parallel among all the savage nations of this continent . . .

For years, Black Bird had been able to practise systematic blackmail on the Missouri traders, British, French and Spanish alike. All goods, even the private merchandise of the *engagés*, had to be opened for his inspection. He took the best third himself and distributed the rest among his men and the dependent tribes at will. Intelligent, cunning and resourceful, he was able to use his long-standing contacts with the British out of Canada to play off St Louis against the northern companies, to blackmail them with his warriors, and to manipulate and direct all the cross-currents of frontier trade and diplomacy. By skill and shrewdness, rather than war, he made all the tribes, even the Sioux, obey his medicine. He had raised his tribe above its natural station and himself to the status McKay accurately captured when he called him 'the Great Prince of the Nations'.

His medicine was strong at all levels. He had first established his pre-eminence as a magician and seer by summoning sixty of his best warriors to a feast of dog soup which they counted a great delicacy. The Great Spirit had granted him the gift of prophecy, he told them, and had warned him that they would all die before daybreak. He had fed them arsenic obtained from French traders. It was this prairie Borgia who had blocked the route north, especially to fire-arms. The intensification of the British effort, confronted now by this lavish Spanish counter-expedition, gave him his opportunity, in an atmosphere thick with rumours of wars and treaties. He exploited it to the hilt.

McKay, with John Evans in ardent lieutenancy, moved resolutely in on him. They harangued his council, denouncing them for offences against the Spanish Father. Now a Company had formed. They would not want for anything any more; they need not go to the English any more; traders would live among them for ever. But if they ever raised their hands against the Spanish again, they would be cut off with nothing. The chiefs begged forgiveness and asked for two hundred muskets to share out among their seven hundred warriors (but they had to be English, not French; the latter blew up in their hands). McKay made his promise.

He immediately set to work on his fort, Fort Charles, anchor of the Pacific chain. Sited on a commanding hill overlooking both village and Missouri, it had emplacements for two large guns and enormously impressed the Omahas. McKay stopped trading promptly at nightfall and totally refused to start again until morning. The Indians, used to trafficking when they pleased, were even more impressed. The Scotsman found a Ponca chief in the village. He denounced him before the men. He showed him a pirogue and, lying in his teeth, said that it had been destined for the Ponca. Now, however, because of their treatment of Lecuyer, the Ponca would get no supplies, no guns or powder. Their women would starve, their men be left helpless before their enemies. The great and terrible Black Bird would help the agents of the Spanish Father punish this wicked people. The Ponca chief left in tears.

All this, however, was merely a preliminary warm-up for the parley with Black Bird. For days McKay and the 'grandiloquent moocher' harangued each other. The Company presented Black Bird with his special medal and letters patent, together with a splendid gift. The Omaha chief was greatly pleased but 'he was surprised at not finding in it a large flag, telling me the English always gave one'. The English were always pestering him to rally to them and tempted him with all those superior goods they had, but he had always let them understand that he had no intention of abandoning the friendship of his Spanish Father. 'However, he believed the latter did not appreciate this affection . . . besides it would be shameful for him not to receive a large banner and a present proportional to his importance . . .' particularly since the English showered valuable presents on him every year and continually invited him to the Minnesota.

Black Bird harped constantly on the largesse of the British, their ceaseless insinuations that the Spanish Father cared nothing for his Indian children, and sent men with bad hearts among them, cheated them, and deprived them of weapons, which they continually spirited past them in secrecy, to their enemies up the river. But he harped no less on his continuing love for Spain, his devotion, his readiness to clear the road,

161

punish the Ponca, and bring the Sioux to peace. If only this Spanish affection could assume a more concrete and visible form and one proper to his standing among the tribes . . .

McKay responded warmly and in fact the two men seem to have established a personal friendship which was to survive the collapse of the Spanish enterprise. McKay promised him rewards and status, broke open the reserved pirogues for presents, and bombarded St Louis with requests for gifts, banners, medals, and suitably gorgeous patents. During 1796, demand after demand went down the Mississippi from St Louis, from a Company already strained to the limit in the Todd enterprise, to climax in the sending of a new boat specially commissioned for Black Bird. His demands were insatiable. Could McKay produce a letter patent from the Great Father who lived across the Great Lake in Europe, to establish his pre-eminence among the red children? McKay, hard-pressed, delivered an eloquent speech on the efficacy of the Spanish Father this side of the Lake, Don Zenon Trudeau who had treated Black Bird's son so well in St Louis. Black Bird, promising to bring the tribes to peace and to open the river, said this could not be done 'without great presents of cloth, blankets, kettles, tobacco, guns and ammunition . . . he was not asking for these articles for himself, but rather for me . . .'. He could not make his authority effective among the tribes without some suitably expensive symbol. Only in that way could the tribes be brought to respect the Spanish flag 'notwithstanding how ordinary it might be, for the Sioux, as well as other tribes of the north, receive only silk flags from the English', who, recollect, had thirty pirogues of excellent goods on rivers only four days' journey away . . .

McKay's prompt response to this blackmail, which was threatening to unhinge the long-term plan of the Company, dribbling away the goods which had been reserved for the far tribes, is understandable. For Black Bird offered a great deal in return. He would, in person, punish the Ponca; he would, in person, lead the expedition to the Arikara. He would, in person, bring in even the terrible Sioux to pardon. He offered McKay the chance of settling with the lower river tribes once and for all. This was precisely the Scotsman's purpose. He was sending out messages and presents to every tribe within reach. He told Breda to bury the remaining goods among the Ponca and deny them access. He heard rumours of a war between the Arikara and the Sioux. The river was impassable, so on 24 November he sent out a select party overland to find the Arikara. They butted into a large hunting party of Sioux out after buffalo and were forced to run for their lives, reeling back into Fort Charles on 6 January. Black Bird immediately renewed his promise to help McKay, paid a ceremonial visit to the fort and offered the expedition his horses. During that critical year, St Louis despatches to New Orleans were full of the great assembly of the tribes which McKay, with Black Bird's help, was summoning for June 1796. Carondelet petitioned for a captain's commission for the Scotsman.

But the price was heavy. The Omaha and other demands were eating into the precious pirogues. McKay's letters to St Louis were imperative in tone:

> We need the aid of the Government to resist and destroy the ambition of foreigners. Otherwise, the ruin of the Company in its infancy is inevitable . . . The intrigue of the English, in order to attract the tribes of the Missouri, has planted such deep roots among these peoples, that it is necessary to apply a prompt remedy, unless we desire to see ourselves exposed to abandon this magnificent country which must some day be a great resource to the prosperity and glory of the state.'

No one in St Louis or New Orleans would have disagreed with him, but the Spanish Father was sick; in his empire 'it was late afternoon, getting on for evening.'

A revaluation of the enterprise had become essential. The first need was elemental. They were clearly stuck at Fort Charles for the winter and they had to stay alive. By late November, there was hardly any maize left in the village; a single measure of it cost a blanket. Work on the fort was held up. The Indians organized a buffalo hunt. McKay sent a party of his men with them. To lead it, he chose John Evans.

Evans left with the hunt on 21 November and was away twenty-five days. Characteristically, he left no record of this experience. All the evidence shows that he got on well with Indians. Few of them, and none of their chiefs, ever seriously blamed him for anything: they knew it was the Spanish Father who failed him as he failed them. By this time, he must have felt himself an old hand at the wilderness trade. Nevertheless, he was of a reflective turn of mind, and one wonders how those four weeks went, in the snowy prairies and sudden blizzards west of the Missouri. Did those Waun-fawr eyes strain for prints of the Madogwys? He had his flute of course, a talent he had perhaps picked up from Iolo Morganwg. By this time, he had little else. He got back just in time to see the Missouri at Fort Charles freeze solid.

McKay and Evans took stock. The trade goods were draining away at an alarming rate; McKay had to stay put at Fort Charles for the great assembly in June. He would clearly be too late at the Mandans the following summer. McKay came to the crucial decision. A party had to leave for the Mandans and the Pacific at once, depth of winter though it was. He sent his report back to St Louis and asked for a boat to carry a fresh load of supplies for Black Bird and the June conference (a request which caused consternation at base). 'Through my fear of arriving late next summer at the Mandans,' he said:

I am going to send out a detachment within a few days under the charge of Monsieur Even (sic) until he meets Truteau, who must have already constructed his fort among the above-mentioned Mandans, if he has experienced no opposition on the part of the English . . . Monsieur Even is to leave there with picked men, who occasion us great expense, in order to visit the head-waters of the Missouri and *La Cadena de Rocas* [Rocky Chain, i.e., Rocky Mountains] and follow to the Pacific Sea, according to the enclosed instructions, of which he carries a copy.

Those Instructions, dated 28 January 1796, make a remarkable document, a model for the more celebrated set which President Thomas Jefferson issued a few years later to Lewis and Clark. They indicate that the sweep and scope of the Evans mission were identical to those of that famous expedition. The central objective was the Pacific. In the Instructions, the first base was to be set up at the Mandans. Beyond them, Evans was to build canoes to descend to the ocean. But in a follow-up letter sent after him a fortnight later, McKay told Evans that if he could find the 'south fork' of the Missouri which Jacques d'Eglise had mentioned (in reality the Cheyenne river) he was to take it and ignore the Mandans altogether. McKay, who thought he was further west and south than he was, still conceived of the Rockies as a single chain of mountains with a relatively easy crossing, but he was more realistic about distances: 'the distance in longitude from the Rockies to the Pacific Ocean ought not to be above 290 leagues, perhaps less,' which meant that the rivers there were either very rapid or had great falls. Beyond the Mandans, McKay knew that a great river came into the Missouri from the south-west; it came directly from 'the Stony Mountains', but he did not know whether it communicated with the waters of the West. 'This river is called River de Roche Jaune or the River of the Yellow Stone' (this is the first mention of the noble Yellowstone).

Evans was to get to the sources of the Missouri, cross the Rockies, keeping as far as possible to the 40° latitude mark until he reached the 111th or 112th degree of longitude. Then he was to avoid waters which would probably curve south towards California, and head north towards 42° latitude until he hit the Pacific shore. There would be a Russian settlement north of California and there were probably others. He was to take careful note of all of them, offer to bring back letters from the sea-captains there and find an alternative route for the return.

And on his progress, he was to be meticulous. He was to keep a daily journal, noting precisely longitude, latitude, route, distance and weather. He was to make a full record of all the tribes and their customs, all flora and fauna, and every detail of topography; 'in case you will be short of ink, use the powder, and for want of powder, in the summer you will surely find some fruit whose juice can replace both . . .'. All portages were to be

164

clearly marked with large notices carrying 'in large letters' the name of Charles IV, King of Spain, 'and below that, Company of the Missouri, the day, the month, the year'. He was to dole out his supplies to the Indians economically, gain intelligence on trade prospects, and carry a good supply of dried meat (jerky). All strange animals were to be noted; if possible samples were to be brought back from the mountains and the seashore (there was said to be a one-horned beast in the Rockies).

McKay gave Evans very detailed instructions on behaviour towards Indians. Be reserved, he said, but show goodwill, and 'always give to your conduct the air of importance', but above all, be prudent:

> You will take heed not to fall in with some parties of savages where there are neither women or children, as they are almost always on the warpath. It would not be prudent to appear at any nation if you can avoid it, unless it be in their villages; and in spite of this be well on your guard. You will never fire any guns except in case of necessity; you will never cut wood except with a knife unless it be strictly necessary; you will never build a fire without a true need, and you will avoid having the smoke seen from afar . . . You will not camp too early and will always leave before daybreak . . . you will always have your arms in good condition, changing the tinder evening and morning, and you will never separate them from you or place them in the hands of savages. When you will see some nations, raise your flag a long way off as a sign of peace, and never approach without speaking to them from a distance. When you will enter a village, stop and ground arms at a small distance until they come to receive and conduct you. Appear always on guard and never be fearful or timid, for the savages are not generally bold, but will act in a manner to make you afraid of them . . . You will recollect that the pipe is the symbol of peace and that when they have smoked with you there is no longer any danger; nevertheless you must beware of treason . . .

Above all, the mission must be kept secret. He was to divulge its details to no one, not even Truteau whom he ought to find at the Arikara or the Mandans, but was to report only to McKay or, if he were dead, to Clamorgan; if Clamorgan were also dead, he was to report to Trudeau in St Louis. The Indians, on the other hand, were to be impressed with the benevolence of 'their great father, Spain, who is protector of all the white and red men', who had sent Evans 'to tell them that, desiring to make them happy, he wishes to open a communication with them . . .'.

It was a wrench for McKay and Evans to part, for they had become close friends. 'I have found the time tedious since you left,' wrote McKay to the Welshman on 19 February, 'however, I begin to get accustomed to live Solletary, I dare say that in the course of some time hence I shall be happy alone as the Indian on the desert'. In his reports to Clamorgan, McKay described Evans as 'a young man of Upright Character on whose Perseverance and Ability I could entirely rely'. Clamorgan, in turn, when he received McKay's report, was excited. In April, he reported to Carondelet that he had sent out the boat for Black Bird which McKay requested: 'pure loss to us, adds a very cruel sum to our expenses; and besides, this will not excuse us from sending him the fine presents upon which he is counting next autumn . . .'. But a skilled and intelligent man was now en route to the far sea and 'it seems very likely that a year from next June [June 1797] I shall be able to announce to you the discovery of the Pacific Ocean by crossing this vast continent and to offer you an exact map of the course of the Missouri which hitherto I have been able to obtain only from vague reports of several *voyageurs*.' John Evans did not disappoint either man in his devotion. He stretched himself to the limit in the service of the Company and the splendid map which he prepared from his two journeys up the Missouri was to prove of critical assistance eight years later to Lewis and Clark themselves.

His first attempt, however, was abortive. He was allotted two of the most trustworthy and experienced *engagés*, Scarlet and Tollibois, and he set out early in February 1796. The party travelled by land, across a bleak and wintry country. They did not get very far; John Evans thought it 300 miles, McKay something over 200. He got as high as the White river, near the Grand Detour, when he ran into a party of Sioux, out on their spring hunt. The Sioux discovered Evans's party near their camp and at once attacked them. Evans and his men fled down the river, chased by the Sioux for a dozen miles before they made good their escape under cover of night and the filthy weather. The men had lost their nerve and the party returned to Fort Charles.

They had reason to be fearful, because the Sioux came swarming across the Missouri that spring in an ugly mood. They finished off the last foothold of the earlier St Louis missions. Truteau had gathered the survivors around him among the Arikara. In the summer of 1795, he had tried to regain the initiative. He had sent presents of tobacco to Ménard and Jusseaume among the Mandans, and promised that the Spanish Father would send an expedition in the spring. But he had run out of goods and could get no further, despite encouraging replies from the Mandans. He and his men holed up through the winter. But as spring approached, party after party of Sioux came over and began to threaten the Arikara. Despite the massive fortifications of their Mandan-like village, the Arikara panicked. The whole tribe took off into the western prairies, leaving the handful of whites exposed. These desperate men killed some cows, made a bull-boat and set off down the Missouri with the ferocious Sioux at their heels. The Sioux hunted them for hundreds of miles right back to the edge of Omaha territory. The shattered party got through to McKay at Fort Charles in May.

It says a great deal for McKay that he held firm through this sequence of disasters. Once Evans was back, he turned to Black Bird once more and sent another *Parole* with presents for the Sioux. After a month, four chiefs of the Sioux finally came in for parley. It is not clear whether this was in fact some substitute for the 'great assembly' scheduled for June. Breda had taken out the special boat for Black Bird from St Louis in April. During May, Auguste Chouteau brought a boat into St Louis from New Orleans loaded with medals and presents destined for the chiefs at Fort Charles. McKay's commission as commandant of the Missouri forts came in during June. But in July, news of Truteau's precipitate flight had reached Trudeau, who reported to Carondelet that 'the total loss of all merchandise' had thrown the Company into chaos and many of its members into beggary. McKay 'did some very bad business' among the Omahas, 'where perhaps he still is.'

At the Omahas, in fact, McKay was wrestling with the Sioux. He was cautious on the prospects. 'I shall only say that this Conference served to open a communication more for the future.' He was right to be doubtful. During the autumn, François Derouin, in a follow-up mission to the Otos, found them in a rebellious mood and hard to handle. He learned from them that, in the summer, the Sioux had taken 150 rifles and six kegs of brandy from English traders to the Omahas. Black Bird was saving the brandy to bring to the Otos for a joint war on the Kansas. Crippled by lack of supplies, McKay's Fort Charles project was crumbling beneath him. At the Sioux conference, however, he secured one vital promise; he seems to have got some kind of clearance from them (at what cost to the supplies one can imagine) for the mission to the Mandans. Once again, he chose John Evans to lead it.

Once again, John was to work to the January Instructions. This time, he also carried a special proclamation which McKay drew up on 27 May. This was directed at all British subjects trading in the region. The King of Spain had granted to his Missouri Company all the land on both sides of the Missouri, from the watershed separating it from Hudson's Bay westward to the Pacific. 'All foreigners whatever (especially all British subjects)' were warned against intrusion, on pain of confiscation of their property and punishment according to Spanish law. All the goods which could be spared were scraped together and allotted to John Evans.

He and his party set out on 8 June. It was slow going. It took them nine weeks to cover the 700 miles to the Arikara village, 'a long and fatiguing voyage', according to Evans's journal. It was probably the survey as well as the difficulties of the river which delayed them. On 8 August, Evans came into the Arikara village on the south side of the Missouri where he was at once stopped. He found them as congenial as other whites had done: 'the nations who had but an imperfect knowledge of the Whites (being yet in a State of Nature)', he reported, 'were of a softer and better

167

Character'; but they would not let him go — they wanted all the goods for themselves. He was stuck there for six weeks. He put the time to good use, making a thorough survey of the Missouri. After a few weeks, he made contact with the far western nations whom Truteau had briefly met, for some Cheyenne and other Rocky Mountain Indians came in. 'Their Chief in a very long and prolix discourse expressed to me the joy they felt to see the Whites, they assured me of their Love and Attachment for the Great father the Spaniard and for all his children who Came to their Country.' John Evans was prompt to develop this significant contact as best he could. More, he worked successfully on the Arikara. No details of the transaction survive, but it is a measure of his merit that he finally talked the Arikara into letting him, and some of his goods, go.

And at long last, on 24 September 1796, he finally got through to the Mandan villages. His entry was something of a triumph. The Indians, joined by some Hidatsa and Wattersoons, crowded around in welcome.

> I gave their Chiefs in the name of their Great Father the Spaniard who inhabits the other side of the great lake and in the name of the Great Chief who inhabits this side of the great lake and also in the name of the Chief who resides at the Entrance of the Missouri, the flags and medals that were given me for that purpose by Mr McKay. Besides those medals and flags I made some small presents, which they received with the greatest of Satisfaction and testified their acknowledgement in the most expressive manner, promising to observe the most sincere attachment to their Great Father the Spaniard and his Chiefs, who have sent to them from so far their children the Whites with such great marks of their Esteem and their Charity for the Red People; they added that they would hear what I had to say and had sent to all their Brothers, and hereafter they would follow my Counsels on all occasions . . .

John Evans deserved his day of triumph. He was the first white man effectively to break the Sioux and Omaha blockade and to plant Spanish authority on the Upper Missouri. The missionary to the Madogwys at last confronted the reality of those 'White Padoucas' who had stared up at him from all those maps back home. There was one further duty to perform. On 28 September, surrounded by the chiefs and their friendly warriors, he marched to Jusseaume's fort. To the cheers of the Indians, he ran down the British flag and raised the standard of Spain, which they had never yet seen.

A week later, back in Europe, the king he now served went to war with the king whose native subject he was.

10

On the rim of empire

As John Evans came into the Mandan villages in the autumn of 1796, the great flights of ducks, geese and swans, whose like no one was ever to see again, were already beating their way south, through the skies of the north-western mystery which winter would turn gun-metal grey. The eagles, grouse and quail, which seemed as numerous as the pestilent fleas and ticks, would stay, along with the bears whose carcasses yielded the oil which was as essential to the Indian economy as the buffalo tallow needed for its pemmican. As soon as the rivers froze, which they often did before the end of November, the ice-houses were full of cuts and sides of buffalo. The Indians drove the docile herds on to the ice, and bunched them until it cracked and they drowned. John Macdonnell of the North West Company once saw 7,000 buffalo corpses drowned and mired along thirty miles of the Qu'Appelle river; the Indians liked their buffalo meat green. The sudden rains would turn bitter cold; and there would be short, whirling snowstorms, until the north-western winter, along the Upper Missouri as ferocious as any winter on earth, gripped the sawtooth bluffs of the frozen river. As well as the ice and snow, there were the abrupt arctic gales, the long windless cold waves which threw haloes round the moon and produced the 'false suns', the sundog.

The fur-traders knew by heart the sounds of the long close-in of winter: the ice groaning and the cottonwoods cracking. This was the season of spirits. On the Qu'Appelle river (the River-that-Cries) one ghost wailed all night. The windigo, a cannibal spectre, stalked the snow; and men saw their funeral hearses before season. It was a time when a man would go a hundred miles through blizzards for the glimpse of a different book. Anything was welcome which would break the routine of half-life, even a wolf pack after a camp bitch. The *engagés*, with many of the squaws joining in, went sledging, and played infinite variants of the snow games of Canada, Scotland and the tribes; Indian ceremonies, with their endless cacophony and murderous brawls, their dancing and their magicians, drew visitors from miles away — and those of the Mandans were peculiarly lascivious. Joseph Garreau, coming in once from months of solitude, paid no less than a full gallon of undiluted wine and a half-dozen knives for one night with a girl who got too drunk to deliver. One *engagé* paid £16.13s.4d. 'for one single touch of a slave girl'.

Mandan girls were celebrated for their good looks and amiability and were said to be more adept than most. They chattered endlessly even while making love — a fact which one later observer cited as further proof of their Welsh descent! John Evans, reared as a Methodist, has left no testimony on the point. Not even his buffalo hunt among the Omahas, however, could have prepared him for the winter of North Dakota — 'such frost I never saw in the States,' said one of Lewis and Clark's men. And most of the seven months that Evans spent with the Mandans were winter months, passed huddled in the smoky, smelly earth lodges with the horses packed in among the families (did he play his flute to them?) or in the cramped and close-breathing company of the French Canadians in the cottonwood fort which Jusseaume had built and which Evans renamed Fort McKay. Without doubt, that killing winter shortened his life.

The Indians were no trouble, at least until his goods ran out together with hope of any more. Nearly everyone who reached them liked the Mandans; they were an open, sunny people, often startling in their fair skin and that lighter-coloured hair which turned grey. The chiefs and leading men, in particular, took to Evans. Black Cat, the senior chief, who was anti-Canadian by instinct anyway, became a close friend. By this time, after the disaster of the 1781-2 smallpox epidemic and their shift from Heart River, they were in truth a good deal less numerous than the Hidatsa who, though they were a tougher lot who rather enjoyed fighting the Sioux, shared the Mandan way of life and were close allies. When John Evans's fellow Welshman, David Thompson the Canadian explorer, reached the area a few months later (strangely enough to make not a single reference to Evans), he found five villages with over 300 of their securely planted beehive earth-lodges ringed with palisades, moats and earthworks. 'The best Quality of Land is found in the Mandaine country,' wrote Evans in his journal; their storage pits were always full.

The central village of the Mandans lay on the east bank of the Missouri about a mile below the mouth of Knife River. It was called Rooptarhe and was the home of the paramount chief *Posecopsahe* (Black Cat). Three miles further south and on the west bank was Matootonha; its chief was *Shahaka* (Big White) with his deputy Little Raven. Jusseaume's fort was sited between these villages and those of the Hidatsa. One branch of the Hidatsa with its own tribal organization, the Wattersoons or Anahaways, was sited in a village right at the mouth of Knife River, to the north of it and on the west bank of the Missouri; called Maharha, its chief was White Buffalo Robe. Two other Hidatsa villages were strung out a half-mile and a mile and a half up Knife River: Metehartan under Chief Black Moccasin, and another whose name is not known under Little Wolf's Medicine.

Those villages certainly looked like the hill-fort settlements of the iron-age British. If John Evans noticed the resemblance, he did not mention it. Nor did he speak of their round skin-and-wickerwork boats and fishing rituals in which later observers saw reminiscences of the Welsh coracles of the river Teifi. And even David Ingram would have had difficulty in making those names Welsh.

John Evans, however, took note of a great deal else. From the Mandans, he secured a wealth of accurate information on the Upper Missouri. He measured the river at their village and found it was 500 *toises;* such a breadth indicated that the sources of the great river were much further off than had been thought. He put the eastern chain of the Rockies at 170 leagues beyond the Mandans. The Missouri rose somewhere in the Rockies at about latitude 40°, flowed north through the mountains and then turned east over giant falls to enter the plains. He knew of the great rivers running into it from the south-west, in particular the Yellowstone. He reported the confused picture which the Indians gave him of the lands and tribes to the west, and he knew that 'it is at these Mountains where the great Meadows and Prairies terminate, the Country then begins to be Absolutely Covered with trees, even upon the Rocky Mountains and it is probable these woods extend to the Pacific Ocean . . .'.

But how was John Evans now to get there? His trade goods were few and were fast running out. The Indians had accepted him and would have gone on accepting him and Spain: they would probably have helped him on towards the Pacific, they would probably have stopped the British, if he had had anything more to offer them than promises. But through that winter, promises were all he had. At that moment the most westerly human spearpoint of European enterprise, John Evans stood at the very rim of empire. But behind him, that enterprise was crumbling, and his lifeline unravelling. At that rim, he stood paralysed. His months of penury, cold and loneliness, were months of misery and frustration. This frustration would be something more than the frustration of a dedicated servant of the Missouri Company. Where now were the White Padoucas, the Madogwys? The months with the Mandans were the hinge of fate for the ebullient young man from Waun-fawr.

They were also months of harassment and mounting fury. For a mere two weeks away, to the north, were the watchful British. At the mouth of the Souris river where it began its great curve south to Mandan territory, was a fort of the North West Company. Two miles up the Assiniboine was the Hudson's Bay Company post at Brandon House. Some way further up that river was another North West Company post at Rivière-Tremblante, Aspin House. From these North West forts, René

Jusseaume had got through to Knife River and raised his fort. The evidence suggests that when Evans occupied that fort, there were no Northwesters there. He does not mention Ménard, who had lived among the Mandans for some time. There might well have been deserters around, however. One Chayé had deserted La Souris in the autumn of 1796; La Grave had quit the Jusseaume expedition. Fotman and Jonquard had gone in 1795. Some of them had set up a kind of free port in the Mandan area, to the rage of both Canadian companies, who were already resolutely thrusting for each other's jugular. If Evans found any illicit traders at the Mandans, he either drove them off or enrolled them (in the following February, John Macdonnell accused him of bribing his *engagés*).

Within two weeks of the Welshman's arrival, however, a small party came in from the North West post at La Souris. Their leader was a Neil or Donald McKay. Evans's description of the encounter is succinct:

> The 8th of October arrived Several men at the Mandaine Village belonging to the Canada Traders that I have above mentioned, they had brought some Goods with them, not having a Sufficiency of men, I did not strive to oppose their arrival, nor of their goods: I nevertheless found a means to hinder their Trade and some days after absolutely forced them to leave the Mandane Territory, I sent by them in the North the Declaration that I had received of Mr McKay . . .

He managed this without too much difficulty. The Norwester McKay was in some trouble and Evans permitted one of his own men to accompany him with a compass. At this point, the Canadian *engagés* thought John Evans a *bon garçon*. McKay was allowed to leave without having his goods confiscated, on the understanding that he would take no more goods there. At that point, clearly, John Evans exercised total command over the Mandans.

This party got back to the La Souris fort around 25 October. Their return caused a sensation. Big John Macdonnell, in command at La Souris, sent the information on to Cuthbert Grant at Rivière-Tremblante. John Sutherland, the Hudson's Bay man at Brandon House 'stept over' the two miles to hear the news. He read James McKay's May proclamation against British traders and listened to what the *engagés* had to say. They reported that James McKay himself had not yet reached the Mandans, 'only a party under a Mr Evans, a Welsh Gentleman, who has come to explore the source of the river as far as the stoney mountains if not to the Pacific ocean in search of mines, some of which is already found'.

An enormous curiosity settled on the Canadian posts. Their surprise and their caution at the unexpected appearance of Evans among the Mandans are patent. There was, further, a genuine human response to the discovery of a 'Welsh Gentleman', and an educated one at that, in this wilderness. The North West Company was most directly affected and had an excuse to hand. René Jusseaume, in his accounting with Cuthbert Grant, had found himself in debt; some of his furs, and his Indian wife, were still at the Mandans. On 5 November, Jusseaume, who was then at the mouth of the Assiniboine on the Red River, sent a letter to Evans. He apologized because he was not able to send him even a single pipe of tobacco, begged the Welshman to look after his wife and asked him to deliver his pelts to Cuthbert Grant. 'My compliments to all the French.'

Cuthbert Grant sent Jusseaume's letter to La Souris with an official letter of his own. This noted James McKay's proclamation, and was prompt to 'withdraw what little property the N.W. Co. has their'; Jusseaume had lost a great deal of money anyway. He warmly thanked Evans for assisting the *engagé* McKay and asked him to forward Jusseaume's goods by the bearer.

These letters reached the La Souris fort by 23 November, when John Macdonnell composed an exquisitely apologetic letter to Evans. 'We are obliged to trouble you with another visit though infinitely against our wills . . .' Jusseaume's 'dearly acquired debt' had to be collected. There were also the deserters — Chayé, who owed three years of his time, and La Grave, who ran away some time ago owing huge sums. Garreau, too, had decoyed a horse and a slave girl from his man McKay — could Mr Evans help in this matter? He approached the question of the mission to the Mandans, which was to be led by the interpreter Desmarais, with the utmost delicacy:

Desmarais Interpreter to the N. West Company is the person that has the little goods sent in charge, which I suppose will only be sufficient to purchase two Horses if requisite to transport the above mentioned Peltries of Jusseaumes' . . . As you know the turbulent spirit of the French Canadians I will tell you that I found it impossible to get any of them to undertake the voyage at this severe season of the year without giving them some articles on credit to be paid in Robes etc. upon their return but I had represented to them that their property ran risk of confiscation, they replied that they heard that Mr Evans was a *bon garçon* and hoped upon asking leave to trade what little they brought that you would not refuse them as they so little thot it would not injure your interests in the least . .'

This exercise in man-to-man diplomacy between experienced traders (who were after all both British), endlessly harassed by the unpredictability of *voyageurs*, was supplemented by some fraternal wilderness assistance:

Please accept as a Small token of my esteem a few trifles I forward you by Desmarais, viz. two European Magazines and a Guthrie's

Geographical Grammar for your amusement, a Powder Horn and Shott Bag, 1 Bottle Turlington's Balsam, 1 Ditto Peppermint, ½ dozen vomits, ½ dozen punges [sic, presumably purges], 1 Lanut and the Compass you had the bonté to let Mr McKay have the loan of. You will please return the Books by any favourable opportunity after perusal as they are not my own . . .

James Sutherland of the Hudson's Bay Company stepped over to La Souris yet again, to add a letter of his own. He too noted James McKay's proclamation, but said that while this might affect his rivals, it would 'very little those from Hudson's Bay . . . I should be glad however to know if we may be permitted on any future occasion to visit the Mandals [sic] and Trade Horses, Indian corn and Buffalo Robes which articles we suppose to be unconnected with the Fur Trade . . .'. He reported to the Company that he had sent this letter to Evans 'barly out of couriositey'. In fact, these most westerly agents of the Canadian companies were consumed with curiosity, distinctly apprehensive and avid for information.

The Desmarais expedition was evidently something of a reconnaissance. No report on it survives, but it seems to have passed off in an atmosphere of courtesy. It reached the Mandans about mid-December and, on the 20th of that month, John Evans sent letters in reply. To Sutherland, he was polite but firm, indeed immovable. He thought the Missouri Company's ban could affect neither of the two Canadian companies, since they had met with nothing but losses on the Missouri. As for Sutherland's request to be allowed some little trading in goods other than furs, Evans said he had no power to grant such a concession, but he thought the trade in buffalo robes would certainly be prohibited, since it was the staple trade of the country. 'However, you will be properly informed after the arrival of the Agent General and Lieut. Mooroch at this post.' He ended on an expressive note. 'Having no entertaining news of any kind to transfer to you, I remain . . .'.

This trip to the Mandans had exposed John Evans's isolation and weakness. By Christmas, the Hudson's Bay men were reporting that their rivals the Norwesters were thinking of 'taking possession' of the Upper Missouri. The Desmarais expedition itself provided an occasion for a further sortie, for the party was ambushed by a band of Pawnees who stole their horses; they were forced to abandon their gear. They started back for the Mandans at once. This time, two of James Sutherland's Hudson's Bay engagés, two 'English lads', Slettar and Yorston, went with them, out of curiosity and hoping to buy a slave girl. Sutherland sent some gifts, 6 lb. of flour, two cakes of chocolate and a little sugar. 'I am only sorry I have not any thing more worthy of your acceptance as my stock is near out, but hope you will take the will for the deed.' It was a friendly, but rather sly letter. 'Although personally unknown to me, as a Country man I was pleased to hear of your welfare. It is not my business to enquire into the causes of your exposing yourself to such dangers and difficulties which from hearsay attends your situateion, it is sufficient for me to suppose that your future views doubtless are adequate to your present hardships.'

This delicate but unmistakable hint at Evans's precarious situation was followed up by a rather less subtle approach. All the news he had, his two men would convey; 'a little from you would be very acceptable such as when you expect the gentlemen from below to your post, what your future intentions are with regards to exploring further up the river and if your agent general be the same Mr James McKay who was formerly a trader here in Red River' (he was). Such queries were no doubt tedious, but 'I suppose a gentleman of your abilities can have no objection . . .'.

Sutherland was right to point to the fragility of John Evans's authority. According to Slettar and Yorston, the encounter at the Mandans was explosive. Some 300 Indians met the party at the village early in February. They carried the traders' sleds on their shoulders 'so fond wer they of the English'. John Evans promptly 'hoisted his Spanish flagg'. He was 'as cival to them as his wretched siteuation would admit', but he would not allow any of them to trade direct with the Indians. He traded the goods himself at a lower price and greatly displeased many of the Mandans. The Hudson's Bay men who took four sleds well loaded with furs back to Brandon House, which they reached on 25 February, thought that Evans had endangered himself.

In that brief but sharp struggle in the depth of a Dakota winter, John Evans had evidently carried the day, but how much longer could he hold the Mandans against this English pressure? And where were James McKay, the Spanish lieutenant, the vital goods and reinforcements? In what was still a courageous (for courage was something John never lacked) but desperate gesture, the Welshman on 6 February addressed two peremptory letters of protest and prohibition to the northern companies. They do not survive, but they were evidently a direct challenge.

Sutherland of Hudson's Bay responded like a gentleman in the service of a gentlemanly company. He at once promised not to bother the Missouri tribes at all; his Company had never yet broken any law. He warned Evans, however, about his rivals. 'I hear you have complaints against some of them and possibe'ly not without reason, and I could say more on that hand, had I the pleasure of seeing you, there is no harm however on your being on your guard against designing people; a word is enough to the wise.' Thanking Evans for some gifts, he hastened to add, 'I was far from meaning to dive or enquire into your affairs any further than you was pleased to intimate only such a sensible man in such a remote quarter of the world is a rare thing and your letters will appear with pleasure before our Governor and Council . . .'. He would find a

175

correspondence with John Evans highly acceptable. 'I should be extremely happy to have the pleasure of seeing you in this or any other country where perhaps something better than we can command at present would cheer our Souls and make us forgit our past cares, and each relate the adventure of the wandering Sailor (or rather Soldier) for as well as you I have been appointed by providence to traverse the wild regions of America for several years past.'

This warm and engaging letter, however, was accompanied by a very different one from John Macdonnell, also written on 26 February. After briefly thanking John Evans for a gift, Macdonnell referred to his criticisms of Jusseaume and his aide Jean Baptiste La France. 'You seem to be as inveterated against the one as the other; they have an opportunity of vindicating themselves from your aspersions in your own presence.' He countered with an attack on the desertion and alleged bribery of his *engagés*. 'Be at bottom of it who will most certain I am that there is most complicated vilainy carried on this year at the Missouri.' Chayé had been debauched last fall and 200 dollars had been offered to the two English men. 'It must give any sensible person no grand idea of your Missouri Company making use of such *Canaille* as I have reason to think many of your *engagés* are,' added Macdonnell, citing La Grave and others. Moreover, he totally rejected Evans's claim to exercise jurisdiction over the Missouri trade. 'British subjects are not to be tried by Spanish laws nor do I look upon you as an officer commissioned to apprehend other people's servants, if you serve a chartered Company, why not show the Spanish Governor's Orders, declarations denounciations or manifestoes prohibiting others from frequenting that country — Then we shall leave you in peace.'

This was a declaration of war. The letter was to go with a party led by René Jusseaume. It took plenty of goods and was clearly intended to win a minuscule frontier struggle of major imperial significance. 'The Intentions of the British Traders,' wrote John Evans to St Louis;

> were Not to spare trouble or Expence to maintain a Fort at the Mandaine Village Not that they see the least appearance of a Benefit to the Mandanes but to carry their views further, they wish to open a trade by the Missouri with Nations who inhabit the Rocky Mountains, a Trade which at this Moment is Supposed to be the best on the Continent of America.

Jusseaume was launching a direct frontal assault on Fort McKay. To resist it, John Evans had nothing but his will and such loyalty as he could command among the Mandans. For hundreds of miles behind him, both his Company and St Louis were in turmoil.

'*Tres Excellent Gouverneur,*' wrote Jacques Clamorgan to Carondelet on 26 May 1796:

Nothing has astonished me more than the underhanded and unfaithful trickery of *Sieur* Robidoux, member of the Missouri Company, who has been shamelessly goaded by malicious envy. I have learned that he has villainously complained to you; that he has acted with the blackest and most evil artifice in order to make me hated by you . . . Most Excellent Governor, for the future impose silence on *Sieur* Robidoux and his bitterness, just as your law imposes upon me never to harm my equals, especially those who, conjointly with me, have sought by new discoveries to render themselves useful to the prosperity of our colony . . . the last of my days will be most glorious if I may see floating as far as you on our miry waters the industrial resources of the sources of the Missouri . . .

Even in his life-and-death struggle, Morgan of the Missouri Company was not losing the grandeur of his imperial vision. But in the summer of 1796, he was having to struggle. It was in April 1796 that Clamorgan had revealed to Carondelet the new direction which the Todd enterprise was taking. In a clear reference to the McKay expedition, he stated baldly that Todd goods had sustained the Missouri Company's enterprises, and added, 'I have acted freely on behalf of some of my partners and myself concerning some advances which the house of Todd has lavished on me.' Throughout April, the orders in support of McKay at Fort Charles, with his planned great assembly of the barrier tribes, were flowing south. Now, Clamorgan proposed to anchor the vast Todd-Missouri Company scheme. He and Régis Loisel were to form the company of Clamorgan and Loisel by 1 May, in partnership with the house of Todd. He had ordered the rest of the shareholders of the Missouri Company to stop trading with all other Canadian companies and work with the Todds alone. They were resisting. Clamorgan asked for an order compelling them to obey and admitting Andrew Todd to the Missouri Company. He repeated his request for a fort on the Des Moines-Minnesota and suggested that Todd be given a trading monopoly with the Sauk-Fox Indians on the Upper Mississippi.

On 11 May Carondelet sent his letters granting Clamorgan his requests. But before his letters had reached St Louis, the shattered Truteau had come in from Fort Charles, with his devastating news of disasters up the Missouri. Lieutenant-Governor Trudeau wrote an angry letter to New Orleans on 3 July. He reported Truteau's story in full, confessed that he did not know whether McKay was still at Fort Charles (by that time John Evans had been on his way north for a month) and denounced Clamorgan. Most members of the Company had been reduced to beggary. Clamorgan wanted 'to usurp everything with the help of Todd, always combining and conducting the operations poorly.' Trudeau no longer had any confidence in him. The only men he could trust were the 'more prudent' Robidoux and Reihle. As a counter, Clamorgan in a few days was able to send down McKay's journal and his Instructions to Evans.

It was in August that Carondelet's letters in favour of Clamorgan reached St Louis. On 4 August Trudeau protested against them, pointed to the ruin of the Company and denounced the avarice of Clamorgan and his selfish collusion with Todd. They were explicitly relying, said Trudeau, on the 10,000 pesos' royal subsidy for the forts. And, precisely on that point, the celebrated resolutions of the Spanish Council of State of May, supporting the original Clamorgan-Todd enterprise, reached New Orleans in September. Clamorgan himself was in the city in that month. He welcomed the news, acknowledged the dispatch of a garrison to the Upper Mississippi and proposed that control now be vested in the consortium of Todd and Clamorgan-Loisel.

At that point, Governor Carondelet was clearly committed to the Clamorgan project. He boasted of having secured the 10,000 pesos' subsidy. Clamorgan's plan moved to its climax. Three of the remaining shareholders in the Missouri Company, who had been supported by Auguste Chouteau, were bought out by Loisel using Todd money and, on 26 October, a formal agreement was registered at New Orleans between the house of Todd (acting through Daniel Clark the New Orleans merchant, speculator and empire-builder in Spanish territory) and Clamorgan-Loisel. Special provision was made for favoured treatment of Chouteau and John Evans's friend William Arundel.

But the triumph was as brief as it was false. Carondelet was about to be transferred, and to be replaced as governor by Gayoso de Lemos. Juan Ventura Morales took over as interim Intendant and he immediately challenged Carondelet's interpretation of the 10,000 pesos' subsidy clause. By his reading (the issue turned on the meaning of the Spanish adjective *su*) the Company was to maintain the 100-man garrison of its forts itself. This precipitated a long and agonized controversy which dragged on for years. Clamorgan never got the money, which knocked one vital prop from under his plan. In that same November (John Evans had just chased off the first Norwester party from the Mandans) Carondelet received Trudeau's letter protesting against Clamorgan's demands. Robidoux was persisting in his opposition. Carondelet wrote to St Louis to annul his own orders.

This loss of nerve was followed by the devastating blow of Andrew Todd's death in the yellow fever epidemic which killed 800 people in New Orleans by December. This disrupted the entire plan. Daniel Clark, with the *Antelope*, several caches of trade goods and a multitude of half-finished plans on his hands, was by the spring of 1797 locked in legal wrangles with Clamorgan and Loisel; Isaac Todd in Canada was disengaging himself from the project. In that spring, as John Evans at the Mandans was confronting the third party from the Canada traders,

Dérouin returned to St Louis with his news of trouble among the Otos, and of Black Bird's plans for a war in alliance with the Sioux. The audacious enterprise which was to have sustained McKay, who was now left isolated and starved of goods at Fort Charles, was shuddering into collapse.

Across this riven scene blew the gales of political upheaval. As soon as news of the peace with France came through during 1796, rumours began to spread that Louisiana was to return to its French allegiance. As war with Britain loomed (it was actually declared on 6 October) the rumours grew more insistent. At this point the French General Victor Collot arrived on his mission to St Louis.

Collot had served during the American war and had been chief of staff of the French *Armée du Nord* during 1792. Appointed governor of Guadeloupe in 1794, he had been captured when the British took the island, but was released on parole to the USA. There he had been detained by a law suit brought by an aggrieved merchant. During his enforced residence in the USA he took the opportunity to inspect the interior, and the Spanish possessions, in the service of France, in company with his adjutant Warin who was killed by a Chickasaw on the Mississippi. Collot hit St Louis like a shock wave. He drew maps, prepared plans for its defence against the British and enthused the local French, who were convinced that his arrival signalled their imminent transfer to the republic. The Spaniards in St Louis and New Orleans quickly followed up his suggestions, hiring the Dutch engineer Louis Vandenbenden to fortify St Louis.

But on Collot's departure, the French underground which had long existed in St Louis came bubbling to the surface. Jean Papin, a mason by trade, born in Quebec but long resident in St Louis, took the lead. Carondelet called him 'a man of system, who writes with talent and perhaps really has some, but a peevish fellow and an enemy of our government'. Allied with him was Louis Coignard, a fur-trader who had married the daughter of a distinguished soldier. They organized a *Society of Sans-culottes* which staged marches and demonstrations, singing revolutionary songs. On the eve of the French revolutionary year, 20 September, they marched around the town, serenading the leading citizens, and especially the clergy, with a 'Happy New Year'! An organized political society, first noticed on 17 October, was credited with sweeping ambitions. They threatened to take Upper Louisiana from New Madrid north into secession, to link up with the English and the Americans. Americans and 'French democrats' would pour over the Mississippi and the British were already entrenching themselves to the north.

In these circumstances, with the Clamorgan plan in disarray, Carondelet decided to strike hard. He appointed a celebrated Irish soldier in Spanish service, Don Carlos Howard, to the command of a strong expedition. He was to pick up two galleys, a galiot and other gunboats along the southern Mississippi, evacuate Chickasaw Bluffs under the terms of the treaty with the USA, and then take a garrison up river to St Louis, suppress sedition and restore order there, and move on to destroy the British posts which threatened the Upper Mississippi. He was, further, to send an armed ship and a small garrison up the Missouri to destroy the British fort at the Mandans and succour John Evans. These orders (which included highly entertaining character sketches of the leading citizens of St Louis) were issued on 26-7 November 1796.

The expedition, which was long remembered in St Louis as the 'year of the galleys', was something of an anticlimax. Charles Howard followed his orders as best he could. He reached St Louis on 27 April 1797 and had little trouble in restoring order. He found, however, that the menacing English posts to the north had already been handed over to the Americans. The nearest English post was now over 800 miles away and he would have to cross American territory to reach it. More important, he reported on 13 May 1797 that James McKay had a few days earlier returned from the Missouri. From what he said, Howard thought that it would be difficult but not impossible to dislodge the English from the Mandans. 'But, in order to accomplish that,' he added in what was by now a familiar litany, 'I should have to be supplied with more aid than I now have.'

Don Diego McCay had told Howard, however, that

Don Juan Evans, who had been sent to explore a route to the Pacific Ocean had crossed the Mandan nation successfully on his way to the Shining Mountains (montañas relucientes) alias the White Mountains alias the Rocky Mountains (Pedrejosas) and that once they were traversed, he believed it would be easy to reach the sea.

Back in Wales, some Welsh were saying that Don Juan Evans had found the Madogwys as well. To Trudeau, McKay was more circumspect. Trudeau described Howard's arrival and actions in a pained letter to Carondelet on 26 May. What he had to report was the complete paralysis of the Company's effort. The Otos and the Mahas had broken out of control. The chief of the former had begged St Louis to cut off all trade in the hope of bringing his young men back to obedience. No goods would go up the Missouri in 1797.

McKay, however, had sent 'a well-educated young man' up to the Mandans. 'At the time of his [McKay's] departure from the said Mahas, he knew that this young man had reached the Mandans, from whence he will start again when the snow melts, to search for the Sea.' Trudeau also repeated his hopes for Jacques D'Eglise, who had committed himself to the mission. A 'very good map' of the Missouri (John Evans's), which Trudeau attributed to McKay, would be sent down as soon as possible.

In this total paralysis of the Company's operations, the withdrawal of McKay was the most serious blow to John Evans. Little is known of the Scotsman's activities at Fort Charles after John Evans's departure. He made a pioneering journey into Western Nebraska, looking for Rocky Mountain Indians. By the spring of 1797, he must have known his mission was spent. He was however as stubborn as John Evans himself. According to Trudeau, he withdrew only when ordered to by Jacques Clamorgan, who blamed him for the Company's losses. He must have left Fort Charles about the time that the well-equipped party of Norwesters came into the Mandan villages led by René Jusseaume, the illiterate but skilled, experienced and ruthless veteran of the wilderness trade who was to serve every mission to the west, including Lewis and Clark's. To meet this threat, John Evans, now a lone and isolated man 1,800 miles from his base, had nothing but his will and spirit.

In these desperate circumstances, his performance can only be called remarkable. A garbled version of the encounter got back to the Brandon House people by 14 April. Evans and the Canadians had almost come to blows when the former tried to prevent the latter from trading and 'not having goods himself set all the Indians out against him, he was obliged to set off with himself and all his men down the river for Fort Charles, the Indians threatening to kill them if they refused being greatly exasperated against them for preventing the Subjects of G. Britain from coming to Trade with them . . .'. This is but a half-truth. The story is best told in John Evans's own prose.

The 13th March 1797 Arrived at the Mandaine Village from the North, a man named *Jusson* accompanied by several Engagees he was sent by the English traders with Merchandizes as presents for the Mandaines and neighbouring nations, so as to be able to break off the Attachment and fidelity they had promised to his Majesty and his Subjects, the said *Jussom* and those who Accompanied him advised the Indians to enter into my house under the Mask of Friendship, then to kill me and my men and pillage my property; several of the Good Chiefs who were my friends and to whom *Jussom* had offered presents; refused them with indignation and shuddered at the thought of such a horrid Design and came and informed me of the Whole. Nevertheless the presents that *Jussom* had made to the Indians had tempted some of the inferior class, who joined him to execute his abominable design, happily for me his presents had not the same effect with some of the Principal chiefs, to undertake Such an enormous crime, therefore many of these chiefs Came to my house to guard me and were resolved to die in the attack if any should be made; this Resolution disconcerted entirely my enemies and totally put an End to their infamous Design. Some days after *Jussom* came to my house with a number of his Men, and seizing the moment

that my Back was turned to him, tried to discharge a Pistol at my head
loaded with Deer Shot but my Interpreter having perceived his design
hindered the Execution — the Indians immediately dragged him out of
my house and would have killed him, had I not prevented them — this
man having refused me Satisfaction for all the Insults he had given me.
Moreover disgusted on the ill success of the Execution of his Black
Designs, left the Mandanes with his men some days after and returned
to his people in the north and bring them the News of his Ill success . . .

One feature of this dramatic encounter, apart from that sense of total
outrage which, after 180 years, still throbs through a prose which distance
had made quaint, is the sheer, stubborn courage of the man from Waun-
fawr. He seems to have challenged Jusseaume to a duel. Most striking,
however, is the equally stubborn loyalty to John Evans which so many of
the Mandans displayed. The tribe was divided, and the division is wholly
understandable. Less easy to understand, in truth, in his desperate and
empty circumstances, is the fact that the chiefs and so many of their men
stood by him, when he had literally nothing to offer. Nothing that is,
except himself. Seven years later, Black Cat was to complain bitterly to
Lewis and Clark that Mr Evans had deceived them. He had promised
them arms and ammunition but he had never come back. The real
significance of this is that in 1797 they took him at his word. Jusseaume
had to retire discomfited. John Evans and his little party, with nothing in
their hands, left the Mandans by agreement, going to fetch the guns and
goods which should have reached them earlier. Speculation is easy, but if
the Spaniards had been able to equip him properly, John Evans, on his
quest for Welsh Indians, might well have made that famous crossing 'By
Land, from St Louis' a decade before Lewis and Clark.

But leave he had to, now. There was no more to be done at the Mandan
villages. He and his party set out, probably in the early days of May. It
must have been an amazing journey, down the swift, ever-shifting river. It
took sixty-eight days. In St Louis, despite his failure, he was given
something of a hero's welcome. After all, he and McKay had done more
for Spain than anyone else. He was warmly received and asked at once
whether he would attempt another expedition towards the Pacific. He
had a duty to perform first. On 15 July 1797, he sat down in St Louis to
write his long-awaited letter to Dr Samuel Jones in Philadelphia. 'I am
ready to supose every body of my friends in that Part of the world has
given me up for dead,' he said. He gave a long account of his first madcap
venture, a much shorter narrative of his march to the Mandans, and a
brief and vivid description of the Missouri. 'I suspect that I shall be
obliged to undertake other voyages as dangerous as the former as there
has allready Solicitations been made to me by government to undertake a
voyage across the Continent,' he wrote, adding, with a flash of his old

spirit, 'which voyage I supose will keep me from having the pleasure of Seeing you, as I think but very little of a trip to Philadelphia at present, having been so far up the Missurie that it took 68 days to come down with the furious Current of the Missurie.'

The saddest duty, however, was the last. Before leaving for William Arundel's house in Cahokia, John Evans reported to Samuel Jones: 'Thus having explored and charted the Missurie for 1,800 miles and by my Communications with the Indians this side of the Pacific Ocean from 35 to 49 Degrees of Latitude, I am able to inform you that there is no such People as the Welsh Indians.'

11

Indestructible Madoc

In July 1797 John Evans told Samuel Jones to address all letters to him at William Arundel's. McKay, however, settled in St Louis. Though the Spaniards asked John to lead another expedition to the Pacific, the Missouri Company was now paralysed. As the Pinckney Treaty with the Americans came into force, the conciliatory Gayoso de Lemos replaced the belligerent Carondelet as Governor. The forward policy was abandoned and Trudeau was told to encourage controlled American immigration.

In these circumstances, Evans was probably hard pressed to make up his mind. He established a connection with two Americans, a Weston at Fort Massac on the Ohio and, more closely, with Maurice Williams who, with two companions called Lemon and Brooks and a black servant, was setting up a trading post in Lorimier's district of Cap Girardeau. In the event, while keeping up his American contacts, John Evans took the job of official surveyor in Upper Louisiana, under Antoine Soulard. Through the winter of 1797-8, he was busy settling Americans around what is today the site of Jackson, Missouri.

His months on the Missouri, however, had undermined his health and he now ran into an avalanche of troubles. He had been promised land near Cap Girardeau, but Lorimier had been forced to withdraw the offer, because the holding had already been earmarked. He had difficulty in getting his pay out of the incoming Americans. He went back to St Louis to brief McKay who was leaving for New Orleans to seek the Governor's patronage and, on his return to his district, he lost most of his property in one of the notorious Mississippi floods and was also robbed. With the threat of a war between America and Spain's ally France, the trickle of immigrants dried up. Weston at Fort Massac ran away from his creditors. Maurice Williams's business was faltering, Brooks seemed to be dying, the black woman was sick and Lemon had disappeared on a mission. 'I must struggle through it as well as I can, it must be a long lane which has no turning . . .'

184

John Evans slumped into one of those fits of nervous depression which had begun to assail him. His spirit broke under the repeated disappointments. He began to drink heavily and to lose his grip on reality. In June 1798 he wrote two very unhappy letters to Trudeau and Soulard, asking for land on Zenon's River (now Hubbell's Creek) and commenting, at twenty-eight years of age; 'a reflection upon the shortness of life and the frowns of Delusive Fortune convinces me dayly of my duty to Live a retired life as soon as I can. For we can scarcely mount the stage of Life Before we ought to prepare to leave it to make room for the next actors.' Before July was out, he was back in St Louis, where he moved into the household of Jacques Clamorgan.

Clamorgan was undeterred by the collapse of his schemes. He was nearly 100,000 pesos in debt, but he was still pressing for another expedition and probably had John Evans in mind as its leader. 'We will march with guns in hand to place, in spite of our enemies, the standard of our empire in the midst of the most distant savage nations . . . We have recruited strong, brave men who we are going to have sent into the midst of danger'; he asked for his 10,000 pesos' subsidy.

Spanish Louisiana could face no more of this; Trudeau talked of 'the absurdities of a veritable madman who enriches himself with dreams'. Even Carondelet was forced to agree that Jacques' schemes were 'only illusions, contradictions and dreams which can never be realized with Morgan's resources alone'. New Orleans, however, retained considerable sympathy for its empire-building demon of a Welsh West Indian. Even Daniel Clark, the Todds' attorney, an Irish adventurer who was to serve as US consul in New Orleans and to cherish his own empire-building fantasies, told his men to go easy on Clamorgan, though he held Jacques in New Orleans by an injunction during 1798-9. By 1800, Clark was himself acting as Clamorgan's attorney. In that year, the former Director of the Missouri Company was awarded the lower Missouri tribes; in 1801, the Ponca; and in 1802 the whole Missouri trade.

In view of this, it seems at first sight strange that New Orleans did not do more for John Evans, who had become something of a hero. 'I have tried to keep to our cause,' Gayoso de Lemos wrote to Spain in November 1798, 'the two most famous travellers of the northern countries of this continent, Don Jayme McCay and Don Juan Evans.' As late as 1801, someone in the Governor's office in New Orleans hurled a thunderous rebuke at the heads of rebellious merchants in St Louis. He berated them for sloth and cowardice, told them to give up trade and take up farming. He denounced them for having undermined the great Missouri Company of 'the worthy and never sufficiently praised *Sieur* Clamorgan'. Central to the indictment was the charge that they had failed to support John Evans. 'You know, sirs, the struggle of *Sieur* Evans, agent of the Company, in 1796 to cause the British flag to be lowered among the

Mandan tribe, when he caused that of His Catholic Majesty to be hoisted, while on his expedition to find the Western Sea. In this, the English were repulsed, with the aid of the savage tribes, who from that hour, acknowledged the standard of His Majesty.' He spoke truth; John Evans had held the Mandans for Spain and they passed, with Louisiana, to the Americans.

Gayoso in fact took McKay into his household in the spring of 1798, and in May made him commandant of San Andrés (St Andrews). McKay petitioned for further assistance in June, presenting John Evans's work as his own; in 1799 he was given the trade of the Omaha. Gayoso intended to use John Evans as a surveyor to fix the frontiers between Canada, the USA and the Spanish dominions — the Missouri again. While waiting for the commission from Spain, he said he had no post to offer the Welshman: 'Not having any position to give Evans, I have preferred to maintain him at my cost, keeping him in my own house in order to prevent his returning to his own country, or for his own convenience, to embrace another cause . . .'.

There may have been more of charity in the amiable Gayoso's attitude than he was prepared officially to admit. By this time John Evans was becoming an alcoholic and unemployable. We do not know when he went down to New Orleans, but it may have been on one of Clamorgan's missions. He was certainly in the city by November 1798, for in that month he wrote an angry letter to Dr Samuel Jones protesting against the publication of his Missouri report in the American press. It may be a sign of his loss of grip that he addressed it to New York. On 20 May 1799, Gayoso sent an unhappy note to McKay:

Poor Evans is very ill; between us I have perceived that he deranged himself out of my sight, but I have perceived it too late; the strength of liquor has deranged his head; he has been out of his senses for several days, but, with care, he is doing better; and I hope he will get well enough to be able to send him to his own country.

On 4 March 1799 Dr Samuel Jones had replied to Evans's rebuke in gentle terms, but the response he received was a shock. It was a letter from Daniel Clark in New Orleans dated 3 August 1799:

The inclosed letter from you to Mr John T. Evans fell lately into my hands and I was induced to open it, that by learning the residence of some of his friends I might advise them of the fate of that unfortunate man who died not long since in this City, after being for some time deprived of his reason. Chagrin and disappointment in his Views contributed, I fear, to hasten his end.

'Is there one thing in the possession of Ieuan ab Ivan that he would not sacrifice to the cause of the Madogion? No, not one: even my precious life

186

would I lay down for their sake.' Poor John Evans had been true to his word. He had lived more in seven years than most men in a lifetime. Now the young man from Waun-fawr was tipped into a lonely grave in a southern city in a Catholic land.

He left one enduring legacy, for in his resolute pursuit of error, he had stumbled across truth. William Richards tried in vain to get hold of his papers. 'The Jealousy of the Spaniards it is said will certainly induce them to secure or destroy them if they are worth anything.' Daniel Clark had reported to Samuel Jones in 1799: 'I believe he [Evans] was possessed of no other property than his Books and Maps of the Country which he had surveyed; these latter will naturally remain for the use of the Government.' In fact, Evans's letters remained in Spanish keeping and ultimately passed to the Archives of the Indies in Seville. His maps and survey material, however, went to the Americans.

The Louisiana Purchase went through in 1803-4, sweeping all those hard-working, frustrated, dreaming, squabbling and forgotten men into the margins of history. The continent passed briefly to France and then to the USA, Brigadier-General Wilkinson raising the flag in New Orleans, and Amos Stoddard in St Louis. 'The Devil may take ALL!' wrote the New Orleans clerk on the last of the Spanish trade licences. In the brief French interval, there was a furious hunt for maps and documents on the mysterious West, but Jefferson's enterprise, of long standing, was more serious. Information had been systematically collected and processed by a small group drawn from the American Philosophical Society and headed by Dr Samuel Mitchill, congressman for New York and editor of the *Medical Repository*. One of the committee was Dr Benjamin Rush who had found the land for the Welsh *Gwladfa* at Beula, Pennsylvania, and was a close friend of Morgan John Rhys. The key material came from McKay and Evans.

Thomas Jefferson sent to Lewis and Clark for their great expedition first a summary and then the whole of the journal of 'the agent of the trading company of St Louis up the Missouri'. This was McKay's journal, which incorporated much of Evans's. Jefferson's famous Instructions to the explorers were modelled on McKay's to Evans. William Clark, one of the greatest wilderness men of them all and one who certainly gave credence to stories of Welsh Indians, had McKay's manuscript *Indian Tribes*. Among William Clark's papers was a note dated 1803: 'Mr Evins's sketches of the Missouri presented to Mr McKay'. There are suggestions that Lewis and Clark had more of Evans's material than has survived. Entries in their journal for 18 and 20 October 1804, with references to 'those remarkable places mentioned by evins' cannot be explained in terms of his map or his section of McKay's journal.

The explorers certainly had John's great map. 'I now enclose you a map of the Missouri as far as the Mendans, 1,200 miles I presume above its mouth,' wrote Jefferson to Lewis in January 1804; 'it is said to be very accurate having been done by a Mr Evans by order of the Spanish government.' One copy had been passed to the President by Daniel Clark in New Orleans, another by William Henry Harrison, governor of the new Indiana territory — 'a copy of the Manuscript map of Mr Evans who ascended the Missouri river by order of the Spanish government further than any other person.' Nine days after sending on the map, Jefferson added the information that Evans had been looking for Welsh Indians and he told the explorers to contact Morgan John Rhys. Jefferson himself boasted that his family had come 'from Snowdon' and he asked his men to keep their eyes open for the Madogwys.

John Evans's sketches, notes and map of the Missouri were of critical assistance to Lewis and Clark. The quest for Welsh Indians had no more remarkable consequence than this. Madoc made John Evans into the last of the Spanish conquistadors, a pioneer of American exploration and as much of a 'precursor' as Morgan John Rhys was to Welsh democracy.

And not even this, the most scientific of American expeditions, could wholly escape the long shadow cast by a small people with a big imagination. In September 1805 the Lewis and Clark party were crossing the Bitterroot mountains in the Rockies. They had gone up a fork of the Salmon river and traversed a hard mountain covered in snow two inches deep. They crossed by Lost Trail Pass over one of the ridges of the Bitterroots and came down a creek to the forks, where they met a party of strange Indians, the Flatheads, who threw white robes over their shoulders and smoked the pipe of peace.

'I was the first white man who ever wer on the waters of this river,' said William Clark on 4 September 1805. He added the following day, 'we assembled the Chiefs and warriers and Spoke to them, with much difficuelty as what we Said had to pass through Several languages before it got into theirs, which is a gugling kind of language Spoken much thro the throught.' Clark himself, though dubbed Red Hair by the Hidatsa, had noted that the Mandans had been 'half-white' and was deeply intrigued. Merriwether Lewis at once began to take down the names of everything in their tongue, 'in order that it may be found out whether they are or whether they Sprang or origenated first from the welch or not.' Two of their men, the celebrated Sergeant John Ordway and Private Joseph Whitehouse, had no doubt: 'these Savages has the Strangest language of any we have ever Seen. they appear to us to have an Empediment in their Speech or a brogue or bur on their tongue but they are the likelyest and honestst Savages we have ever yet Seen . . . we take these Savages to be the Welch Indians.' The logic is impeccable.

For John Evans's report of July 1797, definitive though it might appear to sceptics, proved an anti-climax. In Wales, there had been a flurry of false reports in anticipation. As early as 1795, Job David of Frome heard from his son, who had crossed to America with Morgan John Rhys, that Evans had found Welsh Indians 700 miles up the Missouri who said they had landed in thirteen ships in 1018 (clearly a bunch of heretics). Ben Jones, writing home from the Monongahela in April 1797 reported two Indians at a store on the Mississippi who had needed a Welsh interpreter and who must have come from a cold country because they carried white bearskins, while in the same month William Richards heard that some Glamorgan men had reached the Madogwys and that the Baptist associations in America were sending migrants and missionaries. No wonder the sceptical Walter Davies got angry. Writing of *Whittaker's Etymologies* to William Owen, he commented:

> Can you read it with any patience? I cannot forbear exclaiming frequently as I go on — *Dam the Fool!* — He never boggles at anything. Could you but get him to hunt the Padoucas, I am persuaded he would find them in whatever quarter of the globe you please. He would rouse all the wild cats of America in pursuit and hammer Welsh out of the very Baboons . . .

Others were more committed. Robert Southey kept raising points with William Owen as he built his interminable and intolerable epic poem *Madoc*, while George Burder of Coventry, commissioned by the Missionary Society, was chasing up every scrap of information he could find for a ham-fisted collection *The Welch Indians*, which he published in the summer of 1797. By this time, certainly, the strain was beginning to tell on William Richards; he could not understand why the Welsh in America had not found the Madogwys earlier than this. 'I Beseech you therefore,' he begged William Owen, 'to tell me all you know, without loss of time . . . the suspence in which I am kept is considerably painful to me . . .'.

In December 1797, they heard the worst. Morgan John Rhys passed on John Evans's report; it appeared in the *Monthly Magazine* of 1798 and the new *Greal* of 1800. 'I was always doubtful of the existence of *Welsh Indians*,' commented Morgan John, gilding the lily rather heavily, 'but in my opinion we are left in the dark as much as ever in respect to their existence or non-existence. Those who have asserted that there are such a people may have equal credit in the scale of probability with those who only by superficial research declare they cannot find them.' This set the tone. 'For my part,' wrote Samuel Jones, 'I Keep to my old Text concerning them, that I never knew any thing so likely and at the same time so unlikely as their existence on the Continent.' William Owen pointed out that John Evans had gone sixty-eight days up the Missouri whereas everybody knew the Welsh Indians lay three months' journey up it. The appearance of some Cherokees in London revived the old stories. William Richards had been philosophical at first. 'If he failed in that,' he told Samuel Jones in

189

1798, 'perhaps his journey may not have been quite in vain. Travellers as well as Philosophers, in missing what they were in search of, have often found what amply rewarded their toil and trouble.' A very sagacious comment in the circumstances, but by June 1799 his faith had returned. 'What think you now of the Welsh Indians?' he asked the doctor. 'Our friends here are not yet willing to give them up. Nay, we have pretty good proofs now that John Evans stopt and returned 300 miles short of the confines or limits of their country.' It was that 'superficial research' which was to blame.

In all fairness to these people one has to point out that, on this particular matter, Morgan John Rhys was quite correct when he called John Evans's letter 'very lame'. In July 1797 Evans spent most of his time describing his first, madcap venture up the Missouri. Thereafter, there was simply a summary description of the river, followed by a bare statement that Welsh Indians did not exist. The Mandans were no more than mentioned. 'Mandans' would mean very little to the Welsh at home, but the famous name of 'Padoucas' never even appeared in the letter. From a man whose mission was to find Welsh Indians, this letter read very oddly indeed.

John Evans's letter may have been censored. The Spaniards certainly took pains to discourage unnecessary speculation. 'It is in the interests of His Catholic Majesty,' ran an instruction from Gayoso de Lemos in 1797,

> that the reports of British Indians in Mandan country be denied once and for all. If, however, as seems possible, the subject of association with the Mandans is not mentioned by the British, it might be more expedient to refrain from referring to this tribe, but to relate the denial only to the Padoucas who have already been said by the British to have association with the Welsh.

This was a perfectly comprehensible policy for the Spaniards and they may have tried to enforce it. Certainly, John Evans was angry when he heard that a version of his letter to Samuel Jones had appeared in the American press.

There were persistent reports that he was concealing the facts. An American, Jabez Halliday, who compiled notes on Welsh Indians in 1803, but failed to convince Morgan John Rhys that Mandan bull-boats were coracles (Rhys replying that John Evans had 'emphatically turned down' the Welsh Indian notion), claimed to have known John Evans. He said that the reason John did not go back to Philadelphia was because he had lied about the Welsh Indians. In his cups, Halliday alleged, Evans used to boast that he knew more about Welsh Indians than anyone would ever know now, because he had been paid to keep his mouth shut. In any case, time and disease would soon obliterate all remaining traces of their Welsh ancestry.

That John Evans might have talked like this when drunk is all too likely. It is precisely the kind of thing one might expect him to be saying in the misery of 1797-9. There is no call, of course, to take anything he said in his cups too seriously. The fact remains that there was enough of the ambiguous and the enigmatic about his report home to justify the cool reception it received. It certainly did nothing to stop the remorseless advance of Welsh Indians into the west.

For even as Lewis and Clark were at the Mandans, the Welsh Indian legend came bubbling up in full strength out of Kentucky. Henry Toulmin, a follower of Joseph Priestley who had met Morgan John Rhys on his travels, took down a statement from a Mr Childs who, in turn, had known a Welshman Morris Griffiths who had been a prisoner among the Shawnees for two years. Around 1760, five young men of that tribe took him on a long journey to explore the Missouri. In the midst of the Shining Mountains they met three white men in Indian dress who took them to a nation of Welsh Indians. Their council had discussed whether to put the Shawnees to death and it was Griffiths's intervention in Welsh which had saved them.

This story spread rapidly along the newspaper network after its appearance in the *Kentucky Palladium* of December 1804 and finally lodged, in Welsh translation, in the *Greal* for 1806.

Confirmation quickly reached Dr Mitchill of New York. Some Canadian traders had, about the same time, reached the Missouri some 600 or 700 leagues beyond its mouth (either the Mandans or beyond the Yellowstone). They had met a powerful and hostile tribe of white and bearded Indians. Surely, said the correspondent of the *Medical Repository* for 1805, these must be Griffith's people? Before long, the Welsh Indians became a tribe fifty thousand strong, pure white and Welsh in language, though neolithic in culture, living further up the Missouri than Lewis and Clark 'would probably be able to go'.

In the *Greal* there appeared, at the same time, a remarkable story told by Joseph Roberts, a native of Flintshire who had been a lieutenant in the American army. In 1801 Roberts had been smoking his pipe in a Washington hotel when he turned to berate a laggard Welsh pot-boy in their common language. Whereupon an Indian chief in full regalia had risen from his chair opposite and cried, *'Ai dyna dy iaith di?* (Is that your language?)'. Roberts and the chief conversed at length. Although he had heard of *Lloegr* (England), the Indian had never heard of *Cymru* (Wales) but he spoke better Welsh than Roberts did. He said they had saved their language by forbidding their children to learn any other until they were twelve (which strikes a singularly modern note). The chief showed no inclination to leave his wigwam, not even for Wales, but day after day he instructed Roberts in the medicinal virtues of sundry herbs — and he was merely a secondary prince *(iselradd)*. He said his tribe lived about 800 miles south-west of Philadelphia, which would have put them around the Arkansas.

This cluster of stories registered in the Welsh consciousness at a critical moment. By this time, the Madoc myth was beginning to lose its relevance to a people in turmoil. The war had ceased to be a disputed and divisive struggle against a French Republic, and had become a convulsive tribal rally against the despot Napoleon. Methodism, evangelicalism, and industry were marching across the face of Wales. Men like Iolo Morganwg, Morgan John Rhys and William Richards were already beginning to look like creatures from another time. A Welsh identity which was taking shape in a new age found less and less place for the kind of thinking they had represented. Whatever form 'Welshness' would take, it was not going to be that of the 'nation' which had nourished the Madocians. In these circumstances, Madoc and his Welsh Indians threatened to degenerate swiftly into a historical curiosity.

Moreover, the disappointment of John Evans's mission was soon followed by the return of Lewis and Clark and the apparently massive negative which their expedition had returned to any notion of Welsh Indians. The reports of 1806 would have served merely as a rearguard action had they not been reinforced, at this critical juncture, by the renewed enthusiasm of America. The New World came to the rescue of the Old, in what was to prove a significant and symptomatic conjuncture. In 1812 in Philadelphia, Colonel Amos Stoddard of the US Artillery published a book which virtually established a new orthodoxy for Madoc and his Indians.

Stoddard, who had been a captain at the time, had commanded the American force which took over St Louis in 1804, and had marched over a company from Kaskaskia on 9 March during a cold wave. Merriwether Lewis was already there; he and William Clark set off from Stoddard's fief for the west two months later. Stoddard was also a member of the New York Historical Society and in 1812 published *Sketches, Historical and Descriptive, of Louisiana*. Cogent, well-argued, historical, topographical and sociological, it was an admirable study and well informed, except on the Upper Missouri, on which Stoddard was peculiarly blank. In his chapter on the Aborigines, he expressed the conviction (common enough at the time) that they 'unquestionably derive their origins from some other country'. He cited Phoenicians, Greeks, Egyptians and Jews, but gave pride of place to the Welsh: 'That a colony from Wales arrived in this country in 1170 is much more than probable.' This contention, he agreed, required 'copious detail' to prove; he provided it in his final, seventeenth chapter, 'A Welsh Nation in America'.

Though he knew nothing of John Evans, this was very competently done. He had read David Powel and Hakluyt, and gave an adequate account of the original Madoc story, though he credited the prince with *three* journeys. His real concern, however, was with Welsh Indians. He knew John Williams's *Enquiry* and *Further Observations* and he marshalled the evidence on Welsh-speaking Indians with considerable skill and, indeed, a reasonable degree of healthy scepticism. It seems to have been Stoddard who first deployed that argument which was to prove central to all Madocian historiography: 'It is morally impossible that such a chain of testimony . . . should be fabricated . . .'. He carefully located all the sightings and plotted them geographically. He was the first to publish Oconostota's Cherokee tradition of Welsh Indians, which served to link the scattered references, and he was knowledgeable on ancient remains in Kentucky. Altogether, his picture of possible migrations seemed fairly plausible and must have acquired considerable power from his personal prestige; to the Welsh, it must have sounded at least as 'official' as Hakluyt.

Critical to his location of the Madogwys was his interpretation of Isaac Stewart's narrative as the description of a journey to the Red River *of the South*. He reinforced the Morris Griffiths narrative with a personal reminiscence of his own. In May 1803 he had spoken to a Frenchman employed by the Canadian fur traders on the Assiniboine, 'a few days travel only from the Mandans on the Missouri' (Stoddard's only reference to the Mandans). This man was with a party sent to explore the Missouri. They passed two cataracts and 'much *hard water*'. At the summit of the Shining Mountains they came to a large lake. At the far end was another river running west; the *voyageur* travelled down it for eleven days, to meet a 'yellowish' tribe of Indians with beards and red hair.

Familiar though this story might be to readers of the classical literature (and Stoddard had read Charlevoix), Stoddard used it to construct a plausible enough hypothesis (to those ready to believe) of Welsh-speaking Indians living in a lost corner of the Rockies. Since he was working to the geography of Jonathan Carter (whom he cited), this put them in the 'Mexican mountains' and on the Red River of the South: 'the existence of a people on Red River, speaking the Welsh language, forty or fifty years ago . . seems difficult to doubt'.

Moreover, he confronted Lewis and Clark head on. 'If indeed there be a Welsh or white people in that quarter . . . why were they not discovered by captains Lewis and Clark . . . ? This question admits of a satisfactory answer . . .'. The explorers had chosen the wrong fork at Three Forks (where the Missouri forms). The other travellers must have gone up one of the other forks; Lewis and Clark's own evidence proved that rivers flowed into the Columbia *from the left*, which probably offered an easier route than the northern one they had taken. The explorers had found 'some straggling Indians' near the mouth of the Columbia, similar in appearance to some reported by Vancouver and radically different from other Indians. If a river ran from a great lake to the west, it would join the

Columbia on the left.

Furthermore, Stoddard could actually indicate a tribe which seemed to fit both this location and the general accounts of Welsh Indians. Sixty of them, handsome and of sandy hair, had visited Natchitoches (Louisiana State) for the first and only time in 1807. They were different from their neighbours — pastoral, living in 'tents of a conical figure', migratory and clean. Their language was quite unlike those of other Indians. Their home country was the region about the sources of the Red River, the Arkansas and some of the western branches of the Missouri, in the 'Mexican mountains'. Stoddard called them the Ietans or Alitans. This was the name the Utes applied to the Comanches.

If their Welsh origin could be proved, said Stoddard, 'a multitude of difficulties would be solved'. He drew attention to the many societies which existed among the Indians, 'which apparently resemble our lodges of Freemasons'. In the early days of English history, 'the knowledge of freemasonry was mostly confined to the druids; and Wales was more fruitful of this description of men, than any other part of Europe.'

Stoddard closed his book with a call for exploration and for further study of Welsh traditions. The subject 'cannot be too often revived, nor too strictly investigated . . .'. Many of his readers, whether in America or Wales, would need little further prompting. The Padouca hunt was on again.

$$\widehat{12}$$

Marginal Madoc

William Richards, however, was correct when he wrote to William Owen in 1800, 'I conceived great hopes, one time, of John Evans's adventure being attended with success, but now the scene is closed. And we shall probably never see such another adventurer rise up.' After the death of John Evans, and of Morgan John Rhys's Cambria in Pennsylvania, whose people had been blown away by the winds of the world by 1804, the quest for the Madoc Indians rapidly lost meaning.

'I am taking Madoc to the Court of Owain Cyfeilioc. Will you be kind enough to tell me *where* that Court was? . . . I shall make Madoc present at a Gorsedd in Powys . . .' wrote Robert Southey, addressing William Owen two months before John Evans's letter reached Dr Samuel Jones. In the 1805 preface to his epic poem *Madoc* (as long a labour as any twelfth-century Atlantic crossing) the Poet Laureate could trumpet like an authentic Cambro-Briton: 'Strong evidence has been adduced that he reached America and that his posterity exists there to this day, on the southern branches of the Missouri, retaining their complexion, their language, and, in some degree, their arts.' A mere ten years later, it was becoming harder to swallow this particular leek: 'That country has now been fully explored, and wherever Madoc may have settled, it is now certain that no Welsh Indians are to be found upon any branches of the Missouri . . .'.

There were still sightings from time to time. In 1819, disturbed by persistent reports, the Welsh of Oneida county, New York, sent out John T. Roberts on a mission to St Louis. His answer was as negative as John Evans's and Lewis and Clark's. Forty years later, he gave some brief credence to reports of Welsh Indians near Salt Lake City, and some people never gave up: as late as 1947 the Welsh Indians were identified as the Kutenai Indians of British Columbia. Speculators ran out of likely candidates, however, long before Owen Jones's son got to work on the Crystal Palace for the Great Exhibition of 1851. Such claims were already ringing hollow within a generation of John Evans's death.

Even George Catlin's famous description of the Mandans, which so warmed the hearts of true believers, testifies to a shift to the defensive. Catlin, who was born in Wyoming County, Pennsylvania, had spent his early years 'with books reluctantly held in one hand and a rifle or fishing-pole firmly and affectionately grasped in the other.' Propelled by his father into an eastern law school, he practised 'as a sort of *Nimrodical* lawyer' for a while, 'when I very deliberately sold my law library and all (save my rifle and fishing-tackle) and converting their proceeds into brushes and paint-pots, I commenced the art of painting in Philadelphia.' The arrival of some Indians in the city, 'in silent and stoic dignity', charged Catlin's life with purpose. From 1832, he spent eight years among the Indians, painting, drawing, and recording their lives, as an amateur but enthusiastic anthropologist and linguist.

He spent many months on the Missouri, where he was hypnotized by the Mandans, as Prince Maximilien of Germany and the brilliant painter Karl Bodmer were to be shortly afterwards. Catlin's minute, precise and vivid account of the Mandans captured many minds. His final conclusion, preached not only in the multiple editions of his great work, but on lecture tours through Britain and the USA, was that the Mandans had originated to the southwards. He thought he could trace their settlements at least to the Ohio. He gave qualified support to the Madoc tradition, suggesting that Madoc's people landed at the Mississippi mouth or Florida, and made their way to the Ohio where they finally succumbed to the attacks of a myriad enemies. The survivors, intermarried into the conquering peoples, became despised half-breeds and, in a dramatic severance, formed themselves into a tribe and went on their Long March to the Upper Missouri. Catlin detected traces of their Welsh ancestry in their bull-boats ('exactly the Welsh *coracle*'), their 'whiteness', their unique art of making blue glass beads, their language (he presented a cavalier comparative vocabulary of Welsh and Mandan) and their very name, derived from William Owen's *Madawgwys*.

Catlin was promptly canonized by the Madocians, but in fact, in his argument, the Madoc tradition shrinks. It is another station on the via dolorosa of decline. Characteristically, the appendix in which Catlin recorded his final judgement was headed 'Extinction of the Mandans'. In 1837 smallpox wiped the tribe out. A few dozen survivors were enslaved by the Arikara, and a nation disappeared from history. The 'Welsh Indians' of Catlin were a race of ghosts.

The rapid and remorseless advance of knowledge across the American continent left the Madogwys with no purchase on reality. The quest had to curl back on itself, to spend itself on exercises in imaginative archaeology. There was a limit to the satisfaction to be gained from post-mortems. The essential precariousness of the Madoc myth was exposed, and there was little to halt the inroad of scepticism and indifference.

'An unfounded tradition among the uncultivated natives of North

Wales, respecting the migration of Madog, is still persisted in by certain illiterate Methodist and other preachers,' thundered Dr John Jones of Llandybie, Carmarthenshire, to the *Monthly Magazine* in 1819. ' . . . the whole population of Gwynedd at that time did not equal that of St Mary of Islington . . . the fleet of Commodore Madog, consisting of wickerwork boats covered with hides or tarred blankets, effected a rather extraordinary performance if they were able to leave Ireland on the north and cast these supposed deserters of their country on the coasts of Armorica or Galicia . . .' (he wrote without benefit of Tim Severin's *Brendan* journey, of course).

John Jones was awarded an LL.D. by the University of Jena in Prussia, and was a sarcastic scourge of Madoc. Geography had now become a positive science and had found no trace of this imaginary people of Welsh Indians. As for Madoc, all that the historic bards had recorded was that he had been generous, an eminent fisherman and lost at sea. No more, then, of these mythical tribes of 'Welsh Indians, Madogion or mad-dogs'. Dr Jones died in distressed circumstances in Islington, in the same year as the Mandans.

Before the nineteenth century, there had been little or no overt hostility to the tradition, though indifference there was in abundance. Even Lord Lyttelton and Dr Robertson, those *bêtes noires* of William Jones, had been disposed to grant the story some substance, while discounting any discovery of America, the former supposing that Madoc had made a memorable journey, the latter suggesting that he had reached Madeira or one of the western islands. Cotton Mather believed in Madoc; M. Buache had presented him to the Royal Academy of Paris in 1784. The great explorer Alexander von Humboldt kept an open mind while his compatriot J.G. Kohl proposed, in the style of Dr Plot, that America be renamed Madocia. A tentative attitude, reluctant to commit itself to an outright rejection, has persisted among many American scholars and scholars of America, though not among historians of exploration.

The sheer absence of any hard evidence of any kind, however, together with the increasing visibility of that horrid emptiness, and the parallel draining of the Madoc myth of any purpose beyond the psychiatric, expelled the hero from English discourse and mercilessly eroded his stature even in Welsh. In the dynamic decades of the early nineteenth century, Welsh Indians and, hard on their heels, Madoc himself, visibly shrink in the minds of the Welsh.

Even in the days of Iolo and William Jones Llangadfan, Thomas Pennant had been sceptical and Walter Davies an outright unbeliever. In the new journal *Seren Gomer,* through 1818 and 1819, a lively controversy saw the emergence of a powerful anti-Madoc minority which made its presence felt even in the London-Welsh societies; while the winner of the prize for an essay on Madoc at the Carmarthen eisteddfod of 1823, although accepting that a seafarer Madoc had probably existed, could accept nothing else in view of the absence of positive evidence. 'For if the Welsh language be actually spoken among the Indians of America and there really exist among them ancient Welsh MSS it is truly extraordinary that the fact has not, before this time, been placed beyond the reach of cavil . . . .' Woodward's influential history of Wales of 1854 dismissed the whole tradition and, as early as 1831, an anonymous writer in the *Cambrian and Caledonian Magazine* could boldly assert that the Madoc story 'is not now believed to have any foundation'.

He was a trifle optimistic, but what destroyed the splendid edifice in the first instance was without doubt a brute reality: the straightforward advance in knowledge had proven that Welsh Indians simply did not exist. There were other, equally powerful, forces at work. In the sixteenth century, and in the late eighteenth century, the Madoc myth had served a recognizable and, in some senses, a valid function. Not only did it meet some psychological need; it was itself an integral element of a particular historical conjuncture. In the new Wales of the nineteenth century, this was no longer true. The social transformation, particularly of the south and east, and the onward march of both industrial society and the English language, bred new aspirations, new fears, and new and different mythologies. Madoc quite rapidly became a particular preserve of Welsh-speaking Wales and, as Welsh remorselessly shrank, so did he.

Within that Welsh-speaking world itself, the new thrusts and preoccupations of an awakening people were inimical to the myth. After the great storms of Chartism and the Rebecca Riots, came the Oxford Movement and the 'radicalizing of the Methodists' in reaction; and the Treason of the Blue Books of 1847, when a harsh but accurate government report on education in Wales moved on to a gratuitous, lying and vicious onslaught on the Welsh language and Welsh Dissent, probably at the prompting of an Anglican establishment threated in its very existence. This whipped a species of Welsh nationalism to life. Among some, the response took the form of a shrill, exaggerated and sometimes paranoid Welsh patriotism in which Madoc could certainly find a home, but most intellectuals of this new Welsh nation dedicated themselves to a crusade to register the worth and presence of Welsh literature and history. Coupled with the national obsession with education, the repeated campaigns for literacy and for primary and secondary schools, and the university movement which swept forward from the 1860s, this new Welsh nationalism translated itself into an enterprise to modernize Wales and establish its historical respectability. The first scientific historians of Wales emerged a generation after those of England, particularly with the creation of the university, the national library and the national museum in the golden age of liberalism at the end of the century. Those first professional Welsh historians conceived it their duty, as it was, to purge the history of their country of the myths and fantasies which diminished it in the world's eyes. Scepticism towards Madoc was replaced by something akin to a crusader's hatred.

In such a world, Madoc shrank. He and his story became a minor descant to the increasingly orchestrated cacophony of a people finding a voice. In nineteenth century Wales Madoc survived, but largely as a matter of after-dinner rhetoric and eisteddfod patriotism, of romantic entertainment and children's verse, and sometimes as licensed eccentricity.

If the myth served any purpose at all in the nineteenth century, it was in America with its spasmodic hunger for ancient and distinctive roots. There, often outside but sometimes on the margins of serious discourse, its growth was monstrous. The legend grew into a mighty folk-epic which had Madoc landing anywhere from Newfoundland to the mouth of the Amazon. Leading massive tribes of the Welsh with their Christian Bibles and their advanced culture, and building great forts and cities, the Madocians, although harassed by enemies, pressed on towards the Ohio, even as outrunners founded the Aztec and Inca civilizations to the south. At the Falls of the Ohio, they made their last stand against a host of enemies and went down in frightful slaughter. But unlike other great peoples who had made a similar migration to keep their rendezvous with death in similar style, a handful of the 30,000 Welsh survived. That intrepidity again; and fortunately some were female. Multiplying steadily once more, they moved up the Missouri and into the mist, coming to rest as the Mandans.

Not only did something of this legend pass into the traditions of Indians themselves, such as the Cherokees and the Mandans; a core of it passed into serious scholarship. In 1862, the American Ethnological Society thought there was considerable evidence in support of the Madoc tradition, as it had done in 1841; in 1863, the American Antiquarian Society, presented with a relic of the Welsh Indians, declared that the future would decide; in 1865, the Smithsonian Institution (whose first secretary and archivist was a grandson of Morgan John Rhys) regarded the story as an open question. Benjamin Franklin de Costa, one of the most respected authorities of his day on pre-Columban voyages, published an essay in support in 1891. Some American school textbooks after 1900 carried the bald statement that the Mandans were descended from Madoc's people.

Nemesis struck in 1858. The Llangollen eisteddfod back in Wales offered a prize for an essay on Madoc's discovery of America. Six were submitted, five of which took the truth of the story for granted. The sixth was one of the finest essays in historical criticism to be written in any language. Its author was Thomas Stephens, a chemist and literateur of Merthyr Tydfil ('a self-educated literary druggist' to his enemies). He had already written the first critical history of Welsh literature; and, with a cool and cogent brain, a powerful analytical capacity and a compulsive style, he was one of the sharpest intelligences Wales has produced. Under his scalpel, Madoc was shredded.

Of the three adjudicators, one strongly supported his essay, another was disconcerted and thought it out of order, but proposed that Stephens share the prize with the best author among those who took a reassuringly positive view of Madoc. The third simply resigned. For the eisteddfod committee arbitrarily intervened. Since the set piece was an essay on the discovery of America by Madoc, and since Thomas Stephens's essay was on the non-discovery, they declared that the latter was 'not upon the given subject', disqualified it, and suppressed the favourable adjudication. Thomas Stephens marched to the platform to protest and the chairman ordered the band to strike up. It was, in brief, an unholy eisteddfod scandal, almost as characteristic a feature of nineteenth century Welsh culture as a chapel split.

The scene has often been recalled and taken as evidence of Madoc's hold over the Welsh imagination. While it certainly does testify to the myth's persistence at one level of Welsh consciousness (and in some highly peculiar circumstances — one of the committee was the author of one of the essays), it is in fact evidence of the opposite. The audience at the eisteddfod shouted down the band, demanded a hearing for Stephens and punctuated his speech with applause:

> His ambition was to be the interpreter of the claims of the language and literature of the Principality to neighbouring and continental nations (hear, hear!) . . . he would continue to urge strongly and persistently every merit honestly pertaining to the history and national character of the Kymry (hear, hear!) . . . but he thought it lowered them as a people to be arguing claims which they could not prove and that they were only clouding their own reputation in attempting to deprive Christopher Columbus of the fame to which he was justly entitled (hear, hear!) . . . He, for one, would be content with simple truthfulness; he would never be a jackdaw decked out with borrowed feathers, but would be content with his own plumage, brilliant or plain as that might be (hear, hear!) . . .

and so on to his peroration, which was echoed by the press in its thunders of 'Turpitude! Disgrace!' hurled at the heads of the wretched eisteddfod committee.

Though the eisteddfod managed not to publish his essay, victory went to Thomas Stephens and to that cause which he embraced in memorable words in the final paragraphs of his piece.

> The Madoc story has already done us very serious injury; it has lowered our character as truthful men . . . Let us do our duties, late as it is. Let us

put the legend in its proper place in the list of our 'Mabinogion'. Let us show that we are not incapable either of self-analysis or of historical criticism . . . We inherit and still fluently speak one of the parent languages of the world; let it be our aim to illustrate it worthily and obtain for it an honoured place in comparative philology. We have an ancient literature, which Europe expects us to translate and illustrate: be it our pleasing duty to gratify the expectation. We have an honourable history, as yet unwritten . . . may we seek to study these records, to write our annals honestly and thoroughly and to present such pictures of our forefathers and ourselves, as from their fidelity shall obtain for us lasting honours, when the fables which form the texts of stump-orators have been scattered to the four winds of heaven' . . . Amen I think?

Or as another Celtic writer put it, after he had withered into truth out of the gaudy mythologies of the lying days of his youth, there's more enterprise in walking naked. What person of spirit and sensibility would not stand with Thomas Stephens, shouting above the band? *Y gwir yn erbyn y byd*, after all (Truth against the World), to quote Iolo.

Stephens's essay was finally published posthumously, with a good fighting introduction by Llywarch Reynolds. He timed its appearance with a cunning which gentiles occasionally ascribe to the Welsh. It came out in 1893, simultaneously in London and New York, to coincide with the great Welsh-American eisteddfod held at Chicago under the benevolent dictatorship of a celebrated Welsh-American whose middle name was Madoc.

Since Thomas Stephens, belief in the Madoc legend has had to rest on faith rather than works. The faithful, however, survive and in not inconsiderable numbers, particularly in the USA. In 1950, the American Zella Armstrong argued the case all over again, citing a wealth of new evidence. In 1953, the Daughters of the American Revolution raised their plaque at Mobile. In 1966, Richard Deacon produced a more sophisticated apology. Whatever scholars might say, the Madogwys have gone on thundering over the prairies into our own day.

And whatever scholars may say, the story of Madoc will never die. From the parlour, the 'front room' of the Welsh mind, which two generations of historical scholarship have swept clean and tidy, Madoc has been banished. But late on a quiet evening or in the small hours, you can still hear him, stumbling about in the attic. Probably because of his implantation in openly romantic fantasy, probably because of those haunting echoes of insistent children's verse from the schoolrooms of a Wales that is dying, Madoc still lurks just beyond the edge of consciousness. A man's reach has to exceed his grasp, has it not, especially among what David Lloyd George once called the five-foot nations? In our own day, there has been a certain revival of interest, for reasons both more sophisticated and more desperate. The hard proof of the Icelanders' settlements in Labrador and Newfoundland (and those who scorned Madoc once also scorned the Vikings); the deeper awareness of the sea and its role in human life, of the role of sea-travel in the life of earlier peoples and of those peoples' remarkable capacity for sea-venture; the example of the voyages of Thor Heyerdal, Tim Severin and others; all these have made people less dismissive of predecessors we call primitive, and less disposed to suffer the rather silly arrogance of those to whom history is a mere empiricism imprisoned in properly authenticated documents (a definition which begs a question in its every term). In Wales, certainly, people are less disposed to accept the quite stupefying arrogance of historians who, apparently basing themselves on a single, patently untrue sentence of Gerald the Welshman and in the teeth of evidence massive enough to break the back of Anatole France's old mole of an historian, have rejected Madoc on the grounds that the Welsh have no maritime tradition — itself a myth to dwarf any Madoc!

Now that professional Welsh history has come of age and has fulfilled its first duty, to clear the ground of legend, it is moving into a more sophisticated enterprise — the relocation of those legends in history, the analysis of legend and its function in history, for the history of all peoples has largely been a matter of motor-myths. In our own day interest has tended to shift towards that motor-force, to Spaniards and French and Americans and British blundering into a continent and running off a multi-coloured spectrum of false but directive knowledge. In Wales, it has tended to centre on the Mandans themselves, and on the disappearance of nations; it focuses fears of a loss of historical identity.

But, of course, the biggest myth of all is to assume that the Madoc myth has been a peculiarly Welsh myth. It has been nothing of the kind. It was not Welshmen who first launched it into the world; it was not Welshmen who erected the most elaborate and baroque structures upon it. Among the believers, the Welsh have been a minority. The demands of policy, of expediency and of ideology explain much of this, but they are not enough to explain the myth's persistence and strength in more recent times. There is some quality in the Madoc legend which strikes the resonant frequency of many people. As legends go, it is a genial one, human and humane. It appeals not only to five-foot nations but to five-foot people in every nation. It has that quality which the American Zella Armstrong caught in 1950 when, at the end of her laborious, combative and dedicated defence of the legend, she cried in a kind of defiant despair, 'If the Amazing Story of Madoc is a myth, it is a *good* myth!' *Si non e vero, e ben trovato*.

No matter how many Thomas Stephens stand triumphantly rational on its ruins, the story of Madoc cannot die. There are some plausibilities in it. 'I do not participate in the rejecting spirit which has, but too often, thrown popular tradition into obscurity,' said the great Alexander von Humboldt, speaking of Madoc. 'On the contrary, I am strongly convinced that some facts, hitherto lost sight of, may be recovered . . .' And there remain those unanswered questions which are the sustenance of true believers. That popular tradition of Madoc which Humphrey Llwyd spoke of: where did it come from? Those ten lost sails of Gutyn Owain: where did they go? We do not know, and we shall probably never know.

Sure it is, then, to adapt the words of Humphrey Llwyd, that in some secret corner of many a mind, they will go on for ever, brave and tiny, across a vast and silver sea towards that far horizon with its long, low sliver of island-cloud, rose-tinted with promise in an endless sunset.

Epilogue

It was the wind which got to you first, as soon as you left the car and tried to set up the television camera. It came whipping in from the north across an ice-age lake, slicing into and through everything; it seemed to freeze you from the inside. Then there was the smell, dogs and squalor and stale liquor, a foetid, protecting warmth and the elusive stench of defeat, rasping at the nostrils like pepper. It lay heavy on the scattered huddles of huts, cabins and caravans by the lake, the forlorn Ark of the Lone Man, the ring of cottonwoods grey in the snaking snow-flurries, bolts of cloths thrown across, cigarette packets inside the circle, a sick and shuddering calf with a monstrously swollen eye tethered nearby.

It was a cruel month, for sure, that April of 1976 in Twin Buttes Reservation. Half an hour away across ground like corrugated iron, at the social centre, a sudden burst of light and warmth and welfare workers like a bright modern chapel, they told us there might be a few Mandans left; a young student came in now and then to take down their language. Their memorial was there, in a short main street going nowhere, ringed by muffled and bicycling boys who told us their American names but would not give their Indian ones; a battered and illegible monolith, raised in memory of Four Bears, the last of their chiefs. When the smallpox came, Four Bears, friend of the whites, pronounced his curse on them as he watched his people die, and in seven days fasted to death, going back into his lodge to lie beside the corpses of his family.

It had been a long haul to find what was left of them, following in the footsteps of the Madoc myth and of John Evans. It had begun down in New Orleans, already bright and blazing with sun: donkeys in straw hats, the riverboat by the levee, and all the black and bold beautiful girls in waistcoats and trousers. Hard by the Cabildo was the museum, once the Governor's house where John Evans had drunk himself to death. Along the coast, on the fine white sand, the poet and folk-singer Julian Lee Rayford had talked of Madoc — 'a God to me' — and had chanted his verse:

Over the arches of fear
over the arc of the earth
Madoc sailed out of the dark night
out from the shadows of dread

the dark night of Europe's fear . . .
Came a strange man, not to conquer but to love. Not to
kill but to make happiness . . .

After we had made our obeisance at the brave and silly plaque of the
Revolution's Daughters at the entrance to Fort Morgan, Julian had shown
us his bronze sculpture of Madoc in the white, pillared museum and art
gallery of Mobile; the heraldic gold of helmet and beard and scaly legs
blazing against the tonsured green of the park.

On then, through a country full of legends to the great hilltop ruins
around Chattanooga, to Fort Mountain with its stones and ditches
thousands of feet up over the highway, feeling like the Gaer above
Brecon, down to the Old Stone Fort at Manchester, Tennessee, with its
true believer, the film show in the museum, the imaginative drawings and
the insistent voice: 'Did Maydoc build the Old Stone Fort?' And everywhere the state historical markers — 'White Indians', 'blue-eyed Indians',
'Welsh Indians', 'Maydoc'. On to Cherokee with its Las Vegas strip of craft
shops and men in feathers, the Indian school at softball run by a
Welshman, and the anthropologist who had married a Cherokee, reciting
Oconostota's story.

The trail ran out at St Louis, with its high and graceful arch; as we drove
on along the Missouri an Atlantic of country music battering the car radio,
broken only by the occasional reef of a town rising from the horizon like
an island, we found that John Evans had been forgotten. It is the
memorials to Lewis and Clark which march along that river of legend,
now tamed; they have made poor John into the strangest ghost of the
great river, stranger than the windigo. By one of the dams there was a
scatter of Arikara pottery, and then we were into Bismarck with its
meticulously reconstructed Mandan villages, its replica of the Lewis and
Clark fort, and its Masonic memorial to the explorers as the 'first
Freemasons to enter the territory' (William Arundel and John Evans must
be spinning in their graves). On, finally, to Garrison Lake and into the tail
end of winter; and a lashing tail it was too.

We found a Mandan: Ralph Little Owl, who dressed up in a Sioux
head-dress and chanted what he said was a Mandan prayer at the lake,
told us where the Lone Man's shrine was but would not take us there,
though he presented him as a blend of Noah and Jesus Christ. It was his
nephew who told us most, Ronald Little Owl, known as Sam, and his wife
Evalon, a painter in the primitive style. Her father, Richard Crow Heart,
bright and beady and permanently tipsy, said he had once reared Welsh

ponies and called himself a 'half-assed cowboy'. Both of the younger people were half-Mandan, both had been alcoholics but were now struggling to regain themselves, and both were committed to the Indian revival. They showed us their new-old gear, the wampum beads and much else supplied by a firm in Hong Kong which services that revival. And Ronald Little Owl talked, going over and over the old traditions he was recovering, while our bookish minds clicked like computers, noting discrepancies and deviations, checking silently with Catlin and the anthropologists, as we squatted in a choked and stifling caravan loud with round and black-eyed children and vulpine dogs, sensing as never before the kinship which exists between the historian and the grave-robber.

They came at last, those moments we had half-hoped for, half-feared, when a chill ran through us which was not the wind. Ronald Little Owl rehearsed the Mandan prophecies which had all come true, including one that the old wolves would make the Missouri run backwards (as they have done). The last one, however, he would not tell us — 'it would not be polite.' The language? 'When I die, the Mandan language will have gone.' And the Lone Man? He bent his Asiatic face into the television lights and said, 'The Lone Man was the founder of our people. He was a white man who brought our people in his big canoe across a great water and landed them on the Gulf of Mexico.'

Documentation

On Nootka Sound, David Samwell and the Nootka crisis: J.C. Beaglehole (ed.), *The Journals of Captain James Cook on his voyages of discovery: the voyage of the Resolution and the Discovery 1776-1780,* three vols. (Hakluyt Society, Cambridge University Press, 1967); E.G. Bowen, *David Samwell* (University of Wales, Cardiff, 1974); John Ehrman, *The Younger Pitt: the years of acclaim* (London, 1969).

On Spanish North America and the Mandans: Two fine collections of documents from the Spanish archives:A.P. Nasatir (ed.), *Before Lewis and Clark,* two vols. (St Louis, 1952), and Louis Houck (ed.), *The Spanish Regime in Missouri,* two vols. (Chicago, 1909, reprinted New York, 1971); A.P. Nasatir, 'Jacques Clamorgan: colonial promoter on the northern border of New Spain', *New Mexico Historical Review,* xvii (1942); R. E. Oglesby, *Manuel Lisa and the opening of the Missouri fur trade* (University of Oklahoma, Norman, 1963); A.P. Whittaker, *The Spanish-American frontier 1783-95* (University of Nebraska, Lincoln, 1927; Bison Books, 1969) and *The Mississippi Question 1795-1803* (American Historical Association, 1934, reprinted Gloucester, Mass. 1962); Samuel F. Bemis, *Jay's Treaty* (New York 1923; reprinted Yale 1962) and *Pinckney's Treaty* (Baltimore, 1926; reprinted Yale 1960). Personal visits to Fort Berthold Indian reservation, North Dakota, April 1976, and to Fort Lincoln, Fort Clark and Fort Mandan sites; briefings and occasional papers, especially from Nick Franke, research archaeologist at State Historical Museum, Bismarck, North Dakota; George Catlin's classic, *North American Indians,* two vols (I have used the London edition, 1857); R.H. Lowie, *Indians of the Plains* (Natural History Press, Doubleday ed, New York 1963); Preston Holder, *The Hoe and the Horse on the Plains* (Lincoln, 1970).

On the American continent and its exploration generally, the idiosyncratic but brilliant Bernard de Voto, *The Course of Empire* (Cambridge, Mass., Sentry edn, 1962).

On the Madoc myth and the Tudors: The works of Dr John Dee, viz., his *Famous and Rich Discoveries* in British Library, Reference Division (British Museum) Cottonian MS., Vitellius C. vii; his map and his claim on the dorse in Augustus, I, 1, i and iv; writings in Caligula, A.vi; his printed *General and Rare Memorials Pertayning to the Perfecte Arte of Navigation* (London, 1577); J.O. Halliwell (ed.), *The private diary of Dr John Dee* (London, 1842); P.J. French, *John Dee* (London, 1972); E.G.R. Taylor, *Tudor Geography 1485-1583* (London, 1930). Humphrey Llwyd's history is in B.M. Cottonian MS. Caligula A. vi and in David Powel, *Historie of Cambria* (London, 1584). A critical text is E.G.R. Taylor (ed.), 'A letter dated 1577 from Mercator to John Dee', *Imago Mundi,* xiii (1956). Central are the works of Professor D.B. Quinn, especially (ed.), *Voyages and colonising enterprises of Sir Humphrey Gilbert,* two vols. (Hakluyt Society, 1938) which has Peckham's *True Reporte* and David Ingram's evidence; and D.B. Quinn (ed.), *The Roanoke Voyages 1584-90,* two vols. (Hakluyt Society, 1955), and the collection of his essays in the crucial *England and the Discovery of America 1481-1620* (London, 1974).

Of critical significance to the history of discovery are: Samuel E. Morison, *The European Discovery of America: the northern voyages* (New York, 1971); W.P. Cumming, R.A. Skelton and D.B. Quinn (eds.), *The Discovery of North America* (Elek, London, 1971) with its magnificent maps and illustrations; Geoffrey Ashe (ed.), *The Quest for America* (London, 1971), and the splendid series of Hakluyt Society publications, especially D.B. Quinn (ed.), *The Hakluyt Handbook*, two vols. (1974), the photolithographic facsimile of *Richard Hakluyt's Principall Navigations of 1589* (1965), and E.G.R. Taylor (ed.), *The Original Writings and Correspondence of the two Richard Hakluyts*, two vols. (1935). See also the original Richard Hakluyt, *Principall Navigations* (London, 1598-1600); Humphrey Llwyd, *Breviary of Britayne* (London, 1573); B.F. de Costa, *Myvyrian Archaiology* (New York, 1891); G.W. Dasent (ed.), *The Orkneyingers' Saga* (London, Rolls Series, 1887); W. Dunkel, *William Lambard, Elizabethan jurist* (Rutgers, 1965); and J.H. Harvey (ed.), *William Worcestre, Itineraries* (Oxford, 1969). On the more general Arthurian background: T.D. Kendrick, *British Antiquity* (London, 1950); Glanmor Williams, *Welsh Reformation Essays* (University of Wales, Cardiff, 1967); and Charles B. Millican, *Spenser and the Table Round* (Harvard, 1932; reprinted Cass, London, 1967).

On Irish and Scandinavian voyages: Apart from the general texts above, such as the volume edited by Geoffrey Ashe and the Elek volume, see Tim Severin, *The Brendan Voyage* (London, 1978); the excellent Gwyn Jones, *The Norse Atlantic Saga* (Oxford, 1964) and Tryggvi L. Oleson, *Early Voyages and Northern Approaches 1000-1632* (Oxford, 1964). See also, in a different but related area, the Spanish text of Arredondo of 1742 translated and edited in Herbert E. Bolton, *Spain's Title to Georgia* (University of California, Berkeley, 1925).

On Willem the Fleming: I have found most useful E. Colledge (ed.), *Reynard the Fox and other medieval Netherlands secular literature* (London, 1967); J.F. Willens (ed.), with essay by O. Delepierre, *Le Roman du Renarde* (Brussels, 1837); J.W. Muller (ed.), *Vos Reinaerde* (Leiden, 1939); J.D. Wolters on the same subject (Groningen, 1959); W.G. Hellinga, *Wie was Willem die de Reynaert schreef?* (1950?); E.S. Hartland (ed.), *Walter Map, De Nugis Curialum*, trans. M.R. James with notes by J.E. Lloyd (Cymmrodorion, London 1923); E.D. Jones, 'The reputed discovery of America by Madoc ap Owain Gwynedd', *National Library of Wales Journal*, xiv (1965).

On Wales, Madoc and America: The really critical original sources are manuscript collections in the National Library of Wales: the papers and correspondence of William Owen, Iolo Morganwg and William Jones Llangadfan; a collection in the Historical Society of Pennsylvania in Philadelphia, Mrs Irving H. McKesson Collection, Samuel Jones Pennepek papers; the manuscript journal 1794-5 of Morgan John Rhys, photocopy supplied to me by Mrs Mary Murray Brown of Mount Kisco, New York, and by Brown University Library, Providence, Rhode Island.

For the general history of Wales, see A.J. Roderick, *Wales through the Ages*, two vols. (1959 and reprints, a series of broadcast talks). The standard texts are J.E. Lloyd, *A History of Wales*, two vols. (London, 3rd edn, 1939) on the medieval history, and David Williams, *Modern Wales* (London, 1950; revised ed. by I.G. Jones, London, 1977). The work of Professor David Williams is critical; the quickest appropriation is via the special number of the *Welsh History Review* (1967) devoted to his work.

From a large number of monographs, one may perhaps single out: Gwyn Williams, *An Introduction to Welsh Poetry* (London, 1953); Donald Moore (ed.), *Wales in the Eighteenth Century* (Swansea, 1976); R.T. Jenkins, *Hanes Cymru yn y Ddeunawfed Ganrif* (University of Wales, reprint, 1972, on eighteenth century Wales); D.J.V. Jones, *Before Rebecca* (London, 1973) and David Williams, *The Rebecca Riots* (University of Wales, Cardiff, 1955); John Evans, *Memoirs of the Life and writings of the Rev. William Richards* (London, 1819) and R.T. Jenkins, 'William Richards of Lynn', *Trafodion Cymdeithas Hanes Bedyddwyr Cymru* (Welsh Baptist Historical Society 1930); J.J. Evans, *Morgan John Rhys a'i amserau* (University of Wales, 1935); J.T. Griffiths, *Morgan John Rhys* (USA, 1899; Wales, 1910) and my own 'Morgan John Rhys and Volney's Ruins of Empires', *Bulletin of the Board of Celtic Studies*, xx (1962), and 'Morgan John Rhys and his Beula', *Welsh History Review*, iii (1967); the magisterial G.J. Williams, *Traddodiad Llenyddol Morgannwg* (Unversity of Wales, Cardiff, 1948) on Glamorgan's literary tradition; and the same author's *Iolo Morganwg* (Cardiff, 1956) and his short talk in English, 'Iolo Morganwg' (BBC, Cardiff, 1963); together with the lively Prys Morgan, *Iolo Morganwg* (in English, Welsh Arts Council and University of Wales, Cardiff, 1975). See also Stuart Piggott, *The Druids* (London, 1968); R.T. Jenkins and Helen M. Ramage, *History of the Honourable Society of Cymmrodorion and of the Gwyneddigion and Cymreigyddion Societies* (Cymmrodorion, London, 1951); J.J. Evans, *Dylanwad y Chwyldro Ffrengig ar Lenyddiaeth Cymru* (Liverpool, 1928); and E.G. Hartmann, *Americans from Wales* (Boston, 1967).

On the Madoc myth: The key text is the superb essay in historical criticism, Thomas Stephens, *Madoc* (London and New York, 1893). The best essays in defence of Madoc are Zella Armstrong, *Who Discovered America?* (Chattanooga, 1950) and Richard Deacon, *Madoc* (London, 1966). Important articles are David Williams, 'John Evans's strange journey', *American Historical Review*, liv (1949), and my own follow-up essay, 'John Evans's mission to the Madogwys, 1792–99', *Bulletin of the Board of Celtic Studies*, xxvii (1978).

Index

Acts and Monuments of the Church (Foxe), 35

Adam of Bremen (d.c. 1075) German chronicler, 53

Adams, John (1735-1826) second President of United States, xiii, 108

Alaska, 4

Alien and Sedition Acts 1798, 19

Allaire, Peter, 4

Allen brothers of Vermont, 4

Ambrosius Aurelianus see Emrys

American Antiquarian Society, 199

American Ethnological Society, 199

American Geography (1792) (Morse), 116

American Philosophical Society, 7, 187

American Revolution, 112

Anderson, William, naval surgeon and botanist, 2

Aneirin (fl. 6th-7th cents) Welsh bard, 32, 103

Archaionomia (1568) (Lambard), 55

Archives of the Indies (Seville), 187

Arctic see Expeditions, Scandinavia

Arikara Indians see Indians

Ark of the Lone Man (Mandan shrine), 9, 10, 12, 13, 204

Arkansas River, 15, 16, 134, 192, 194

Armes Prydein, Welsh polemical poem, 31

Armstrong, John (12758-1843) American soldier and diplomat, 6

Armstrong, Zella, champion of Madoc, 201, 202

Arthur, King, 3, 34, 35, 36, 39, 53, 55, 58, 60, 61, 64

Arthurian legends, 51, 54, 55, 62, 63

Arundel, William, frontier merchant, 152, 158, 178, 183, 184, 205

Asser, Welsh monk, protégé of King Alfred, 34

Assiniboine Indians see Indians

Astoria, 2

Astrolable ('the priest with the'), 58, 61, 62, 63, 67

Ayllón, Lucas Vazquex de (c. 1475-1526) Spanish explorer, 44

Bacon's Rebellion, 78

Bahamas, 18, 63

Bala, Wales, mecca of Welsh Methodism, 94

Bale, John (1495-1563) English ecclesiastic and dramatist, 36

Baltimore, 147, 148

Baptists, 96, 112-14, 141

Bardarson, Ivar, Greenland administrator, 59

Beatty, Rev. Charles, Irish minister in Pennsylvania, 81-2, 118, 134

Beckworth, Major George, 5, 19

Behaim, Martin (1436?-1507) German cosmographer, 58

Bella Coola River, 6

211

Bennett, Major-General, of Virginia, 75

Berkeley, Sir William (*c.* 1608-77) British colonial governor of Virginia, 75, 76

Bible (The Book) of the Welsh Indians, 82-4, 128, 140

Bible, Protestant Welsh, 33

Big Sandy Creek, Colorado, heartland of Welsh Indians, 126

Bimini Island, 44, 63

Binon (Beynon), Welsh trader with Indians, 128-9

Bismarck (North Dakota), 205

Black Bird, Omaha Indian chief, 23, 28, 29, 159-63, 166, 167, 179, 182

Black Cat (Posecopsaha), Mandan Indian chief, 141, 170

Black Moccasin, chief of Metehartan (Hidatsa) Indians, 171

Bligh, Captain, 2

Blount, William (1749-1800) American politician, 5, 17, 125

Bodmer, Karl, explorer and artist, 9, 10, 196

Book, The *see* Bible

Borough, Steven (1525-84) English navigator, 64

Bossu, American traveller, 8, 16, 129, 130

Bounty, the, 2

Bourbon River, 17, 133, 149

Bourgmond, Etienne de, French adventurer, 13, 14

Bowdler, Miss and Mrs (of Bath), patrons, 130, 139

Bowles, 'General' William Augustus, self-styled Indian chief, 4, 5, 18, 20, 125-7 134, 139, 144

Bradford, John, antiquary and poet, 79, 98

Bradshaw, William, supposed author of *The Letters of a Turkish Spy*, 73

Brandon House, Hudson Bay Company post, 15, 171, 172 175, 181

Brant, Joseph (1742-1807) Mohawk chief, 19

Bravo River *see* Rio Grande

Brazil, 124

Brechfa, Ieuan, writer, 49

Breda, Antoine, Louisiana trader, 29, 152, 162, 167

Breviary of Britayne (1573) (Llwyd), 37, 43

Bristol ventures, 56, 58, 60

Britannia (1586) (Camden) 36, 37

Britannia Descriptionis Fragmentum (1572) (Llwyd), 37

British History (*c.* 1147) (Geoffrey of Monmouth), 34, 35, 36, 47

British Remains (1777) (Owen), 87, 123

British Sailor's Discovery or the Spanish Pretentions Confuted, The (1739) (anon.), 67, 78

Brut y Tywysogion (Chronicle of the Princes) (?Caradoc), 47

Buffalo-hunting, 10, 140, 163, 169, 170

Building design of Indian lodges and villages, 10

Bull-boats, 10, 190, 196

Burghley *see* Cecil

Burnell, Richard, trader, 134

Burial tombs, 127

Burke, Edmund (1729-97) British statesman and philosopher, 87, 115

Bylan, Morgan Blaen *see* Morgan, Maurice

Cabot, Giovanni (1425-*c.*1500) discoverer of mainland of North America, 39, 42, 64, 66, 67

Cabot, Sebastian (1474-1557) explorer, 64, 66, 67, 123

Cadog, saint, 47

Cadwaladr, Arthurian legend, 45

Cahokia, 23, 154

California, 1, 4, 164

Calvinists, 113

Cambrian and Caledonian Magazine, 198

Camden, William (1551-1623) English scholar and historian, 36, 67

Canada: colonization of, 5; resources of, 25; traders, 2, 5, 9, 14, 19, 20, 25, 29, 172-4, 178, 191

214

218

43, 64, 75, 131, 191, 195; *Silurian*, 127; Siouan, 10; Welsh words in American and Mexican language, 43, 47, 69, 71-4 *passim*

Las Casas, Bartolomeo de (1474-1566) missionary, 20, 62

Laski, Count, Polish mystic, 45

Las Salinas mines, 22

Le Page du Pratz, a founder of New Orleans, 13

Lecuyer, Louisiana trader, 28, 29, 158, 161

Ledyard, John, mariner and explorer, 2

Leland, John (*c.* 1506-52) English antiquary, 36

Lemos, Gayoso de, Governor of Louisiana, 21, 178, 184-6 *passim*, 190

L'Espion Turc (Marena), 73

Letters of a Turkish Spy, The (1687-93) (Mahmoud, nom-de-plume), 73, 74, 77-8

Lewis, Meriwether (1774-1809) American explorer, 2, 6, 9, 14, 25, 84, 129, 164, 166, 170, 181, 182, 187, 188, 191-3 *passim*, 205

Lhuyd, Edward, antiquarian, 77-8

Lisa, Manuel (1772-1820) pioneer Missouri fur-trader, 25

Little People in the North (Eskimos), 57, 60

Living conditions of early Plains Indians, 10-11

Lloyd, Charles, brother of Thomas, below, 75, 77, 78, 80

Lloyd, Richard, 123

Lloyd, Thomas, William Penn's deputy, 75, 76

Lloyd, William (1627-1717) Bishop of St Asaph, 77

Llwyd, Humphrey, historian, 37, 40, 43-9 *passim*, 54, 61-4 *passim*, 66, 67, 203

Llywarch Hen (fl. *c.* AD 700) Welsh poet, 32

Llywarch Hen (1792) (Owen), 104, 108

Lobo Indians *see* Indians

Lodges (earth), 10, 12, 170, 194, 204

Loisel, René, partner in Clamorgan and Loisel Company, 157, 177, 178

London Corresponding Society, 110, 115

London-Welsh society *see* Gwyneddigion

Lone Man, 10, 12, 204, 205, *see also* Art of

Lorimer, Louis, French trader and commandant at Cap Girardeau, 22, 26, 150, 151, 184

Lost Brothers, xiii, 104, 116, 142, 155

Lost Colonists of Roanoke, 44, 71, 77

Louisiana, 1, 4-7 *passim*, 13, 14, 17, 19, 20, 87, 149, 179, 185; expedition of 1794-5, 28-30; warfare, 26

Louisiana Purchase, 20, 151, 187

Loyalists, 19

Lundy Island *(Ynys Wair)*, 52, 54

Lyttleton, Lord George (1709-1773), 90, 197

Mabinogion, The, Welsh tales, 32, 54, 63, 67, 201

McDonnell, Big John, trader, 14-15, 169, 172, 173, 176

McGillivray, Alexander (*c.* 1739-1793) Creek Indian chief, 5, 18, 124

McKay, James, fur-trader and explorer, 14, 15, 23, 29, 141, 152, 153, 155-68, 173-5 *passim*, 177-80 *passim*, 182, 184-7 *passim*, *see also* Expeditions, John Evans

McKay (Neil or Donald) trader, 172

Mackenzie, Sir Alexander (*c.* 1755-1820) Canadian explorer and fur-trader, 6, 8, 129, 132, 136

Madoc legend, 31, 34-5, 44, 48, 68-88, 102, 116, 122, 123, 143, 192-3, 197-203; American rebirth, 199; authentic emergence into history, 45-6; death of the myth, 197-203

Madoc, Welsh prince, xiv, 30, 34-5, 39-55 *passim*, 71, 72, 74, 87, 88, 107, 110, 111, 116, 119-20, 124, 197; discoverer of America, 40, 66, 70-3, 199; discoverer of Mexico and Peru, 124; Jacobin appraisal, 89-105;

Oto Indians *see* Indians

Ouachipouenne *see* Indians 'White'

Oviedo Y Valdés, Gonzalo Hernandez de (1478-1557) Spanish historian, 44

Owain Glyn Dŵr see Glendower

Owain, Gutyn (fl. 1460-1500) scholar, 47, 48, 71, 203

Owen, Hugh, educational pioneer, 141

Owen, Nicholas, historian, 87, 123

Owen, William, scholar, 104, 105, 108-9, 110-11, 115, 118, 122-7 *passim*, 130, 133, 135, 138, 139, 142, 143, 146, 148, 189, 195, 196

'Oxford Minorite', supposedly Nicholas of Lynn, 58, 59, 60, 62, 64

Oxford Movement, 198

Pancane, chief of Miami Indians, 26

Pacific, search for overland routes to, 5-30, 140-83

Padouca *see* Indians, Comanche

Padouca Gazette Extraordinary (Williams), 130

Padouca Hunt (1792) (Samwell), 107, 127

Panana see Indians, Mandan

Pananis see Indians, Arikara

Panton, Leslie and Company, British company in Florida, 5, 18, 157

Panton, Paul, patron, 127

Pantycelyn, William Williams (1717-91) Methodist founder and hymnwriter, 79

Papal Bull (1493) dividing the New World between Spain and Portugal, 40

Parry, Blanche, 43

Patagonia, 119

Peace of Paris (1763), 14

Peckham, Sir George, 40-3 *passim*, 45, 67

Penn, William (1644-1718) Quaker founder of Pennsylvania, 75, 76

Pennant, Thomas, patron, 127, 139, 197

Penninc, Celtic poet, Flemish version

of *Gawain*, 50

Pennsylvania, xiii, 80-1, 86, 112-13, 195

Perez, Juan, Spanish explorer, 1

Peru, 124

Peter Martyr Anglerius (1459-1525) Italian historian, 44, 72

Philadelphia, 112, 138, 182, 192, 196

Phrysius, Gemma, Flemish cosmographer, 37

Piega Indians *see* Indians

Pinckney Treaty (1795), 6, 18, 20, 21, 184

Pitt, William (1759-1806) English statesman, 4, 109, 110

Plains Indians *see* Indians

Plains, The, 13

Platte River, 13, 159

Plot, Dr, FRS, 78, 197

Pocahontas romance, 72, 76

Poems Lyrical and Pastoral (1791) (Williams), 130

Poetry, Welsh heroic, 32

Poitiers fragment, 51, 65

Polo, Marco (1254-1324) Venetian traveller, 60

Ponca Indians *see* Indians

Pond, Peter, explorer of the Northwest Territory, 131-2

Portell, Thomas, Commandant at New Madrid, 22, 149, 150

Powel, Dr David, chaplain to Sir Henry Sidney, 40, 44, 45, 47, 64, 67, 78, 79, 80, 192

Pownall, Governor of Canada, 132, 148

Pratz *see* Le Page du Pratz

Preideu Annwfyn (Taliesin) Arthurian poem, 63

Price, Sir John of Brecon, 36, 45

Price, Richard (1723-91) Welsh philosopher, 99, 112

Priestley, Joseph (1733-1804) Dissenting clergyman, 115, 116

Principal Navigations, Voyages and Discoveries of the English Nation (1589, 1598-1600) (Hakluyt), 43, 49, 56, 59, 61, 67